# Seventy Years In Dixie

## Recollection and Sayings
### of
# T.W. Caskey and Others

by

F.D. Srygley

**Truth**
Publications

*Taking His hand,*
*Helping each other home.*
TM

ISBN 10: 1-58427-165-5

ISBN 13: 978-158427-165-9

First Printing: 2006

**Truth Publications, Inc.**
**CEI Bookstore**
**220 S. Marion St., Athens, AL 35611**
**855-492-6657**
**sales@truthpublications.com**
**www.truthbooks.com**

# PREFACE.

Since the days of early childhood, I have eagerly listened to the life-story of every one who has been willing to confide in me. In this particular, I have been "no respecter of persons." I have given interested and impartial attention to all sorts, ages and sizes of men and women, as they told the stories of their lives in their own way. I have listened to old men and young men, sick men and well men, wise men and foolish men, good men and bad men, rich men and poor men, married men and single men, town men and country men, free men and bond men, serious men and funny men, religious men and worldly men, white men and black men, drunk men and sober men. It did not occur to me when I was listening to all those strange life-stories, that I was accumulating a fund of unclassified information, which, in due course of time, would ooze out of me upon a defenceless public, in the form of a book like this, "but such is life." In gratifying an abnormal curiosity, I simply accumulated more facts than an over-burdened memory could retain or a feeble intellect could digest. The only remedy, so far as I could see, was to disgorge my over-loaded mind of this mass of unprofitable information, in the form of a volume like this. This is my explanation and apology for imposing another book upon the public.

If I thought that readers would find as much pleasure in the perusal of this volume, as I enjoyed in gathering up the information which it contains, I would count myself as one of the popular authors of the nineteenth century, in advance, and advise my publishers to bring out a large edition of the book—at their own risk and without any expense to me!

I know not what estimate a discriminating public may put upon this volume, but it is a relief to me to rid my mind of the matter which these pages contain, anyhow. I have meditated upon the strange stories here given to the public, many an hour when I ought to have been engaged in better business. I have, at times, reflected upon the marvelous changes that have taken place in this queer world within the memory of those yet living, till my head would positively grow dizzy, and I would, for the moment, feel utterly lost

(3)

in the rapidly changing scenes through which my mind was wandering.

Some philosophers say that, if a man would be happy, he must live in harmony with his environments. But, in view of the marvelous changes which have taken place during the last seventy years, it would seem that the man who seeks happiness according to such philosophy would have a hard race, to keep pace with his environments. Indeed, it is difficult for any man, in such times of rapid mutations, to know what his environments are. To try to understand your environments in such an age, is like an effort to study the geography and topography of a country by looking out of the window of an express train, as you dash along at the rate of sixty miles an hour. Your head becomes dizzy, and you soon conclude that environments change so rapidly that it is impossible to fully understand them, if, indeed, you have any at all.

He is not a philosopher who would seek happiness by an effort to put himself in harmony with such rapidly changing environments. If there be any truth in the philosophy, the environments with which we must harmonize in order to find happiness, must be something less changeable than the fads, fancies, customs and sentiments of this fickle age and generation. To seek happiness by a hard race to keep pace with such environments, is to act the folly of the discontented slaves of fast life, who always make haste to worship at the shrine of the latest gods of fashion. There is no real happiness along that route. The peace which passeth understanding must come from anchoring the soul to something more sure and steadfast. To put it all in the fewest words possible, the nearest way, and the only way, to true happiness is stated in this one sentence: "Thou shalt love the Lord thy God with all thy soul, and with all thy strength, and with all thy mind; and thy neighbor as thyself." These two things are the same, and must ever remain the same, in all ages, among all peoples, and under all circumstances. And, "On these two commandments hang all the law and the prophets."

There is no fiction in this book. It is mainly the story of the life of Mr. Caskey, but such things as are not parts of the story of his life, are, nevertheless, real incidents in the lives of other veritable persons.

My young friend, J. D. Kelley, of Nashville, Tennessee, is entitled to all the credit for illustrating the book. Whatever merit there may be in the pictures, both in the matter of their conception and the manner of their execution, is due wholly to his genius.

I indulge the hope that the reader will, at least, be able to while away a few hours in the perusal of this volume. And I have failed to accomplish the object on which my heart was chiefly set in the preparation of the book, if there are not passages in it which will draw the reader's heart into closer sympathy with suffering humanity.

Finally, I beg to suggest that the changes portrayed in the book, and the blindness manifested by the wisest of men in grappling with problems that solved themselves, in due course of time, contrary to all the theories, plans and philosophies of would-be leaders—all these things ought to convince us that there is a wisdom above man, and superior to all men combined, that guides the world in its progress. If I can but fix this thought firmly in the mind of one of the humblest denizens of earth, I shall consider the labor of preparing the book well spent.                                    F. D. SRYGLEY.

Nashville, Tennessee, March 1, 1891.

# INDEX.

## A

## B

(6)

## C

## D

## E

## F

## G

## H

## I

## J

## K

## L

## M

# INDEX TO ILLUSTRATIONS.

# CHAPTER I.

I attended a religious convention many years ago, which, as well as I now remember, was called a Christian State Meeting. It assembled in a little inland Southern town, and was largely attended by the brethren from the rural districts. There were but few railroads in the South then. Fort Worth, Texas was but a village of a few hundred inhabitants, Dallas was scarcely more than a country town, and Birmingham, Alabama was not so much as named till many years afterwards.

I may not have the name of that old-time annual gathering of Christians exactly right, but no matter. It was not a corporate body or a chartered institution anyhow, and though it assembled every year, it could hardly be said to have "a local habitation" or "a name." It was neither an organized body nor an authoritative convention. It assumed no prerogatives over Christians or churches; neither did it attempt to settle any question of doctrine, or, inaugurate any form of ecclesiasticism. It was simply an undenominational mass meeting of Christians. Those in attendance were, in the main, preachers, but still there were women and laymen enough to give variety to the assembly. Those who were present came not as delegates from churches, neither did they claim to represent anybody but themselves in the meeting. To use the phraseology of the time and country, every man "went on his own hook." They assembled, not as delegates with "letters of authority," but as brethren. Each one brought into the meeting his own ideas and zeal, and from the conglomeration of individuality every man filled himself with such things as were congenial to his nature, just as men do at a picnic or a barbecue.

The meeting had a chairman, whose principal duty seemed to be to tell the audience when to pray, what to sing and when to adjourn. The chairman also enjoyed a good joke or a sally of wit, and at all proper times he pitched the fun and led the laugh for the convention. He also had a tender heart and a loving soul, and many a time did he lead the audience in a gush of religious pathos or pious tears. He had no committees to appoint and no questions of parliamentary usage to settle. Every body was all the time in a good humor, and no body ever got out of order. It was simply a revival, a prayer-meeting, a love-feast, a social gathering and an experience meeting all in one. The chairman was a privileged character. In fact they were all privileged characters. He would stop the proceedings of the convention to tell a funny story, and then every body would laugh. At another time he would be moved to relate a pathetic incident—his voice would grow tremulous with emotion, tears would gather in his eyes and flow freely down his radiant cheeks, his lips would tremble, his speech would fail—and then sobs and sighs would be heard in all parts of the vast assembly. Again, he would announce a song, and everybody in the audience would join in the singing with a strength of voice and earnestness of expression which would put professional city choirs to shame.

The songs they sang were, for the most part, old and familiar words set to simple melodies. Everybody knew the words, and anybody could sing the tunes. "Amaz-

"HOW FIRM A FOUNDATION."

2

ing grace, how sweet the sound," was a favorite with
them all, and " On Jordan's stormy banks I stand," was
scarcely less popular. "Am I a soldier of the cross,"
was in great demand, and " How firm a foundation "
was never tabooed. The exercises were varied, but always religious and deeply earnest. They sang, and
prayed, and preached, and exhorted, and discussed questions, and told their experiences.

The preachers in attendance were, in the main, a
cheaply-dressed, hard-worked, poorly-paid, saddle-bags
crowd of earnest, God-loving, Bible-believing, self-sac-
rificing men. There were but few rich and fashionable
churches in the country then. Hence, town-preachers
and city pastors were conspicuous for their absence in
that great meeting. There was but one "plug" hat in
all that assembly, and it was worn by the president of a
college who was there from a distance on a business trip
in the interest of his school. And yet there was no
lack of native ability or scholarly attainments on the
part of the preachers in that meeting. Many of them
were graduates from good colleges and universities in
older States, and not a few of them were masters of a
style of vigorous and pathetic oratory, that would have
commanded the attention and aroused the emotions of
cold and formal city audiences who had nodded and
shivered for years under the methodical logic and soul-
less rhetoric of automatic pastors, who claimed a higher
order of culture than the preachers in that meeting
ever aspired to.

Those preachers were men long used to the inconveniences and hardships of country life. It required
men of strong native ability and impressive delivery to
succeed as preachers in this country in those days. The
idea that old and cultured countries require a higher order

of talent than new countries, to insure success in pulpit work, is a mistake. In old countries, where society is well organized, churches are perpetuated largely by inheritance. Children accept the doctrine and join the church of their parents, because that is generally conceded to be the proper thing for them to do. The ability of the preacher and the plausibility of the creed are things

THE OLD WAY OF BUILDING UP A CHURCH.

of little moment. In old countries, churches gain more by generation than by regeneration. Not so in a new country. There are no established churches or social castes in new countries. Preachers are not back-ed by old prejudices or time-worn traditions in their work. They stand upon their merits, and they must build upon the convictions of their hearers. Their only hope of success is in the strength of their case. Their doctrine must be plausible, and their style, both convinc-ing and persuasive, or they will inevitably fail.

Preachers in such a country as this was in those early days are at still another disadvantage. The people who moved to this country in those days did not come, as a rule, to seek religion. Whatever else may have prompted them to come here, it is safe to say it was not particularly an interest in religious subjects. An incident in the mass meeting referred to will illustrate the difference between the old way and the new, in religious work and worship. It will show how far the methods relied on, to establish and build up churches in the early days of a country, differ from the plans adopt-ed, in religious work, by people who are further advanced in the ways of fashionable society.

There was one typical pastor in that meeting. Ele-gantly dressed, dignified in bearing, fluent in speech and polished in manner, he was certainly " a thing of beauty " if not " a joy forever." He was as much out of harmony with his environments as a daisy in a des-ert, and he evidently felt that he was a harbinger of refinement crying in the wilderness of barbarism. He had done service as a city pastor in other States, and he came into that meeting as a sort of missionary of re-finement, to prepare the way for æsthetic taste in the worship of God. He had a sickly little pastorate, in an ambitious little town, and those of his flock, who ac-companied him to the meeting, felt justly proud of his good clothes and stately airs. One day he delivered a set speech to the meeting on the subject, " How to build up a church." He laid special emphasis upon the social qualities of a pastor, as an element of success in building up a church. In his characteristically attractive style, he told the convention that a minister ought to be a good "mixer;" he explained the advantages of pastoral visiting from house to house; he emphasized the importance of personal acquaintance with every member of every household; he insisted that the preacher ought to be a favorite with all the children; he urged that the pastor should carefully cultivate the friendship of young people; he showed that it was important for the pastor to keep himself and his church well to the front in all benevolent enterprises, public gatherings, temperance movements and social festivals. And, last of all, he showed how necessary it was for a preacher to cultivate the acquaintance and friendship of leading families in the bounds of his charge, and, to visit regularly all the members of his church, especially those who seemed cold and indifferent as to their religious duties.

When the young pastor took his seat, an aged man of dignified bearing and confident air took the floor, to express his convictions as to "How to build up a church." He was tall, slender, long-limbed, limber-jointed, frail-bodied and angularly-shaped. His nose hooked over his capacious mouth in a way that suggested penetrative inquisitiveness, and he hooked the front finger of his right hand over the little finger of his left, as if fastening the subject down for dissection after the manner of a saw log in a lumber mill. He spoke with impressive earnestness and in a well modulated voice. As well as I can reproduce his speech, by the help of copious notes, taken at the time, it was as follows:

"I beg leave to differ from the brother who has pre-

ceded me on this question. What I understand to be
of greatest importance as an element of success in building up a church, he has entirely over-looked, or design-
edly ignored. I refer to the material of which churches
are composed, and the manner in which that material is
brought into the churches. There are certain kinds of
people in the church, who have been brought into it by
certain kinds of schemes, who cannot be kept in it without some man eternally trotting at their heels. When
I find such stock as that in a church which I am preaching for, I give them plainly to understand, that, if they
haven't religion enough to come out to the Lord's house
and worship their God, without being driven up every
Sunday like a parcel of stray cattle, they may jump
over the fence and starve to death in the wilderness.
Brethren, I'm not coming down from intellectual work
in the pulpit, to make a common herd-boy out of myself. If I must do such work as that, I will quit preaching and hire out to some man to herd sheep or cows.
Church members who cannot be brought out to the
house of the Lord, except by pastoral visitations, are not
worth standing room in a potter's field anyhow. I have
recently had some valuable experience myself in pastoral visiting. I tried it, in a sickly little church
in a fashionable town. I tramped the streets through
dust and heat for three miserable days, hunting for
the lost sheep of the house of Israel. I was assured that the Lord had some stray sheep in that
God-forsaken town, but, after searching the place
diligently, I found only one old wanderer on the mountains of sin, wild and bare, and he had grazed on the
devil's commons till he couldn't tell clover from sneeze
weed. He had lost his bell, shed his fleece and herded
with the goats till he wasn't worth driving home.

Brethren, let me speak freely about this professional pastoral visiting, as a means of building up a church. The sick and the poor, the troubled and the distressed,

"COULDN'T TELL CLOVER FROM SNEEZE WEED."

the fatherless and widows, in their affliction, ought to be visited, not only by the pastor, but by all the saints. No one is readier than I to encourage and practice such visiting. But this is an entirely different thing from professional pastoral visiting, such as we are advised to depend upon, to build up the church. I do not believe that a church can be built up in any such way. Numbers may be added to its membership, but can you increase the zeal, deepen the piety, or strengthen the faith of members in that way? I think not. Those who love God and walk by faith, in the religious life, do not gauge their zeal in the church by the personal popularity or 'mixing' qualities of the preacher. If I have studied the Bible to any profit, it teaches us to rely upon the gospel as 'the power of God unto salvation.' Pastoral visiting and clerical clap-trap may popularize a church and fill it with the irreligious and worldly-minded, but such things will neither convert sinners nor add to the spirituality of the worship. 'God is a spirit, and they that worship him must worship him in spirit and in truth.' If you can convert sinners and build up churches by humoring spiritual weaklings and flattering simpering sentimentalists, in pastoral visiting, without preaching the gospel, you may as well throw away the Bible, get a fashionable preacher and rent hell out for a calf pasture. People who attend the meetings of the saints from the love of the pastor, and who neglect their religious duties unless they are coddled by the pastor, have neither faith nor piety, and their pretended worship is but a hollow mockery which will militate against the piety of any church and prove a stench in the nostrils of our God. Without faith it is impossible to please God. It is every man's inalienable right, as well as indispensable duty, to study the Bible for himself and to formulate his own faith from the teaching of the Bible. The Bible is a revelation from God, made, not to priests, pastors or councils, to be interpreted and handed out to the people, but to each individual soul, with no mediator between the soul and its God, save the Lord Jesus Christ. Sinners are justified by faith, and saints walk by faith, but the faith that justifies the one and leads the other is not a mere admiration for the pastor or his church. It is faith which, Paul says, comes by hearing and hearing by the word of God. The man who studies the word of God carefully for himself, and who forms thereby a faith which works by love and purifies the heart, is a Christian, a disciple of Christ. He has been delivered from the powers of darkness and translated into the kingdom of God's dear Son. The idea that such a Christian will absent himself from the assembly of saints, or grow indifferent as to other religious duties, or privileges, simply because the pastor does not call around regularly, to kiss his baby and gossip with his wife, is contrary to reason and an insult to common sense. The effort to build up the church by clerical schemes and pastoral visits has always diverted attention from the importance of faith which works mightily in the heart by love to the saving of souls. In every age it has, when followed to its logical result, led to a greater effort to build fine houses and strong organizations, than to convert sinners or save souls. The history of religion shows that the effort of an organized, professional ministry in the Catholic hierarchy has always been to save the church and let the devil take the sinners. Professional pastors, in that iniquituous system, have, indeed, been fishers of men, in all ages of the world, but they have always cast their nets and baited their hooks for such men as they thought could give most money and social prestige towards supporting the ministry and building up the church. Hence, there has always been more joy, among such clergymen, over one dives, who walks stiff-necked and unconverted into the organization, than over ninety - and - nine penitent Lazaruses, who are truly converted to the saving of their souls. Let us beware how we infringe upon primitive Christianity, in adopting the plans and poli-

"FISHERS OF MEN."

icies of Rome.   Let us beware lest we, also, exalt money and social influence above piety and humble devotion in the church. Such a policy may build costly houses, sustain fashionable choirs and attract the frivolous and ungodly, but it will never convert sinners or maintain a spiritual worship in the church. True faith to-day is the same as in apostolic times, and will bear the same fruit. Paul says, Moses, by faith, ' refused to be called the son of Pharaoh's daughter, choosing rather to suffer affliction with the people of God, than to enjoy the pleasures of sin for a season.' 'And what shall I more say, for time would fail me to tell of Gideon and of Barak, and of Samson, and of Jepthah; of David also, and Samuel, and the prophets; who, through faith, subdued kingdoms, wrought righteousness, obtained promises, stopped the mouths of lions, quenched the violence of fire, escaped the edge of the sword, out of weakness were made strong, waxed valiant in fight, turned to flight the armies of the aliens. Women received their dead raised to life again, and others were tormented, not accepting deliverance, that they might obtain the better resurrection. And others had trials of cruel mockings and scourging, yea, moreover of bonds and imprisonments. They were stoned, they were sawn asunder, were tempted, were slain with the sword. They wandered about in sheepskins and goatskins, being destitute, afflicted, tormented. * * * They wandered in deserts, and in mountains, and in dens and caves of the earth.' It may be claimed that some of these glorious achievements of faith in olden times were miraculous, and that, therefore, such things are not to be expected, as the fruits of faith, in these modern days. This is readily granted. But, touching all the ordinary fruits of faith, it is claimed that those who have the same faith now, will manifest it in the same way, and to the same extent, and this will build up the church now infinitely better and faster than

pastoral visiting and organized routine work. Did the
church prosper in those early days of Christianity?
Great multitudes were obedient to the faith, and, notwithstanding the persecutions which afflicted the saints
in every nation, the church flourished as it has never
flourished in any other age. It even passed into a pro-
verb, 'that the blood of the martyrs has become the seed
of the church.' Were those saints of old humored, and
petted, and flattered, and coddled by the professional
visits of pastors, who prided themselves on being good
'mixers,' to get them to assemble for worship in caves
and dens of the earth at midnight's secret hour? Were
churches then built up by the popularity of pastors, the
artistic performance of godless choirs, the imposing appearance of costly houses of worship, the wealth and
social position of leading members, or the worldly at-
tractions of the services? Ah, no. Those were the
blessed days when sinners were converted and saints
controlled by *faith.* Those were the days when the poor
had the gospel preached to them. The church put no
premium upon wealth in those days. Those who started
out to seek the kingdom of heaven were glad enough
to distribute their worldly possessions in good works,
for they were given to understand, in very plain words,
at the very out-set, that wealth was an incumbrance
which effectually and forever barred the gates of
heaven against them. The call was then to those who
labored and were heavily laden. The blessing was upon
the poor in spirit, who humbled themselves before the
Lord. The command was to go out into the highways
and compel the poor to come to the gospel feast. The
rich, the proud and the self-righteous were put aside.
'It is easier for a camel to go through a needle's eye,
than for a rich man to enter the kingdom of God.'

'Ye rich men, weep and howl for your miseries that shall come upon you. Your riches are corrupted and your garments moth-eaten. Your gold and silver is cankered; and the rust of them shall be a witness against you, and shall eat your flesh as it were fire. Ye have heaped treasures together for the last days. * * * Ye have lived in pleasure on the earth, and been wanton ; Ye have nourished your hearts as in a day of slaughter.' Ah, brethren, the saints of God had deep convictions and soul-moving love for God and for each other in those days. With such convictions, and such faith, and such love to-day, they will build up churches and convert sinners all over this broad land. The best way to build up a church, therefore, is to return to the apostolic order of preaching and worship."

By enquiring, I learned that the speaker, who delivered this remarkable address on 'pastoral visiting,' was Thomas W. Caskey, of Mississippi. His speech was, to my mind, the most impressive part of the whole convention. In fact it is about the only speech of the convention that I can clearly remember now, after the lapse of many years. I was introduced to Mr. Caskey then, and our acquaintance soon ripened into close, confidential friendship. He is now in his seventy-fifth year, and I consider him, in many respects, one of the most unique characters the South has ever produced. He has a distinct recollection of men and things extending back to 1820, and he has been connected in some way with almost everything of importance in the history of the South for more than half a century. Born of poor parents and brought up under all the disadvantages of frontier life, he gradually worked his way upward through all the grades of society, to a position in the first circle of Southern aristocracy before the war. He has been a blacksmith, farmer, preacher, politician and soldier. As a laborer, he helped to clear away the primitive forests, in the days when the country was sparsely populated, and infested with all manner of wild beasts. He has lived in the cabins of the poor in pioneer days; he has moved in the highest circles of aristocratic society in times of Southern magnificence. He "stumped" the State of Mississippi as a politician, in the great political excitement of 1860; and followed the "lost cause" to its grave in the last ditch. For many years he was the personal friend of the late Jefferson Davis, and he loved him as a friend to the day of his death. He flourished as a Southern planter in possession of a magnificent cotton plantation in Mississippi, in the famous times of Southern prosperity before the war, and he suffered, with the rest of the people of the South, through the weary period of ruin and desolation, which was the common lot of every part of the Southern country during the years which immediately succeeded the war. To use his own unique words, he has been "on all sides of the world—on the top side and the bottom side, the good side and the bad side, the hard side and the soft side, the right side and the wrong side." The story of his life is the history of almost every phase of the Southern country and people during the last seventy years.

I have tried to gather the fragments of the true lifestory of this remarkable man, and in the following chapters I give the result of my labors.

Much that I give was written by him, and appears here in almost the exact form of his original manuscript. Parts of the story I have reproduced from my own recollection of conversations, speeches, sermons, lectures and addresses I have heard from him. In some places

I have stated facts and incidents from my own experience and observation, by way of more fully bringing out the history of some peculiar phase of Southern life, in connection with the story of his life. So, the following chapters may be described as seventy years of Southern life-history, embracing the various stages and phases of material development and social customs, as compiled from the combined experiences, observations and recollections of Thomas W. Caskey and myself.

Throughout the book, I have thought best to use the first person, which gives the story the *form* of a personal narative. This is a mere matter of taste and convenience, and should not confuse the reader. Let it be understood, once for all, that it is a single, continuous, personal narative in *form only.* As to the *facts*, they are taken from the stories of several lives—still, they *are* *facts*, nevertheless.

# CHAPTER II.

To begin at the beginning of the story of my life, I am reliably informed that I was born in Maury county, Tennessee, January 12, 1816. I am compelled to rely upon the statement of others for this bit of information, for, good as my memory is, I confess that I have no well-defined recollection of that, to me, important event. The reader may consider my birth a matter of very small moment, anyway, but it is an event in which *I* have always felt a profound interest. Without it, I never could have amounted to much in this world, no matter how much energy and perseverance I may have manifested. And yet, I cannot say, positively, that it has been a very great blessing to me, after all. Only the light of eternity and the righteous judgment of God, can determine whether the world is the better and I will be the happier, in the great hereafter that ever I was born.

Not only is my memory blank, as to when and where I was born, but I have no distinct recollection as to why that event ever occurred, to mark an epoch in my wild career. I frankly confess that I have no well-defined idea, to this good day, as to why I was born, though I have been studying that question, off and on, ever since the early days of my childhood, when my Presbyterian father began to teach me the Shorter Catechism. The language of that old relic of defunct theology, which my father always insisted was an explanation of why I was born, was, in substance, "that man's chief .

end is to glorify God and enjoy him forever." I confess
that the connection between that statement and the
reason I was born, was never at all clear to my childish
mind. In my childish way of thinking, I remember
how I puzzled my brain over this grave, theological
problem. I would say, over and over, to myself, "If
man's *chief* end is to glorify God, I wonder what his
*other* end is for?" I would think, and think, and think,
till my little head would ache, and my poor little motherless heart would grow heavy and sad with the burden
of my troubles, but still I could not see a single ray of
light, or hear a whisper of love, to guide my weary soul
through all the deep, dark mysteries such questions and
answers, in the catechism, opened up all around me.
Why was my hungry soul fed on such dry crusts of
speculative theology, when my little heart, which had
never tasted the sweets of a mother's affection, was literally starving for a whisper of tenderness and love?
Why did they not tell me plainly and simply, that Jesus
loved little children, and said, suffer them "to come
unto me, and forbid them not : for of such is the kingdom of God?" Why did they not tell me, without any
catechetical foolishness about it, that the loving Savior
took the blessed little children "up in his arms, put
his hands upon them, and blessed them?" There would
have been comfort, joy and peace, to my lonely,
troubled soul, in such precious words as these. I could
have loved, and I would have delighted to serve, such a
blessed Savior as this, if he had been offered to me in
his own tender nature, without the hard questions and
deep mysteries set forth in the catechism. But I had
no time to think about Jesus and his love. I had to
learn what the catechism said about the chief end of
man. And finally I began to say to myself: "I won-

3

der which end of a man *is* his *chief* end, anyhow." And
the next time I appeared before my austere father,
to recite my lesson in the catechism, my answer showed that I had spent my time in wondering and speculat-
ing, rather than in memorizing the answer written
down in the book. With his usual gravity my father
read out the question: "What is the chief end of
man?" And with more promptness than discretion, I frankly gave it, as my opinion, that man's
chief end was his *head*. My father took this as
a bit of youthful and impious impertinence, and proceeded to give me a sound thrashing for my smartness.
That question is still an open one between me and the
Presbyterian fathers. I have never yet seen any good
reason to change my opinion, and they have not
thought it proper to change the answer to that question
in the catechism. So we are still divided in opinion on
that point. In this little difference between me and
Presbyterian theology, my father very promptly sided
with his adopted church against his own motherless offspring. This aroused in me a strong prejudice against
the whole catechism fraternity, and from that day to
the end of my boyhood's theological course, I never
saw a catechism, short or long, that I did not devoutly
wish it were shorter at both ends and not quite so long
in the middle. But in those days, every son and every
daughter of a Presbyterian father or mother, had to
learn both the shorter and longer catechisms, no matter
how intense and well-grounded might be the feelings of
prejudice against those theological documents.

Looking back over my checkered career, I feel
that I have demonstrated, by more than seventy
years of eventful experiment, that the first clause in the
answer to that famous question, as written down in the

Shorter Catechism, is not correct. I cannot feel that my poor, unworthy life has in any way glorified God. To me it is a precious thought, that God will glorify me, if I believe on his only begotten Son, but it is not in my heart, nor do I find authority in the teaching of the Scriptures, to claim that my life or conduct has, in any way, affected the glory which God had before the world was.

I entered this world by the sacrifice of a noble, blessed mother's life—she died in giving me birth—and I hope to enter the glorious world above, where trouble comes not, through the sacrifice of another purer, nobler and higher life—the life of my ever precious Savior. But I do not claim that I have glorified God, or that I can glorify him, by such a life as I have lived; much less do I believe that God will save me because of any works of merit which I have done.

Of the first years of my babyhood, I remember nothing, though I was always told that I had a remarkable memory. This tradition concerning my memory had its origin in a little incident that occurred in my early childhood. I heard older persons relate certain events, which were very interesting to me, so often, that I repeated them to my playmates and declared that I could remember them distinctly myself. For this remarkable development of a rather precocious memory, I was heartily laughed at, and informed that the things took place two or three years before I was born. Had they told me this sooner, they might have kept me from thus making a fool of myself almost the first thing I did in life, but perhaps this early beginning in a life-time occupation was well enough. Had not this hereditary tendency of my nature manifested itself at that early age, there would have been left the more innate foolish-

ness to ooze out of me in riper years, and it might have
cropped out in directions far more harmful and none the
less embarrassing to me.   I do not think I intentionally

"TURNED UPSIDE DOWN."

prevaricated about those incidents in my early childhood.   I had heard them repeated so often that I verily
thought I remembered them.

I am asked to relate some of my earliest recollections. I think I can recollect some things which occurred in my third year—I *know* I can recollect things that occurred in my *fourth* year. The first thing I remember is the churning my old black mammy used to give me on her knee, to stop my yelling, when, perhaps, the milk drawn from my bottle had curdled on my little stomach. I did not know then, nor do I yet, why she thus churned and wallopped me. I don't understand why this barbarous treatment of babies still prevails in this enlightened country. Why should a sick baby be treated worse than a horse or a dog? When animals are sick and suffering, they are allowed to lie down and rest, or turn and tumble about, as nature may prompt. But when a helpless little babe is suffering, it must be trotted up and down, turned over on its back, then tumbled over on its stomach, turned up-side down, wrong end up, and every other imaginable way, except inside out.

The more it is pounded, twisted and jolted, the louder it squalls, and no wonder. Finally, the poor, anxious, exhausted mother gives up in despair and the much worried, shamefully abused little darling drops into sweet and refreshing sleep.

Dark clouds lowered o'er my cradle, and misfortune has ever been my lot. I have been unfortunate mentally, morally, physically, politically and financially. Unfortunate, mentally, through ignorance, morally, through wickedness, politically, by being always on the losing side, financially, by being three times ruined—"dead broke"—through no fault of mine, and physically, by suffering, at different times through life, all of Job's afflictions, with small-pox thrown in. I have always thought that the devil was the author of that loathsome, painful, death-dealing disease, and I hold that the old serpent never has done a meaner thing than to originate that detestable plague among men. It came near carrying me across the river, and even that would have been scarcely worse than to spoil my beauty as it did. I have never been considered a beauty since I had the small-pox! One, and only one, of Job's misfortunes I have escaped, and for that I am profoundly thankful to— my wife! I have never had a mean, quarrelsome wife, and, God being my helper, I never will have one. I would not have such a wife for all the temporal good-fortune that crowned Job's latter days. I have had grievous troubles in society from my very youth up. I was too poor, and too ignorant, and too "unpolished," to associate with what the world called the best society, in early life. By the way, the "unpolish," I am told, has not been entirely rubbed off yet! I served my time as a soldier, but there, too, I lost all save honor, and as I never kept much of that on hand at a time, the little I saved is hardly worth the mention. And, worst of all, when I was a soldier, I got most ingloriously thrashed. All that is left to me on that line is my limited stock of honor, my self-respect, and the consciousness that I always did what, at the time, I earnestly and sincerely believed to be my duty.

But my life has not all been storms, clouds, darkness, trials, disappointments, conflicts and troubles. I have had days of brightest sunshine as well as of darkest gloom. I have had prosperity as well as adversity; clear skies as well as lowering clouds; joy and gladness as well as sorrow and sadness; victory as well as defeat. Mine has not been an even, uneventful life, though it has, perhaps, been an unimportant and an unprofitable one to the world.

The cradles in which babies were rocked in those

days, in the circle of life in which I was born, would be
something of a curiosity now. I saw mine many years
after I had ceased to use it. The model cradle of 1816
was simply half of a hollow log, with a bit of clapboard nailed on each end, to keep the youngster from
getting out of the thing and causing trouble. This
simple arrangement was placed on the dirt, or puncheon

" GENTLY ROCKED THE YOUNG HOPEFUL."

floor of a log cabin; the infant, carefully wrapped in
quilts, or in the fur skins of wild animals, was placed in it,
and the mother or nurse, seated near enough, to touch it
with her foot, gently rocked the young hopeful through
sweet dreams of innocent infancy, to the cares and
trials of maturer childhood.

Of all the cradles ever invented, the old time, hollow-log variety, on a puncheon floor, or a dirt floor, unquestionably had the strongest proclivity towards perpetual motion. It almost rocked itself. Once started, it would rock on for hours with only an occasional help by a gentle touch of the maternal foot. A thick cloth pad was fastened on each side of the cradle near the top to prevent the concern from capsizing. I doubt whether inventive genius has made any real improvement, except in looks, upon this rude cradle of my childhood. I know *I* have never been rocked in an easier going concern.

# CHAPTER III.

## BLACK MAMMIES.

Like other children, who were brought up at the South in those early days, by parents who owned slaves, I had a black mammy. In my case, such an arrangement was a necessity, for my mother died at the time of my birth, but a little later in the history of the country, a black mammy was an indispensable piece of furniture in many of the aristocratic households where there were infants to nurse. For the benefit of those who are not informed as to the customs and institutions of the old-time South, it would, perhaps, be well to describe this relic of ages past.

A black mammy was not exactly a nurse. She had the care of all the children of the household, in a certain sense, from earliest infancy till they were somewhat advanced into the maturer years of boyhood and girlhood, but not exactly in the capacity of nurse. She was rather a foster mother. She took charge of each child of her mistress, at birth, and she brought them all up so far as a general supervision was concerned, and in many cases she nursed them at her own breast. She was a motherly, even-tempered, child-loving old soul with an inexhaustible supply of songs, stories, traditions, and superstitions with which to amuse and entertain her young charges. She always lived in a cabin near the family residence, and devoted her time largely to the children. The real mother of the children gave them careful and constant attention and superintended their training in a general way, but she took upon herself very little of the burdens and drudgery of bringing them up.

A nurse was an entirely different thing from a black mammy. The nurse was the children's guardian and companion when they went out for exercise, on visits, or to seek diversion and recreation. A nurse was younger, more tidy in dress, and every way more comely, than a black mammy. The black mammy was the highest authority in the nursery in all matters pertaining to the management of the children. The nurse was subordinate to her, and even the real mother of the children humored her superior claims of authority far enough never to needlessly make an issue with her in the government of the nursery.

The relationship between a child and its black mammy was both intimate and affectionate. Any Southern man would resent an injury to his old black mammy, as a personal insult, as long as he lived. Distinguished men of the old-time South never visited their old homes without tenderly greeting the faithful old slave whom they had known only as mammy, in early childhood. It was no unusual thing for Congressmen and Senators to sit on a rude stool in the old mammy's log cabin, and listen with courteous patience, if not with deep interest to her story of what had "been gwine on since you been lef' de ole place."

The husband of the old mammy was a person of no ordinary importance in the domestic economy of a Southern home. His own children always called him daddy, and everybody else called him uncle. He took upon himself the general management and over-sight of everything about the house, and the entire household depended upon him to keep everything

straight. He superintended the gardening for the master, looked after the carriages and horses, took care
of the ladies' driving harness, attended to the flowers and shrubbery about the mansion, and watched

"NO MORE INTERESTING COUPLE COULD BE FOUND."

over the children about the premises. He always
had a supply of strings, nails, fishing rods, mar-
bles, and tools, to mend broken toys, for the boys. He
delighted to hunt, fish or engage in any kind of sport
with the boys, and was never happier than when he was

working to gratify some whim of the girls, in arranging things about the place. He was always busy, though he was never required to do any regular manual labor. Younger negroes were at his command, to do any work which was committed to him, and he never was expected to do anything more than superintend it. Still, he was industrious by long-established habit, and he was as busy as a hen with one chick, from early dawn till late at night. Everybody about the place loved him devotedly, from the master to the mammy, and he was eminently worthy of their affection. No more interesting couple could be found, in all the South, than an old daddy, ax on shoulder, leaving his cabin for the regular duties of the morning, and his old spouse, pipe in mouth, giving him the accustomed lecture, about matters and things in general, as he trudged away.

My grandfather bought my old black mammy, from a Massachusetts slave-ship, when she was only six years old. She was just from the dark continent then, and not a word of our language could she speak. She was about forty-five years of age, when I was born. If there can be a feeling in the human heart stronger than a mother's love for her first-born, that feeling burned in the deepest depths of her passionate, African heart, for me. Her skin was as black as night, but her heart was as white and as pure as the virgin snow. I don't believe she ever saw the day, from the time I was placed in her swarthy arms, when but a few hours old, to the day of her death, in my eighteenth year, that she would not have laid down her life for me. For her tender care and motherly love, and for the sleepless nights she passed in ministering to the wants and in trying to alleviate the pains of the poor, motherless little waif, I have never ceased to give her the unstinted devotion and adoration of a grateful heart. \

In my later boyhood, after I was old enough to take care of myself, and was taken from her charge, I often went to see her, and spent my Sundays with her. I loved her better than any other person or thing in the whole world. She loved me as devotedly as I loved her, and she always saved, for me, apples, cakes, homemade candy, and such other delicacies as she knew I was fond of, and which she could in anyway obtain. She would never eat such things herself, no matter how much she might hunger for them. She always saved everthing of that kind for me. As long as she lived, my Sunday visits to her lowly and lonely cabin were great feast-days as well as occasions of hearty enjoyment of tender, loving, motherly companionship with my faithful old mammy. She patiently heard the story of my successes and reverses in life, and she was always ready to weep when I told her I had failed, or applaud me with enthusiasm when I could tell her I had succeeded, in any of my undertakings. But the blessed old soul walked entirely by faith touching all my plans and prospects in life. It was a comfort and an inspiration to me to tell her about them, and she always listened to me with the interest of genuine affection, but it was all beyond her comprehension. Her mind was too weak to understand my purposes, no matter how hard I might try to explain them to her, but she had unbounded faith in *me*, and always expressed herself as perfectly confident that everything I attempted would, in the end, come out just as I had ordained that it should. And on that faith she would have acted, if I had assigned her any work to perform in the matter of consummating my purposes, though her action, in fulfilling the work assigned her, had brought her suffering indescribable and even death itself. I have often thought that her faith in me, and her love for me, aptly illustrate the faith we short-sighted mortals should have in God, who lays all the plans of the world's progress, and in his own way accomplishes his wise, but inscrutable purposes.

When my grand-father bought her from the slaveship, he took her away from all the other Africans who were brought over with her. She could not speak a word of English at that time, and until she learned our language she had a lonesome time of it. She soon forgot her native language, except to count ten in it, and this much she taught me when I was a little toddler at her knees. I suppose I am the only living man in the civilized world to-day, who can even count ten in her peculiar dialect.

I love to linger upon the memory of that faithful old slave. Hers was the dusky hand that rocked my baby cradle. Oftimes tears from her loving eyes fell upon my baby face, as she soothed me, and crooned me to sleep in the silent, and to me, suffering hours of night. In my melancholy retrospections, I often think of her now, with tearful eyes and weary heart, and wonder whether she ever comes from her far-off home in the glory land, to watch over her old-time, wayward charge. Does her glorified spirit ever hover about me now, with the old-time tenderness and love, and long to help my weary soul onward and upward to that better land?

While strolling through a Southern forest one balmy evening in early spring, not many years ago, I came upon a lonely, dilapidated negro cabin nestling among the trees. To me, it was a precious souvenir of the sweet long-ago. The full moon, just rising, cast long, wavering shadows over the moss-covered roof, and briars clung about the long-deserted walls. Whippoor-wills chanted their lonely solo in the forest, a mocking-

"WALKING TOWARDS THE CHURCH WITH MY SWEETHEART."

bird warbled his medley from the top of an oak, mag-nolias perfumed the air, and owls hooted dolefully in the distance. To me, the whole scene was full of deso-lation, and, by contrast, reminded me of the blessed days gone by. And there, by that lonely cabin in the woods, I thought long and seriously of my old black mammy, and, amidst such environments, I wept and prayed away some of the sorrows and burdens of my weary heart.

Poor old mammy! The last time I ever saw her, we met one Sunday at church. I had moved to town, as an apprentice, to learn the trade of a blacksmith, but I visited the old home in the country about twice a month. I always met the faithful old soul at church, on these visits, and she never failed to put her black arms around my neck and kiss me in a perfect transport of joyful emotions. The last time I met the dear, faithful, loving old soul, I was walking towards the church door with my sweetheart, when she, unceremoniously, rushed up to me; and in the presence of the young lady, threw her arms around my neck, as usual, and pressed a motherly kiss on both my cheeks.

I then did one of the meanest things of my life—a thing which has caused me feelings of humiliation, shame and heartful regret during all the years of my life since that memorable day. I deeply deplore it, even now, after the lapse of more than half a century, and I would give world's of wealth, if I possessed it, could I but correct that mistake of my boyhood days. My crime was simply base ingratitude. I blushed for shame that I should be thus kissed, by an old negress, in the presence of my young lady friend. I have never yet fully recovered my self-respect, when I think how I blushed to be kissed and loved by one who had so nobly earned her right to a mother's affections and privileges, by all she had done for me during my helpless, infant orphanage. It was mean and contemptible in me. But I will yet atone for it, in a measure, if I am so fortunate as to meet her ransomed soul on the glory-gilded shore of eternity. In that sweet by-and-by, I will walk right up to her, and if her face is as wrinkled and black as it was when last I saw it, I will, nevertheless, throw my arms around

"BY HER GRAVE IN THE WOODS."

her neck and, before God, Christ, the angels and assembled universe, tenderly press a loving, repentant kiss upon her cheeks. I wept bitter tears, when I stood by her humble grave in after years, and thought of all her love and devotion to the helpless waif, and then re-

membered that cowardly blush of shame at her kiss of
love the last time we ever met on the storm-swept shore
of time.

And there, mid the stillness of nature, by her grave
in the woods, I solemnly vowed to cherish her memory,
to strive to imitate her love and labors for the motherless and homeless suffering little ones of this sorrow-
blighted world, and to labor and pray earnestly and
continually, while I live, for the amelioration of the
sufferings of her down-trodden race. {And here, now,
with all the earnestness of a loving, grateful heart,
I deliberatelv record that vow, and seal it with a penitent tear.

Devotion to those old mammies and daddies is one
of the marked traits of Southern character. Throughout the war, and during all the hardships of the country immediately after the war, those faithful old
negroes remained true to their white friends and former
masters, and, in all my travels through the South, I
have never found a case in which they have been cast off
or neglected by their former owners. They have never
ceased to occupy their old-time place in the Southern
families. They still live in the old log cabins near
the country residences, and they take all the interest
of absolute ownership in everything connected with
the old plantation. They feel great pride in the old
family name and reputation, and delight to tell how
" I fotch up dese yer chilluns to be 'spectable an'
hones'." They have a contempt for " all dese yer
smart Ellick niggers w'at growed up sence freedom
come out," and they never tire of drawing contrasts
between " de laz'ness o' dese yer young bucks " and
" de way dem fiel' han's use ter hump deyselves fer
me an' de ole boss 'fo' de war." Those specimens of

the negro race are too old and feeble to labor now, and yet they are bountifully supplied, with all the necessaries and comforts of life, by their white friends. They have very retentive memories, and their descriptions of old times in Dixie are remarkable for fullness of details, and for little incidents, that serve to bring out the history of that period more completely and satisfactorily than even the most painstaking historian could write it.

# CHAPTER IV.

## THE OLD HUNTERS.

There is a remarkably strange and deeply interesting period of Southern history just behind my earliest recollections. In early childhood, I knew well the people who had lived through those earlier days, and from constant association with them I learned so much about the country and the customs of life, with which they were perfectly familiar by life-long experience and observation, that the history of that period seems a veritable part of the story of my own life. I refer now to a time before there were any slaves, of consequence, in all the country where my life has been spent, and before there were even any farms, worthy the name, in that section.

The changes that have taken place in the appearance of the country itself, since those early days, are not less wonderful than the revolutions that have been wrought in the manners and customs of the people. All my childhood, youth and early manhood were spent in constant association and friendly companionship with middle-aged men and women who were contemporaries with the Indians in this country before any homes were built or any farms were cleared. The South of those days differed widely from the South of the present time, even with respect to the very appearance of the face of the country itself. The hills and the valleys, the creeks and the rivers are all here now just as they were here then, of course, but how marvelous are the changes that have taken place in them!

So far as my observations have gone, the South consists of level bottom lands and fertile valleys, bordered by rough mountain regions. In early days, when first the country was vacated by the Indians, it was all timber lands. There were no prairies in the South worthy the name, in comparison with the great prairies of the West. To clear away the heavy forests and put the lands in cultivation, was a huge undertaking. The valleys and bottoms were covered with dense cane-brakes and other growth of small brush-wood, matted together with a perfect network of vines and briers. The impenetrable jungles, in those bottoms and valleys, were infested with wild beasts and ugly vipers. Above all this dense undergrowth towered an unbroken forest of mammoth trees. There were regions of such country, miles in extent, where no ray of the sun had touched the face of the earth for many decades. Across these jungles, wild beasts had beaten a few narrow, zig-zag paths, but beyond those narrow ways it was impossible to penetrate the thickets, even on foot. Leaves and other decaying vegetable matter, many inches thick, covered the whole face of the earth. Streams of water were crooked, sluggish and loathsome. Ragged, rotting drifts choked the channels of the creeks, and seriously interfered with the proper drainage of the country. Such obstructions caused the streams to over-flow their banks and submerge the low grounds contiguous to them, forming disease-breeding swamps, ponds and lagoons.

The uplands and mountain regions were more inviting. The forests were not so dense, and there was no undergrowth to obstruct the view or impede travel. Over these higher, table lands, in the mountain country, one could drive a wagon for miles without any road.

In those uplands, the experienced woodsman, on horse-back or afoot, habitually ignored all roads and took his journey by the nearest route across the open country. The streams of water were brisk, clear and pure. Forest fires annually destroyed the decayed, but thoroughly dried, vegetable matter from the face of the earth. Thus cleansed, and warmed by the rays of sunshine which came down through the slight foliage of the scattering trees, the earth produced an abundance of grass and other vegetable food for deer and other herbivorous wild animals. Innumerable springs of the purest of water burst from the sides of the mountains and went laughing away over beautiful water-falls to the loathsome valley of death below. The mountain air sighed through the tree-tops as pure and sweet as the breath of a maiden; squirrels gamboled in the forest trees; turkeys gobbled and strutted on the mountains; eagles screamed from their lofty perch on towering cliffs; and doves cooed their story of love on every hill and in every dale.

The first settlers of the country occupied the uplands and mountain regions. The bottom lands were considered too low and swampy for human habitation, at that early day, and for years afterwards they were carefully avoided on account of unhealthfulness. But when the necessities of increased white population, and the importation of thousands of slaves, crowded the people down into those bottoms, it was discovered that the lowlands of the South were by far the most valuable part of the country for farming purposes. When the forests and undergrowth were cleared away, and the channels of the streams straightened and freed from obstructions, the whole face of the country was transformed as if by magic. Improved drainage soon converted swamps, ponds and lagoons into cotton, rice and sugar plantations, and the sunshine changed malarial lowlands into healthful settlements.

It required considerable capital and labor to open up a farm in the bottoms then. Such an enterprise, like the building of a railroad at this day, called for men of means and business capacity. Those vast scopes of rich agricultural lands remained in unbroken forests till wealthy slave owners moved upon them with mules, negroes and supplies from older states.

The first settlers of the country, who occupied the mountain region, were not farmers. They were hunters by profession. Their homes were rude log huts, with clapboard roofs, dirt floors and wooden chimneys. Those who assumed aristocratic airs among the early mountaineers floored their cabins with puncheons. One cow, a few articles of wearing apparel and household furniture, a long flint-and-steel rifle, a shabby old pony and a pack of dogs, constituted the in-

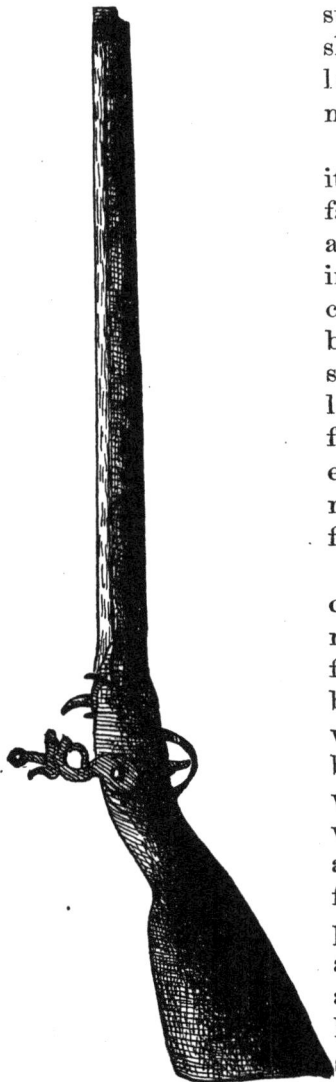

FLINT-AND-STEEL.

ventory of personal property of an average mountaineer.

Comparatively few young people, of this day, have
ever seen a flint-and-steel gun. The one here illustrated was the celebrated rifle of Daniel Boône, which is
now the property of the Tennessee Historical Society.
It may be seen at the rooms of that society in Nashville,
Tennessee. The principal peculiarity of those old-time
guns was the process of igniting the powder and dis-
charging the load. Caps and cartridges were unknown
in those days. The lock of a flint-and-steel gun was
much the same as that of any other gun, except that a
small piece of flint was fastened to the hammer, which
struck against a bit of steel when the hammer fell.
The piece of steel worked on a hinge and was knocked
back when the flint struck it, exposing to the sparks,
struck from the contact of the flint and steel, a small
quantity of powder, called the "priming," in a little
cavity called the "pan," immediately under the bit of
steel. There was a small hole, called the "touch-hole,"
connecting the "pan" with the interior of the gun.
When the sparks ignited the "priming," the "touch-
hole," if everything worked right, carried the "flash" to
the powder within, and so fired off the charge. Pre- •
pared flints for such guns were an article of merchan-
dise in those days, which could be bought in any store.
Occasionally the flint would fail to strike fire, in which
case the remedy was to wet it with the tongue; hence
the saying, "lick your flint and try again." A "flash
in the pan" was a case in which the "touch-hole" failed
to carry the flash to the powder so as to discharge the
load. This frequently occurred on account of the
"touch-hole" being stopped up. If the "priming,"
or the "pan" happened to get wet, it was difficult

to get even a "flash in the pan," and next to impossible
to get a shot fired off. When the powder in the "touch-
hole" got damp, the gun would "hang fire." That is,
after the "flash in the pan," the damp powder in the

"SHE SPUTTERED AN' SPOOTERED."

"touch hole" would burn very slowly, with a great
sputtering and fizzing, like a piece of ordinary fuse,
till the fire reached the dry powder in the charge, when
the load would go off with a bang. This was very annoying, and usually resulted in a wild shot, if nothing

MOUNTED ON HIS OLD PONY.

more serious. It required a man of good nerve and considerable practice to hold a steady aim, at any time, with the "flash in the pan" but a few inches from his face, and when the old gun would "hang fire" in earnest, the best of marksmen would shoot wide of the mark.

An old mountaineer once told me how his old gun hung fire one day when he deliberately aimed at a chicken but a few yards away. He said:

"She sputtered, an' spootered, and sizzled till the chicken got tired waitin' an' went over in the field to hunt June bugs. I had both eyes shet, fur the sparks wuz jest a b'ilin' out'n the tech hole, an' I dasn't take 'er down from my shoulder, 'cause I knowed she'd go off *some* time that day, an' when she *did* go, I knowed she'd git whatever wuz before 'er. So thar I wuz, as blind as a owl, an' a dodgin' the sparks worse'n a blind mule in a yaller jackets nes', an' 'bout that time a old sheep trotted out before the gun, jest as she went off, an' got the whole load right behind the shoulder, an' keeled over deader'n a shad."

In those days there was no need for an old hunter to make anything on the farm, but a little corn for bread. The horse and the cow fared sumptuously, winter and summer, "on the range," and the gun and the dogs, with the help of the man and his pony, were good for an abundance of meat from the woods. Mounted on his old pony, the original mountaineer would go sneaking through the woods with his gun on his shoulder and his dogs at his heels, in search of game, while the faithful wife, with the help of her children, cultivated a few vegetables and a patch of corn, milked the cow and attended to other domestic duties.

When the corn was harvested, there was no such

thing as a grist mill in all the country, to convert it into
meal. At a much later date, settlers in that country
carried corn twenty to thirty miles to mill, on horse-
back. The very earliest settlers prepared corn for the
table by either boiling it into hominy or beating it to
meal, or, rather, to dust, by hand, with a pestle in a
mortar. The mortar was a small basin hollowed out of
a rock. The pestle was a smooth stone something near
the size of the basin in the mortar. A few of those old
mortars may yet be found in possession of the very old
people of the country.

I have been fortunate enough to find one, from which my

" MEAL-MAKING MACHINERY. "

artist drew the picture here presented. It is simply a
large, rough rock with a cavity, or basin, hollowed out
in it, large enough to hold about a gallon of shelled
corn. Imagine a man seated on the ground, the mortar
between his knees and the pestle in his hand, and you
have in mind a clear picture of the meal-making
machinery of this country less than a century ago. It
was a slow process, of course, but there was no demand
for any great hurry in the business then. No body
seemed to have any ambition to get rich, and there was
nothing for a man to do but pound meal and hunt deer.

The meal which they made on those old machines was not equal to the best grade of patent flour made in this day, as an article of diet, but it answered all the purposes of fashionable bread-stuff with our fore-fathers.

When there was a scarcity of corn, and the grinding in the mill, or rather the pounding in the mortar, became low, the dry meat from the breast of wild turkeys, and venison hams thoroughly dried, made pretty fair substitutes for bread. I knew old people in my boyhood who had used such substitutes for bread weeks at a time, and yet they told me that life was more enjoyable then than it is now, with all our patent flour and improved cooking. In traveling through the mountains of the South several years ago, I found several specimens of old mountaineers and first settlers of the country. They still lived in the simple style of the good times of old, and it was always their delight to talk about the country and its inhabitants as they knew them in the day when old hunters flourished in the land. From such specimens of old times as those I discovered in the mountains, the imagnation, aided by their descriptions of men and things in olden times, can easily picture life among the mountains in Dixie before the days of slavery and wealth.

There were no post-offices, no mails, no schools, no newspapers and no stores in that country in those days. Such things existed, to some extent, in more populous regions forty or fifty miles away, but what did they care for such little conveniences of civilization fifty miles away, when perhaps a fine deer might be found just over the hill not forty rods off. Those mountains contained mineral wealth inestimable, then, as they do now, of course, but what did those old hunters care for a coal field or an ore bank worth a few millions of dollars, when they were liable to get a good shot at a fine turkey any moment.

One of the old settlers was particularly interesting to me. He lived in a little log cabin at the foot of a great mountain. He settled there soon after the Indians left the country. All the land about his cabin, that could be cultivated, was in cotton fields when I was there, but he remembered exactly where the old ziz-zag path ran, that was beaten out by deer and other wild animals in passing from the mountains to the cane-brakes in the bottoms, while the country was yet in the woods. He showed me where he sat under a tree in his yard one evening many years ago, and counted twenty-eight deer leisurely walking, single file, along the path from the bottoms to the mountains. He showed me the exact spot where the wolves caught a calf several months old about three o'clock one afternoon, many years ago. The place was in the middle of a cotton field when I was there.

He told me he once heard Andrew Johnson make a political speech to a great crowd at a barbecue in Tennessee. Mr. Johnson was, himself, one of the old settlers, and knew exactly how to touch the tender spot in the hearts of the old mountaineers. The current of public sentiment was decidedly against him at the barbecue, but he took his chances on creating a reaction in his favor among the old settlers. "Fellow citizens, the first time I ever saw this country, I cut my way through the cane-brake with a large hunting-knife near the spot on which I now stand." Such was the eminent statesman's opening sentence. That went straight to the hearts of the old settlers, and completely turned popular feeling in Mr. Johnson's favor for that day. The old hunters gave a yell of approval which wakened the echoes for half a mile around. The opposition weakened perceptibly at this unexpected demonstration, and Mr. Johnson made one of his great speeches, which swept everything before him. When that old mountaineer told me about it years afterwards, he could remember nothing of the great speech but the sentence I have quoted, but he grew enthusiastic in praise of "Old Andy," and showed his readiness to vote for him or die with him, if need be, in furthering any measure that might have been coupled on to that little initiative sentence of his speech. The fact that Andrew Johnson cut his way through a cane-brake with a hunting-knife did not demonstrate to my mind that his platform in that canvass was favorable to the best interests of the country, but I did not express myself on that point to my old friend, the mountaineer. It was interesting, to me, to hear an old settler enthusiastically describe "Old Andy's" speech one moment, and the next instant tell, with equal enthusiasm, how he had killed scores of deer on the very spot where Birmingham, Alabama is now built, before anybody lived in miles of that place.

One of the leading characteristics of those old settlers is their preference for old times. They are not highly educated, they take no interest in books, they rarely receive a letter, and never read a paper. In style of dress and habits of life they adhere closely to the old ways. They are men of vigorous constitutions, robust health, erect forms and sprightly movements. Though well along in the seventies, they enjoy perfect health, and look as young as more modern men at fifty. One of them, in his eighty-second year, mounted an old horse and rode forty miles across as rough a mountain country as I ever navigated on horse-back, and at the end of the trip seemed as sprightly as a school boy.

"NO USE FUR THE INFERNAL TOWN."

Speaking of old times, one of the old mountaineers said:

"I wuz offered a hundred and sixty acres of land once right whar the town of Iuka, Mississippi, now stands, fur a old one-eyed hoss I had that wuz wo'th about thirty dollars them days."

I asked him if he had not always regretted that he did not make that trade. He said:

"Well, I don't know's I've got any use fur the infernal town with all 'f its highfalootin' ways, an' I tell you what, that thar hoss was a spang up nag fur a still hunt them times."

I tried to reason with him. I told him that the whole town would be a magnificent property for one man to own, and that if he only possessed it, he would be one of the richest men in all the country. But it was no use. He merely said:

"Well, that's all owein' to a man's taste. I tell you what *my* feelin's is about sich things. If *you* had sich a hoss now as that wuz, an' this country had the game in it what it had them days, an' *I* owned that whole everlastin' town with all 'f its fine clothes an' Sunday fixin's, you'd git a even swap out'n me mighty quick 'f I couldn' git it off'n my han's fur any better price. That's *me*, right up one side and down t'other."

Those old hunters often clothed themselves in garments made from the skins of wild beasts, even in my own recollection, long after other people began to wear humespun Sunday clothes. Their fashionable suits consisted of coon-skin cap, panther-skin vest, buck-skin breeches and raw-hide moccasins. Those old men were not noted for cleanliness of person or neatness of toilet. They never dreamed of such things as comb and brush for the hair, or razor for the beard. Some of them may have taken a bath secretly now and then, but I have not

5

been able to find a well authenticated case of such a departure from uniform custom.

They had their preachers and their religion, and, though their theology was decidedly crude, their worship was commendable for its earnestness. They usually had a sort of church conference on Saturday, to transact church business. On such occasions they held a kind of church court for the trial of all who stood accused of violations of church usages. An eye to business and a hope of immortal glory, in about equal proportions, seem to have constituted the motive of the average hunter in attending the Saturday meetings of the church. Every hunter would take his gun and his hounds with him to meeting, with the hope of making up for any lack of spirituality in the worship by securing a nice venison, for Sunday, on the trip. In that sparsely settled country, an average congregation would consist of, say, fifteen families. The country was healthful and the people were prolific, hence an average household would consist of probably seven persons, two of whom would be infants, and a third, too young to keep quiet during the services. It would be a rather low average to say there were five dogs to the family. From this it will be seen that a congregation of fifteen families would contain forty-five babies and seventy-five dogs, with only sixty adults to police the mob.

The preaching was a kind of sing-song exhortation, made up principally of death-bed stories and blood-curdling descriptions of a decidedly literal hell. Very few of the old hunters had either Bibles or hymn books, and not many of the preachers could read. Preachers claimed to be called of God to the ministry, and any effort to prepare a sermon was, with them, a species of infidelity, in that it showed lack of reliance upon God, and undue confidence in human wisdom. Such were the old hunters—a generation of people who preceded the first agricultural inhabitants of the country. Their occupation was to take the world easy and enjoy life, but the main purpose of their successors was to build houses and open the country for actual cultivation.

# CHAPTER V.

## HOW THINGS HAVE CHANGED.

The revolutions that have taken place in all parts of the South, during the memory of people yet living, can be best understood, perhaps, in the light of the changes in some particular and well-known locality.

I can remember when hunters killed deer in sight of the hill on which the capitol of the State of Tennessee now stands. All the lowlands around the city of Nashville, Tennessee, including much of the territory now inside the corporate limits of the city, were covered with dense cane-brakes, and the lands contiguous to the river below Nashville, where now are some of the finest farms in the South, were considered too low and swampy for cultivation. Such land could have been bought for a few cents an acre.

Nashville was scarcely more than a boat landing on the west bank of the Cumberland river. There was not a house east of the river, and the whole territory now occupied by East Nashville, down to the very bank of the river, sold for fifty cents an acre. In those days capitol hill was out in the country near Nashville, and all the territory South of Broad Street was either in cultivation or covered with native forests and dense thickets. The present site of the Maxwell House was in the woods, and untutored, if not untamed, Indians were plentifully scattered over all parts of the country.

There is a man living in Nashville, Tennessee, at this

writing, who claims the distinguished honor of having
been scalped by the wild Indians, when he was an infant.   I have investigated this case of hair-breadth
escape from Indian massacre as well as I could, and,
while I am not willing to vouch for the truthfulness of
the tradition, I have not a doubt but that the man himself firmly believes it.   Though he was present himself
when the scalping was done, according to every version

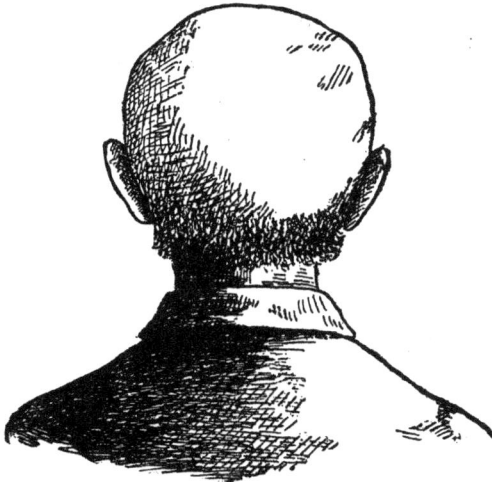

"ONE OF THE OLDEST LANDMARKS."

of the story I have heard, the scalping itself is but a
tradition with him, as well as with the rest of us.   He
was but a few months old when he passed that crisis in
his eventful career, and, of course, he remembers none
of the particulars of the case.   Even if the tradition is
true in every detail, the wound healed long before he
can remember.   So the strongest case he can make out
in favor of the scalping theory must forever rest, main-

ly, upon hear-say testimony, corroborated by his glisten-
ing bald head.

There is no denying the fact that the whole top of
his head is as hairless as an egg, but even that does not
fully substantiate, to my entire satisfaction, the tradition
that he was scalped when an infant. There are probably ten thousand other men, now living in Nashville,
whose heads are as bald as his, but all those shining
pates are not monuments of indian cruelty. Still, there
is something peculiar about this particular bald head,
above all others in Nashville, and that is the fact that
many people, not overly credulous, consider it one of
the oldest landmarks, of its kind, in the whole country.
This is as much as I feel authorized to say in favor of
the truthfulness of the tradition that Nashville yet
has one citizen who has been scalped by wild Indians.

The story of this scalping, as it has been given to
me, is, that the Indians murdered the entire family, save
one little girl, probably too small to walk, and an infant
boy at its mother's breast. As the two children were
unable to walk, they were not murdered, but were left,
presumably to die from cold and starvation. The living
and the dead were all scalped alike. The two children
were found, by some hunters, in time to save the life of
the infant boy, but his baby sister was too far gone to
revive, and she soon died.

While there is, in my mind, some doubt as to the
truthfulness of this strange story, I am frank to confess
that, if the Indians didn't scalp this old man when he
was an infant, it was their own fault. There were wild
Indians here in great multitudes when he was born, and
they undoubtedly did scalp many people about that

time. As he was an infant at his mother's breast, according to his own statement of the case, they couldn't have found an easier job in the scalping business than to have raised his hair, and from the pride he takes in the vague tradition concerning the matter, I am sure they would have won his eternal gratitude and placed him under lasting obligations by making him an example of their fiendish art. But the mere fact that there were Indians here when he was an infant is abundantly sufficient for all the purposes of this book, as showing the marvelous changes that have taken place in this country since our oldest citizens were born, whether we accept the tradition that this particular old man was scalped when he was an infant or not, and this fact can be substantiated by many infallible proofs.

At the foot of a great mountain which borders one of the most beautiful and most fertile valleys in the South, an old settler identified a spot, not many years ago, as I was traveling with him over the country, which suggested to him a story in which I was deeply interested. He said:

"When I fust come to this yer country, I was a drivin' of a wagon loaded with meat, an' my team gin out right here one evenin', an' I had to strike camp. Thar wuz n't a livin' bein' in ten mile o' this place then, an' you couldn't a stuck a butcher knife to the handle in the cane-brake that covered the whole face o' the yeath. I br'iled some meat fur supper, an' 'bout the time I got ready to go to sleep the wolves got a scent o' that br'iled bacon, an' let loose a howl that wuz awful enough to wake the dead. At fust, thar didn't seem to be more'n a dozen of 'em, but it wuz n't long before the woods wuz alive with 'em. They come a howlin' frum the four quarters o' the whole keration, an' sich another

fuss as they made no man ever hearn before.  If thar
wuz one wolf in that gang, thar wuz a million.  Did
you ever hear wolves a howlin'?  Well, sir, it is the
awfullest, scarin'est thing a man ever hearn.  Thar I

"A ROARIN' FIRE."

wuz in the middle o'the woods, with a million o' hungry
wolves a howlin' aroun' me, an' not a blessed thing to
fight 'em with, and not a livin' bein' in ten mile o' me,
to help me fight 'em.  The night wuz as  dark  as

a pile o' black cats in a dungeon, an' the wolves made
sich a fuss I could n't hear my own pra'rs. I wus jist
from the old settlements then, an' did n't know that
wolves wuz all fuss an' no fight. Thar aint no more
danger in a wolf than a lamb, onless it is awfully
crowded with hunger, or pushed into a corner whar it
can't run. But I did n't know that then. It wuz the
fust time I'd ever had any dealin's with the sneakin'
things.

"I cut an' carried logs an' piled on the wagon, to
cover up the meat from wild varmints, before night, as
I did every evenin' when I camped, so I knowed the
meat wuz safe. But I tell you what, I thought my
time 'ad come. I wuz determined to have a good light
to die by, so I piled on bresh, an' made a roarin' fire. I
soon found out that a wolf is powerful skittish about a
light, so I piled more bresh on the fire, an' kep' 'er a
boomin' all night. Them wolves would come so close
to me that I could see the'r eyes a shinin' an' hear
the'r teeth a snappin', an' I looked fur 'em to make a
bulge fur me an' scoop me in every minute, but they
did n't. But if that wuz n't the longest night I ever got
through you may shoot me. Them wolves kep' a howlin' an' I kep' the fire a boomin' the whole blessed night,
an' not a wink o' sleep did *any* of us git *that* night."

It may add something to the credibility of this remarkable wolf story to say I have been intimately ac-
quainted with the chief actor in it from my childhood
up. I have always considered him a man of more than
average veracity. He is still living, though somewhat
advanced in years, and all the old people, who knew the
general condition of the country at the time he avers
that the wolves made the attack upon him, by night, in
the woods, think there is nothing improbable in the

main facts of his story. As for myself, I have always discounted the story as to the number of wolves he heard that night. This, however, is only an opinion of his, drawn, evidently, by an excited imagination, and it does not at all affect his credibility as to the main fact that there were wolves there in great abundance. Indeed it is a circumstance which goes far to strengthen his testimony as to the presence of the wolves. It shows that his imagination was in a peculiar state of perturbation which nothing but the howling of a gang of hungry wolves, under just such circumstances, could have produced.

I am no stranger, myself, to the effect which the howling of wolves in a· dense forest at night will produce upon the whole nervous system of a lonely, belated traveler. I have heard such things under similar circumstances myself. The man who, under such circumstances, can be induced to place his estimate of the number of wolves engaged in such a serenade at anything less than a million, is not listening to such music for the first time in his life, certain.

It occurs to me that my friend, the old settler, used a pretty vigorous metaphor as to the density of the canebrake "which covered the whole face o' the yeath" at that time and place, but I give it as my opinion, based upon a personal knowledge of several parts of "the face o' the yeath" in this country about that time, that the expression is allowable under a liberal construction of the laws governing figures of speech. The whole country was then, compared with its present condition, uninhabited, covered by cane-brakes and unbroken forests, and infested with wolves, panthers, bears, deer and other wild animals.

I can remember well when the Indians were removed

by treaty, from a large district of country west of Huntsville, Alabama, to the Indian Territory. No effort had been made to open farms or build homes in all that region of country up to the time the Indians were removed. Immediately after the departure of the Indians, however, the country was opened for settlement, and when the white people began to pour into it, they found it full of all manner of wild beasts. Wolves and panthers were so numerous that they were considered a barrier to the settlement of the country, and to rid the land of them the State paid a bounty for wolf scalps and panther scalps for the first few years after the Indians were removed. By the law of the State, any man was allowed three dollars for each wolf scalp he would take, to be paid out of the State's funds. Wolf hunting was a lucrative industry in this country in those days, with those who understood the business. But notwithstanding the wolves were very numerous and very annoying, they were remarkably shy and hard to catch. They would commit terrible havoc among sheep, hogs and young calves, and howl defiantly at your very door, by night, but they would not show themselves by day.

The old hunters invented many different plans to catch them in traps, and occasionally they would get a good shot at them in daylight, but an inexperienced hunter almost invariably made a complete failure in a wolf hunt.

Any of the old settlers in this country will tell you that the wolves howled and the panthers screamed around their lonely cabins in the woods every night. Sheep had to be put in houses, or in pens surrounded by high picket fences, every night, hard by their owners' cabins, to save them from the wolves, and many settlers kept young calves under their cabin floors at night, to protect them from wolves and panthers.

Young people these days have no idea what hardships their forefathers endured in the early settlement of this country.

One of my most intimate acquaintances and confidentials friends settled in the mountains of North Alabama, west of Huntsville, soon after the Indians were removed from that country. He was a poor man, and he had to seek employment, in order to support his wife and two infant children, till he could get his land cleared. Wealthy slave owners were then opening farms in the rich valley of the Tennessee river, and to them he was compelled to go for employment. There was no one nearer than that who would pay him wages for work. It was twenty miles from his little log cabin in the mountains to the place in the river bottoms where he was engaged to split rails, for fifty cents a hundred, and board himself. He camped in the woods and did his own cooking from Monday morning till Saturday night. His regular task was to fell the trees and split fifteen hundred rails a week. When it is remembered that farmers in the same country now pay from seventy-five cents to a dollar a hundred for splitting rails, and that the best rail splitters will not make over nine hundred rails a week, the difference between "*now*" and "*then*," will be readily understood.

This poor man would chop fire wood around his cabin in the mountains all day Sunday, carry it on his shoulder and stack it by his cabin door, for his wife and children to burn during the week, eat supper at his humble home Sunday night, and walk twenty miles through the woods to his camp in the river bottoms. By daylight Monday morning he would be at work in the bottoms, and till late Saturday night he would work unceasingly from early dawn till late at night, do his own cooking in his camp, and sleep by a fire in the woods. And all that time his wife and two little children were in that lonely cabin in the mountains, twenty miles away, with but a few neighbors nearer than three miles. The wife worked as hard as the husband, with cards, wheel and loom, making clothing for her little family. Every night wolves would howl and panthers scream around her cabin in the woods, and often she would not see a soul in human shape, except her own helpless children, for several days at a time. After supper at his camp in the river bottoms Saturday night, the husband would walk twenty miles to his home in the mountains, to spend Sunday with his family, occupying the day mainly in chopping and carrying wood to last them another week.

This aged man and his faithful wife are still living, and their younger child, of those days, is now a middle-aged man, and one of the leading business men of the new South. Their labors and hardships, in those days are not over-drawn, nor was theirs an exceptional case. What they suffered and accomplished may be taken as a fair sample of what prevailed all over this country during the first half of this century.

The country was infested with raccoons, minks, foxes and other vermin for many years after the wolves, panthers and other wild animals of larger size were exterminated. Those pestiferous little wild creatures subsisted largely upon poultry and certain kinds of vegetables, and their frequent depredations were a great drain upon the scant resources of the country.

Raccoons were particularly fond of green corn, and where they were very numerous they would destroy vast quantities of it, in a few nights, when it was in the stage known in agricultural parlance as *roasting ear.* The 'coon would climb the corn, break down the stalk and eat the ear. In many cases a 'coon would eat but a few bites of an ear after the stalk was broken down, but the breaking of the stalk and the biting of the ear, at that stage, completely ruined the corn. Hence, a single 'coon would destroy several bushels of corn in a very few nights. And in the early settlement of the country, a little patch of but a few acres of corn, surrounded by a heavy forest and a dense thicket in the bottoms, would often be visited by scores of 'coons every night. Such dire destruction of corn soon brought grave disaster upon the 'coons. It at once marked that obnoxious little wild animal as the open enemy of the human race, and the entire country straightway began to wage a relentless war of extermination against the whole raccoon tribe. Good "'coon dogs" soon came to be highly esteemed in every family, and the regulation "'coon hunt" occupied the time of all the male inhabitants of the country the better part of the first half of every night. And in cases of great emergency the 'coons were given another round by dogs and hunters a couple of hours just before day-light in the morning. While men and boys followed dogs through fields and forests on a "'coon hunt," women and girls applied themselves diligently to work every night with cards, wheels and looms, till a late hour, and every member of the family was out of bed and at the post of duty—men and boys after 'coons and women and girls at the wheels—full two hours before day-light in the morning.

The commerce of the country, in those days, was largely a barter business between fur dealers and 'coon hunters. 'Coon skins were valuable for their fur, and hunters could readily exchange them for powder, lead, flints and such other articles as they needed in their humble homes, and could get from fur dealers. Thus a pest of the country was converted into a blessing for the people.

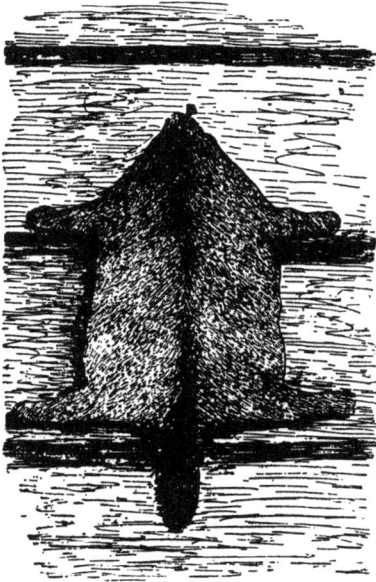

"FRACTIONAL CURRENCY."

It now seems doubtful whether the country could have been developed without those little animals which at one time were universally regarded as an unmitigated evil and blighting curse in the land. This has often been the case in the progress of the world under the guidance of Almighty God. "Every bitter has its sweet." There are roses among the thorns. "Every creature of God is good, and nothing to be refused, if it be received with thanksgiving." But wherein did the despised 'coons prove to be a blessing to the people? After all, the blessing was not in the nature and habits of the *'coon*, so much as in the value of its *hide*, but who can say that the hide would have been so valuable if the 'coon had been less obnoxious in its habits?

The commercial value of 'coon skins was the basis of the whole financial system of the country in those early days. There was no money of consequence here at that time. 'Coon skins constituted the fractional currency in many places. By common consent and tacit agreement, if not by legislative enactment, they were recognized as a legal tender in certain sections of the country. The value of everything was determined by the number of 'coon skins it was worth. Marriage license were paid for in 'coon skins, preachers and public officers were remunerated for their services in the same currency, and drinks were exchanged for them in public saloons at regulation rates. Every man who had anything to sell promptly stated how many 'coon skins he asked for it, and each family counted their 'coon skins with as much pride of wealth as a miser counts his bank bills. To say a man had the 'coon skins was equivalent to saying he had the cash, and it was as common to estimate a man's wealth in 'coon skins then as in dollars now.

The method of preparing such skins for market or for use as a circulating medium, was very simple. As soon as the skin was taken from the animal it was stretched tight and tacked to the walls of a log cabin, to dry. It remained in that position till thoroughly dry, when it was ready for market or for use as fractional currency. When well stretched, a skin would dry thoroughly, in favorable weather, in a very few days. They were always tacked to the log walls on the outside of cabins and above the reach of dogs. If left within the reach of dogs, they were liable to be pulled down and devoured by a hungry cur.

The walls of almost every cabin in the country were well

"I'VE GOT THE 'COON SKINS."

nigh covered with 'coon skins tacked up to dry and awaiting to be used. The greater the number of 'coon skins on the cabin walls, the richer the man who lived in the house. When the family wished to purchase anything, the recognized purse-bearer of the household would walk out and pull down the necessary number of 'coon skins to pay the bill.

6

An old story is told of a young couple who went to the county seat to get married, which aptly illustrates the customs of the country in those days, whether the story itself be regarded as fact or fiction. Dressed in their best apparel, the blushing pair stalked into the clerk's office and called for "marryin' papers." The law required every applicant for marriage license to file a bond, with approved security, for the execution and return of the license, for record, before the clerk was allowed to issue such papers. Under the law, therefore, the clerk was compelled to ask the prospective benedict who would go on his bond for the license. The young man, not understanding the law, considered this a reflection upon his credit, and promptly responded with considerable emphasis and earnestness:

"Bon's be hanged! I don't ask no man to go into any bon's fur my license. I do n't want to marry on a credit nohow. I've got the 'coon skins to lam right down fur the license as soon as you git 'em writ out."

# CHAPTER VI.

Some of the commonest articles of food, of my boyhood days, would be a great curiosity to the young people of this fastidious age. I often sigh for a taste of the old-fashioned Johnny-cake, which was the joy of my heart in early childhood. I have not seen one of those now historic cakes for more than fifty years. The process of making them was very simple, and the machinery necessary to their manufacture, exceedingly crude and inexpensive. The essentials of Johnny-cake making were a bit of clapboard, dressed to a smooth surface with ax or drawing-knife, a quantity of soft corn-meal dough, a hot fire and a skillful woman to manipulate the ingredients. It would be easy enough to find all those things now, save the woman. Modern progress has carried us far beyond this simple and wholesome diet of our forefathers, and woman's sphere has been raised far above the level of Johnny-cake baking. The manufacture of such bread has long been a lost art.

The process was simply to put the soft dough on the Johnny-cake board and stand it before the hot fire, supported by a chair, at an angle of about forty-five degrees, till the heat of the fire baked the cake thoroughly done and crusty brown. I have a distinct and pleasing recollection that the woman always spread the soft dough upon the board with her bare hands, leaving deep prints of her delicate fingers upon the cake as she patted it down and spread it out to the proper thickness. It required no very vivid imagination to see something really ornamental in such finger prints on the brown crust of a well-baked Johnny-cake, especially when the fair cook was known to be the belle of the neighborhood and the idol of your heart.

The origin of Johnny-cakes is not known. Probably the early white settlers in this country learned the art of making them from the Indians. There is a theory that the Indians of olden times were accustomed to bake a quantity of such cakes, when preparing to make a long journey, to eat along the way. It is thought by some that they were, therefore, called journey cakes at first—that is, cakes to take on a journey. This name, it is supposed by those who accept this theory, was, in course of time, corrupted into Johnny-cakes.

I do not claim to be an authority upon the origin of Johnny-cakes, but with becoming modesty I do assert that I thoroughly understand the process of making them. I feel half inclined, at times, to convert my pulpit into a kitchen, and feed the flock on Johnny-cakes instead of theology. I would doubtless increase my congregations and advance my salary by the change, for the world runs wild over anything new in the pulpit these days, and churches encourage, flatter and liberally support everything that creates a sensation and draws a crowd. When Christians exchange the grace of giving for frolics and festivals, why may not preachers use Johnny-cakes in lieu of the gospel?

Speaking of Johnny-cakes reminds me of a bit of Southern history and legislation which richly deserves a place in these reminiscences.

In years gone by, there lived, near the present site of Columbia, Tennessee, one John, whose surname was

Cake. By a not uncommon turn in the current of human events, this Mr. John Cake, who, for short, was called Johnny Cake, fell desperately in love with a young lady whose Christian name was Pattie. He courted her and was promptly rejected on the ground that his name, which was already a joke and a by-word wherever he was known, would be, more than ever, the theme of wags and the humiliation of generations yet unborn, if she should consent to exchange her own maiden name for it. That she loved him devotedly she neither denied nor attempted to conceal, but she positively would not consent to go waltzing down the ages with him, bound together by the indissoluble ties of matrimony, to be jeered and ridiculed by cheap wags and vulgar. wits. Who that had any appreciation at all of the ridiculous, she argued, could fail to see a side-splitting joke in the connubial union of Johnny Cake and Pattie Cake? It was not his fault that his name was Johnny Cake, she freely admitted, nor was she to be blamed for the ill-luck which led her parents to name her Pattie, but she and her lover were both to be pitied, she contended, as the helpless victims of grave misfortune, and hopeless sufferers under a dispensation of unkind providence, which had forever separated two hearts that beat as one, by giving them names which could not be united without making them living examples of a burlesque of fate. The man was importunate, the woman obstinate. The situation became serious. Misfortune begat sympathy. John Cake's name ceased to be a neighborhood joke, and began to be considered a personal calamity. The lovers pined, wags looked serious and the whole community gravely discussed the situation. A petition to the legislature to change Cake's name was finally written by some practical sympathizer and signed by the whole community. The next legislature changed the name, the couple married and "lived happily together ever afterwards" as Mr. and Mrs. J. C. Mitchell.

Ash cakes were also in general use when I was a boy. To me, they were not as palatable as Johnny-cakes, but older people considered them far more healthful. Children were often required to eat them on sanitary principles. Ash cakes were made by putting soft corn-meal dough, pressed into thin cakes between the hands, into the hot ashes under the log fire on the hearth, to be baked. A considerable quantity of ashes, with some small coals, and a reasonable amount of other dirt and trash, always adhered to the cakes. All such foreign matter had to be eaten with the cakes, of course. It was supposed to be beneficial to the health of children, to eat all the dirt, ashes and charcoal that stuck to the cakes. I am now of the opinion that the ash cake cannot be successfully defended on sanitary principles, but the argument in its favor, based on *economy*, is simply invulnerable. Ashes and dirt may not be as healthful as plain corn bread, but they are certainly cheaper. And after all, the important question with me in early boyhood was not to improve my digestion, but to get something to digest. My digestive apparatus was always up with its work and clamoring for something to do. Corn cakes, dirt, ashes and charcoals, all eaten together for supper, would be digested during the night without causing even a dream, so sound would be my slumber. But, really, to speak the truth in soberness, ash cakes were not at all ill-flavored, after one became accustomed to eating them.

Another kind of bread which I very highly appreciated in those days, was a kind of corn light bread. It was made of corn-meal, somewhat on the same general plan we now make light yeast bread out of flour.

We had no cooking stoves in those days. Indeed, we were not overly well supplied with cooking vessels and utensils of any kind. It was doubtless the lack of such things, in the main, which gave the ash cake and the Johnny-cake such wide-spread popularity. A skillet for frying, an oven for baking and a pot for boiling, constituted the outfit of cooking vessels in the best equipped homes.

Corn light bread was always baked in the big flat oven, over a few live coals, on the hearth, before a log fire. Good coals for baking were the joy of every woman's heart, and every boy knew exactly what kind of oak bark made the best quality of such coals. The thick, heavy bark of an aged black oak ranked high as raw material for the manufacture of baking coals. The bark on rails made from such trees would be thoroughly dry, well seasoned, and easy to remove in a few months after the rails were made. The rails were ten feet long, and the bark could be pulled from them with all ease, by hand, in strips from three to five inches wide and full ten feet in length.

To gather bark from rails along the fences around the fields, for cooking purposes, was the daily employment of every boy who was too small to do regular manual labor on the farm. Boys of that age wore neither shoes nor hat. A single garment and a slouch sun-bonnet constituted the wardrobe of such masculine juveniles. The garment was a long, loose dress, made of heavy, home-spun cloth and cut with a very decided *feminine bias*. Thus clad, the fragile bark-gatherer had no protection for his feet against thorns, briers, bull-nettles and sharp rocks, and when he was so unfortunate as to disturb a colony of bumble bees or yellow jackets—a not infrequent piece of ill-luck—the wide spreading skirts of his only garment served only to hive the infuriated insects around his bare body, as they madly rose from their nest in the ground beneath his feet.

Lizards, scorpions and black snakes always seemed most numerous along the fences where bark of the best quality was most abundant, and though perfectly harmless within themselves, they excited terrors indescribable in the breast of every defenseless bark-gatherer.

A lizard would not bite, but it had sharp claws, a rough skin and an ugly look. It delighted to sun itself on the top rail of a fence, in hot weather, and it sought protection from cold and rain under the loose bark of the rails nearer the ground. It perhaps had no feeling of either friendship or enmity towards the boy who so frequently disturbed its repose in quest of bark for an impatient mother, but it was a great coward, and when once thoroughly stampeded it completely lost its wits. In sheer fright it would often dash headlong under its tormentors skirts without a thought as to the impropriety or danger of such a course. The boy who could suffer a sharp-clawed, scaly-skinned lizard to climb his bare anatomy and not go almost into spasms from fright, was blessed with steadier nerves than I ever possessed. In my experience, such escapades always resulted in a thoroughly frightened boy, a squashed lizard and a rent garment. In my fright I would convulsively seize the lizard, with a death grip, through the folds of my garment, throw my bark in every direction and run across the field, screaming as though a thousand demons were at my heels. When completely exhausted from running and fright, I would release my hold upon the lizard, which would fall to the ground dead, and mashed to a pulp, by my convulsive and long-sustained grip. My bonnet would be lost, my dress torn, and all my feelings of manly courage completely evaporated.

At our house, corn light bread was always baked in large quantities on Saturday, to keep from ".breaking the Sabbath," as it was termed, by baking bread on Sunday. This was a common custom, especially in all Presbyterian families. Hence, that particular variety of the staff of life was frequently called Presbyterian bread, and to this day I can distinctly taste that old fashioned bread whenever I read or hear a straight old Presbyterian doctrinal sermon. True, those old pones were not as short as the Shorter Catechism, as long as the longer, as hard as predestination or as tough as original sin, but, according to my thinking, infinitely better than all of them combined.

"TOWER OF STRENGTH."

I did not know then, nor do I understand yet, how the baking of a little bread could possibly damage "the Sabbath," but the old Presbyterian women of that time had very decided convictions of their own on that point, and religious convictions, with those old-time women, meant something more than a mere formal display of light-hearted, routine worship on Sunday. Their convictions controlled their conduct and governed their families. One such woman, with her religious dignity and unyielding powers of discipline, would do more to incorporate the doctrines of her creed in the daily deportment of an entire neighborhood, than a whole denomination of flippant worshipers and vague, liberal, worldly-minded and speculative preachers these days. Theoretically, the church creeds of that day were probably not as perfect as the religious doctrine of these progressive times, but somehow, church members seem to have measured out better in their practices, according to their creeds, then than now. Every old woman in the land was a great tower of doctrinal strength in those days.

We never had any kind of warm bread at our house on Sunday till my sisters were large enough to have beaux. One Sunday, when their beaux came home with them from meeting, they fried some batter cakes, against my step-mother's solemn protest, and all that evening and the next day the dear old woman's face was as long as a moral law and as blue as her Presbyterian theology.

Women all did their own cooking and house work in those days. They even spun the thread, wove the cloth and made all the clothing for their families, with their own hands. And in fact it was no unusual thing for them to assist the men in the clearing, or do a few hours work every day in the crop, in cases of special emergency. Every family was supplied with cards, wheels and a loom. There was no such thing as manufactured cloth of any kind for sale in stores in a country so new, and a sewing machine would have been re-

garded as a miracle of the first magnitude. The hum
of spinning wheels and the clatter of cards made music
in every home from early dawn till nine or ten o'clock
at night.

" CARDING."

Every girl in the country had a public record as to the
number of " cuts " she could card and spin in a day, and a
girl's position in society, and popularity with young
men, depended materially upon her reputation for

neatness and industry in general household duties.

There was not even a cotton gin in existence. We had to pick the seed out of the cotton with our fingers.

After the seeds were picked from the cotton, it took an expert carder and spinner a whole day to make thread enough for the warp of a yard of cloth, and another day to spin the woof. When the carding and spinning were done, .the thread had to be "dyed," " sized," " warped," " beamed," " harnessed," " sleyed," (pronounced slade) and "woven." These words may, or may not, be found in the dictionary. I have not taken the pains to look them all up. But they were all in common use in every family in this country fifty years ago, and each had a specific, technical meaning which represented a part of woman's work in making cloth.

It required at least three days hard work under that regime to make a yard of cloth, than which a much better quality of goods can now be bought for six to ten cents a yard.

In carding, a woman sat in a straight-backed, home-made, low chair, without cushion, arms or rockers. It is difficult to imagine a more uncomfortable seat. She held a card in each hand, and by raking them together in a series of quick jerks, she thoroughly cleansed the cotton of all motes and then made it into rolls as large as a man's thumb and as long as the cards. These rolls were carefully placed in a heap on the floor beside her, one by one, as fast as they were made, till a sufficient number of them were carded to spin a " cut." The rolls were counted as they were made, and every woman knew exactly how many it took to make a "cut" of thread. When the requisite number of rolls were made, the woman would lay aside her cards and take the wheel to spin them. This gave her a change of position and work, which was really a relief and a rest. It may be well to explain here that a "cut" was simply a thread one hundred and sixty yards long, and that a woman would card and spin about six "cuts" in a day.

A card was simply a bit of board made of some kind of hard wood, about ten inches long, four inches wide and one-fourth of inch thick. One side of the board was covered with soft leather in which fine wire "teeth," about half an inch long, were thickly set. Over these "teeth" the cotton was spread, and the vigorous raking of the "teeth" of a pair of cards together, over the cotton, as explained above, was called carding.

Worn-out cards were used for both curry-combs and hair brushes. Whether this was because old cards were really better, or only cheaper, than anything else then in use for currycombs or hair brushes, is, to this day, an unsettled question in my mind. It was clearly a matter of economy to curry your horse or arrange your toilet with that which could be no longer used in any other way, but still old cards may have been better adapted to such purposes than anything else then in use, as well as more economical, for aught I know to the contrary. I was too small to form any opinion upon the merits of the question myself, and a friend of mine somewhat older than myself, used to evade the question entirely, by frankly confessing that, in his boyhood days, he never curried a horse or combed his own hair, except under protest, and the few times he was *compelled* to do either, he wanted nothing better than an old card for the business, unless a card without any "teeth" at all could have been adopted. He thinks that such a card would be a decided improvement even now, in the estimation of such a boy as he was, over anything, ancient or modern, in the way of a currycomb or a hair brush, because it could be rubbed over a horse with less work, or drawn over his own head with less pulling of his tangled locks, than anything else ever used for such purposes.

The question as to the respective merits of old cards and hair brushes was extensively discussed in every home about the time the change was made in these toilet articles, but one party to the argument was so man-

" OLD CARDS."

ifestly influenced by *pride* and the other by *economy*, that it was more a wrangle of antagonistic *spirits* than a logical discussion of the merits of the question. In every case economical parents stood for the old cards, while fashion-loving children clamored for the real hair brush. The one contended that the old cards were in every way much better for the hair than a hair brush, while the other petulantly retorted that it was a shame and a disgrace to use an old card for such a purpose when the leaders of fashion in every neighborhood were known to have real hair brushes.

Thus, with much wrangling and some unpleasant feelings, the old cards gradually and steadily lost ground till in every home they finally gave place to more fashionable, if not better, toilet articles.

Few things were more common than worn-out cards about every home in my boyhood days. They could be seen in almost every ash heap, they were sticking in the cracks of every stable, they were piled away in every closet and lumber room, and they were thrown promiscuously upon every idle table or shelf, in or about the house.

The carder's rolls were drawn into thread by use of a "wheel." Each roll would make a thread several feet long, which, when drawn out to the proper size, and well twisted, was "run up" on a "broach" upon the spindle of the wheel. The rolls were thus "spun," one by one, each being attached, by the rapid twisting of the spindle, to the one last drawn into thread, till the "broach" grew to be a ball of one continuous thread about large enough to measure a "cut." It may be well to explain that the word "broach" was used in a local, technical sense not given to it in the dictionaries.

In "filling quills" a woman could sit on a high bench or stool, beside the wheel; but in regular "spinning," she had to stand, or rather walk back and forth, as the rolls were drawn into thread, twisted by a vigorous turning of the wheel, and then "run up" on the "broach."

The hum of a wheel could be heard several hundred yards, and it was a familiar sound in every home from before daylight in the morning till nine or ten o'clock at night. One pair of cards and a wheel gave employment to two women. One carded while the other "spun," and they exchanged places and work every "cut."

" A WHEEL."

Picking the seeds out of cotton with the fingers was an every-night, after-supper job in every family. The cotton was parcelled out in "tasks" to each member of the family, and no one was allowed to go to bed till the "task" was done. After a hard day's work, the whole family would sit and pick seeds out of cotton as they

drowsily nodded around a big log fire in an open fire-
place, till late into the night, and then be out of bed
and at work again long before day-light the next
morning.

Sometimes the young people would combine business
with pleasure by meeting at night from house to house
and having picking bees. At such gatherings, the cotton would be first spread before the fire, to dry thor-'
oughly, so that the seeds could be picked out with ease
and rapidity. The quantity to be picked would then be
apportioned, in equal parts, to each of the pickers,
when a spirited contest would begin, each one striving
to get his parcel picked first. Whoever won in the race
was awarded the championship as the fastest picker,
and allowed to kiss any girl he might choose in the
crowd. The kiss always assumed the outward form of
a joke, with the boy, and it was as uniformally resented
as an unpleasant ordeal, by the girl, but there are well
authenticated cases in which each party threw into it a
fair degree of genuine sentiment under cover of mere
formal submission to a social custom. It was often but
the first public expression of the mating instinct, to be
quickly followed by a romantic courtship and a happy
marriage. There was no *logical* connection between the
championship as the fastest seed-picker, and the privilege of kissing the choice girl, in the company, of course;
but when were young people of opposite 'sexes ever
known to conform to the principles of logic in their deportment toward each other? The custom was not
founded on reason, or perpetuated by logic. It rested
solely upon the consent of the parties. No one knew
whence it originated, or cared ever to see it end. It
gave satisfaction because all parties liked it, and it was
not disturbed because no one cared to see it modified or

7

abolished. But for the fact that changes in social customs and general environments have provided other and better methods of giving expression to the mating instinct, boys would yet be straining every nerve to win the championship at picking bees, for the privilege of publicly kissing the girl of their choice. Times have changed, but human nature is the same.

Every boy could not be the fastest picker at a picking bee, nor could every girl be the choice of the champion. Society anticipated this difficulty, and neatly solved the problem by providing a few simple games to be engaged in at the close of every bee, by all the boys and girls in attendance. The boys would "choose their partners" and march with them in a circle around the room, singing simple ballads with all the force of their powerful lungs. It is difficult to imagine a more hilarious scene than a dozen strapping boys, such as the habits of life peculiar to that age and country produced, each with a timid girl by his side, and all stalking in a circle about the middle of a little log cabin, vociferously singing "Hog Drivers" or "Old Sister Phœbe," no two of them singing in the same pitch, half of them without a tune and all of them badly out of time. As musical entertainments, such exercises were a failure, but the fact that they gave every boy a chance to kiss the girl of his choice, and every girl an opportunity to vaguely indicate the boy she most admired, was a feature which commended them to public favor, and secured for them universal popularity.

Besides those songs and "marches," with kissing as a sort of doxology and benediction after each, they would play "Grind The Bottle," "Frog In The Middle," "Puss Wants A Corner" and "William Trimble Toe." In each of those games were appropriate places for kissing. A boy would do more public kissing, and with a a greater zest, in a couple of hours at one of those old picking-bee frolics, than some men do during half of their married life—the latter half, of course.

Balls were unknown, and even plain dancing was rigidly proscribed by church members of all denominations, but the ungodly and the sinners often defied the authorities of the church and gave themselves over to a season of delicious enjoyment in the winter hoe-down. The principal difficulties in the way of such amusements were the lack of houses in which to hold forth, and the scarcity of girls to make the hoe-down interesting. There were but few heads of families who cared to insult the churches and tempt heaven by opening their houses for such amusements, and scarcely any parents were willing for their daughters to break over the limits of propriety acknowledged by the preachers and rigidly enforced by a healthy public sentiment. But occasionally a great tide of worldliness and sin would sweep over the country, swamp the church, set the old women to drinking stew and gossiping, the old men to taking grog and fighting, and the young people to making love and dancing. Such wild out-breaks of wickedness would be followed by a general reckoning in all the churches, in which some transgressors would repent and be restored, others would remain stubborn and be expelled, and many would back-bite and vow vengeance.

Such tidal waves of unmitigated wickedness, in the winter, were always followed by a general revival of religion the next summer. The prodigals would return to the churches, bringing scores of new converts with them, preachers would rejoice, saints would shout, everybody would tell a bright experience of grace and zion would prosper.

An old-time costume of a fashionable belle would be a curiosity to this generation. There were but few women financially able to buy any part of their wardrobe. Indeed there was very little they could buy but imported silks and other grades of costly goods. There was but little material for wearing apparel of any kind manufactured in the United States, and imported goods were entirely too expensive for the poor inhabitants of this frontier country. Every woman manufactured her own goods and made her own garments. The various kinds of material used in the manufacture of goods for women's wear were wool, cotton, flax and tow. Occasionally a reigning belle and ambitious leader of fashion would make jeans and exchange it for silk or other kinds of imported goods, and thus rig herself in a costume that would create a sensation throughout the country.

No powers of description can do justice to the fashions of those days as respects the peculiar styles and shapes of women's garments. Fashion plates were unheard of, and even an illustrated book or paper would have been, to us, the wonder of the world. There was not so much as a ladies' journal or household paper known in all the land. We had no methods of travel but walking, riding on horse-back and moving in wagons. The day of newspapers had not yet dawned, and mail facilities were exceedingly meager. There was absolutely no medium by which ideas of any kind could be communicated from one settlement to another except in the head of a horseman or footman, and such receptacles of thought were too small to transmit more than one idea of diminutive proportions at a time. The inhabitants of any section rarely ever saw or heard about anything which took place beyond the limits of

their own neighborhood. The styles and fashions of
every community, therefore, had at least, the merit of
originality. And if by chance two women from dif-

"WALKED BESIDE HIS SWEETHEART."

ferent neighborhoods, a few miles apart, were thrown
together, their costumes, as respected everything new in
the style of each, differed as widely as the fashions of
different continents.

No pictures of the fashions of those days have been preserved. Artists painted the portraits of the rich, and thus handed down to on-coming generations the styles of higher circles of society in that obscure age, but who has ever seen a portrait which gave the backwoods fashions of frontier settlers? Artists were too rare, portraits too expensive and early settlers too poor for such an enteprise. Such fashions exist only in the memory of those who were eyewitnesses of their majesty. They differed so widely from anything this generation has ever seen, that the fancy of my artist, aided by the very best verbal description I could give, has failed to produce anything which remotely resembles the cut and make of either male or female apparel in those days.

That was a Bible-believing, church-going, God-worshiping generation. Few people in all the country were ever absent from the log meeting-house of the neighborhood on Sunday. Men, women and children all walked to meeting. This saved us the trouble of saddling or harnessing horses at home, and effectually protected us against any disturbance from a loose horse in the midst of a long sermon at church. We could also add to the joys of our religion, the satisfaction of the reflection that the poor, tired brutes were getting a day of much needed rest from the drudgery of dragging a heavy plow through rooty ground during the week.

Each boy walked beside his sweetheart and carried her Sunday shoes in his pockets. The preservation of such shoes was a problem of the first magnitude with us. Not every girl in the neighborhood could afford a pair of fine shoes for Sunday wear, and the favored few who could display such extravagance knew well the cost of their vanity.

There were no ready-made shoes for sale in stores. Every neighborhood had a professional cobbler who

PUTTING ON SUNDAY SHOES.

made fine, calf-skin, lined-and-bound shoes, for Sunday wear. The male members of each family made shoes of coarser grade for every-day use.

If a girl aspired to fine, Sunday shoes, she had to make cloth to barter with the neighborhood cobbler. Every pair of Sunday shoes, therefore, represented long days and weary night-hours of hard work with cards, wheel and loom.

We often walked four or five miles over rugged hills and rocky roads to meeting on Sunday. A few such tramps would have measured the natural life of a pair of Sunday shoes which had cost weeks of anxious toil and self-denial. Every boy knew well what his sweetheart's Sunday shoes had cost her, and he knew, too, that every scratch or rent in them, from a sharp. rock or an awkward step, would bring her sorrowful tears and sad repining for many gloomy, dreary days to come. It was, therefore, with feelings of tenderest affection that I always put the Sunday shoes of my best girl in my pockets Sunday morning as we started from her home to the little log meeting house some miles away. There are well authenticated cases in which other boys' sweethearts made the journey with bare feet over rocks and hills while the gallant beaux carried both shoes and hose in their pockets, but *my* girl invariably wore her coarse, every-day shoes on such tramps.

When we came near the meeting house, we would all call a halt, and each girl, seated on a log or a rock by the roadside, would put on her Sunday shoes and give her wardrobe and toilet a general touching up, by the help of her girl companions. They had no mirrors on such occasions, but each girl depended upon the eyes and the suggestions of the others in making her toilet. While the girls were engaged in this purely feminine exercise, the boys stood by as interested spectators.

In all this, there was not the slightest embarrassment or sense of impropriety on the part of either boys or girls. It never occurred to us then that we would live to see the day when the whole programme would seem supremely ludicrous.

# CHAPTER VII.

## OLD-TIME DENTISTS AND DENTISTRY.

I knew nothing about town-life in the days of my early childhood. In fact there was scarcely any such thing as town-life then. The country was new and rough, the people were rougher and fashions roughest. Everything was crude and unpolished. A dentist or a dancing master would have been a greater curiosity than a whole menagerie.

If a tooth became refractory and began to jump and throb with pain, there were various methods for extracting it. Professional tooth-pullers, of whom every neighborhood had at least one, used a pair of coarse, heavy pinchers made of rough bars of iron or steel in a blacksmith shop.

Sometimes a non-professional substitute for a regular tooth-puller would fasten a stout string, or cord, to the disaffected grinder and lift it out of its socket by a vigorous jerk.

Another popular method of extracting a tooth was to set a nail, or iron spike, against it, and make short work of the whole business by a heavy blow with a hammer.

For decaying teeth there was no remedy. False teeth were unheard of, and the art of filling teeth was unknown. When teeth ached, they were removed; when they decayed, they were lost.

The negro preacher explained how people got on

without teeth, in a sermon on the text: "And there shall be weeping and gnashing of teeth."

When the text was announced an old brother in the amen corner said:

"Hol' on dar brer Jake. What dem folks gwine do whar aint got no teef ter *mash*?"

This was decidedly a hard question, but the dusky parson was equal to the emergency.

"Dis tex', brer Joe, am not to be implied to dem whar aint got no teef ter mash. Dey dat got teef ter mash, mus' mash, as de tex' say, an' dey whar aint got no teef ter mash, mus' gum it."

In those days boys and girls were dressed exactly alike till they were five or six years old. You could not determine the gender of the biped by looking at head, feet, or dress. As to head and feet, if the weather permitted, both were bare. Children were not considered worth shoeing till at least six years old. The hair of boys and girls under six years of age was cut short. A six-year-old girl with long hair would have been a subject of general remark.

In winter, boys and girls under six years of age wore a heavy, homespun, woolen frock which came down to their heels. The head-gear of both boys and girls was an old Virginia poke, or sun-bonnet.

I have a distinct and rather painful recollection that my head-covering was once made of flaming red cloth. I was sent one morning down the hill to the spring, about two hundred yards from the house, to bring some water in a cedar piggin. The piggin was thought to be adapted to my age and size, but I confess that when I filled it with water and trudged my weary way, with bare feet, over frozen ground, up that long, steep hill, I was painfully conscious that there was a mistake somewhere in the calculation, either as to the size of the vessel or the strength of the boy. I was about six years old, and next to my flaming red head-covering, the most conspicuous thing about our humble home was an unusually large turkey gobbler. It is either a tradition or a fact, that gobblers have a natural antipathy to things of a red color. The gobbler referred to had such prejudices, either natural or acquired, and through his foolish whim we both came to grief. As I was returning from the spring that cold, frosty morning, we met in the narrow foot-path, and from his maneuvering I readily understood that he was on the war path. He had often followed me about the place before, and a few times he had made hostile demonstrations, but on this particular morning he seemed unusually belligerent. Making a flank movement, he hurled himself upon me with all his power from the rear, as I passed him. We toppled forward, and boy, water, piggin, turkey and all went down together with a crash. I ingloriously fled from the field, leaving him master of the situation and in possession of the spoils. But I vowed vengeance, nursed my wrath and bided my time. One morning I was told to go out to the barn and look for some eggs. I complained that I was afraid of the gobbler, but was shamed for my cowardice and told to defend myself. "A great big boy like you afraid of a turkey! The yard is full of rocks. Can't you rock the gobbler off?" This was my long-wished-for opportunity. Off to the barn I went, and when I got to the barn-yard gate I prepared myself for the conflict. I gathered up the long skirts of my frock, so that, in case of defeat, I would not be cumbered in retreat. I filled my bosom, for pockets I had none, with rocks carefully selected as to weight, shape and size, for effective execution. Thus equipped, into the barn-yard I boldly marched and on came the foe. I took good aim and let the missile fly, with all the strength of my little arm.

Where it would have struck I know not, had not the old fool dodged his head right into the pathway of danger and death. That fatal dodge sealed his doom. The

" ON CAME THE FOE."

stone struck him about two inches below the head, and broke his neck off as short as a pipe stem. Flushed with victory, I dragged his ponderous carcass in triumph at my heels, and, in the sweet enjoyment of injury avenged, I satisfied a boy's keen appetite by feasting on his carcass at dinner.

I remember well the first pair of pantaloons I ever

had. They were not intended for every-day use, but designed for dress parade and Sunday show. Strange to say, they were made of " store " goods.

My sister, instigated by pride, and led on by worldly ambition, purchased cloth and made herself a " store-bought" dress. It was a flimsy material, of white ground, with yellow butterflies dotted over it, at long intervals, but it attracted the attention of the entire community, gratified her vanity and excited the envy of her rivals. It commanded for her a position among the leaders of fashionable society, till decidedly the worse for wear and badly faded, when it was transfigured, so to speak, into my first pair of breeches. With those pantaloons I wore a hunting shirt, or long, loose over-garment, made of the same material. I cannot describe the pride I felt when dressed, for the first time, in such fine apparel.

About that time I exchanged my long-detested, old sun-bonnet for a seal-skin cap, and the cups of my pride and joy were full. With much difficulty I prevailed upon my step-mother to intercede with father, to buy that cap. My strongest argument with her, in favor of the cap theory, was a suddenly acquired aptness to lose bonnets. They were altogether too girlish in expression of countenance to suit my boyish taste. So I began to stuff them into an old hollow cedar log by the wayside, between our home and the field in which I daily labored. I told mother I lost the old bonnets. Thus I took my first lesson in wilfully dodging the truth—vulgarly called lying.

Mother gravely doubted the truthfulness of my stories, and used the rod freely in the hope of picking a flaw in my testimony, but I endured the punishment with a heroism worthy a better cause. Each flogging widened the breach between my affections and the feminine head-gear of my childhood, and left me more than ever determined to continue the boycott against the bonnets. I knew well the cost of a bonnet, to my belligerent mother, in hard work and raw material, and felt sure I would win in the end if I could only endure the stripes and firmly hold my position. No boy ever made a braver fight for what he considered his rights, or won a victory better deserved or more appreciated. My father could have saved me from that continual strain upon my veracity, and the daily wear and tear on important parts of my anatomy, by investing seventy-five cents in a cap, but money was scarce and bonnets were cheap—that is, they were *made*, not *bought*.

The dear woman finally capitulated, and I got the long-coveted cap. But during the siege no less than thirteen bonnets "bit the dust" and went to their long home in the capacious hollow of that old cedar log.

Dining-table furniture was both crude and scarce. Plates, spoons, bowls and dishes were made of pewter, and knives, of material scarcely better, for carrying an edge. I well remember the first "crockery dishes," as they were called, we ever owned. A tide of aristocracy swept over the country, and we had all our pewter plates melted and remolded into milk basins, and vegetable dishes. We then bought some blue-edged deep plates, with cups and saucers to match, and up we went in the social scale. In our humbler days of pewter plates, we drank coffee from tin cups and milk from squash rinds, but now we assumed aristocratic airs, drank coffee, tea and milk, alike, from "store-bought crockery cups," and looked down with feelings of pity upon the poverty-cursed "*masses*" around us! As for myself, I was more conservative than aristocratic in my early childhood, and hence I clung to my old squash rind and pewter spoon, against the strong current of fashionable innovations, as long as my days of milk and mush for supper lasted.

Our knives would not hóld an edge when brought in contact with the hard surface of our "crockery plates." The first time we tried to dine in state, with our new dishes, father's knife failed and his patience went to pieces. It was with no small difficulty that my sisters got his consent to exchange pewter plates for "crockery dishes," at first, and when his knife failed, his whole soul rose up in bitter protest against the innovation. He indignantly threw aside his disabled knife, and shocked our newly-donned aristocracy by calling impatiently for the old butcher-knife which was made in the black-smith shop. He declared that, if there were a pewter plate on the place, he would not eat another mouthful from the abominable substitutes. He denounced the spirit of pride and extravagance which encouraged such innovations, and predicted that if the churches did n't control such impious ambition, heaven would rebuke the whole world by a universal calamity of some kind. In

"WE DINED IN STATE."

his vexation and righteous indignation, he declared he would have every ounce of pewter on the place molded into plates the next time the tinker came round, but before that dignitary made another trip the progressive members of the family had managed to pacify his conservative spirit, and pewter plates had to go.

It may be necessary in this connection to explain that tinkers were men who went from house to house, afoot or on horse-back, carrying with them tools and molds, for repairing or making all kinds of pewter vessels. Every piece of damaged or disabled pewter ware was carefully saved till the tinker came his regular rounds, when it was repaired or remolded into some other kind of vessel.

In the change from the old order of things to the new, pewter plates went first. Pewter spoons held on a spell longer, but by and by the rising tide of innovation took them too, and with them went the tinker, whose business since that time has been a lost art.

Every family had an' abundance of poultry, pigs and puppies. The last named animals were never eaten, though I did not then know why, or do I yet fully understand. It certainly would have been *economy* to eat them, and no argument was more convincing to that poverty-burdened generation, than the logic of economy. But there was a popular prejudice against such diet which effectually protected the whole canine tribe from a fate so deplorable. This unreasonable prejudice still prevails in the best society, but enterprising manufacturers of market sausage, it is thought, have long since outgrown the silly whim.

Dogs have always been prolific animals, and in my boyhood days the production of puppies largely exceeded the demand. Dogs cannot live without something

8

to eat, and, if they are not fed, instinct, or self-preserva-
tion, which is commonly called the first law of nature,
will lead them to pilfer cupboards, larders, hens' nests
and sheep folds, for subsistence. A hungry dog was a
disgrace to his owner, and a constant menace to the
whole community. But the resources of the country
were absolutely inadequate to support such a canine
population as would have replenished the land in a
few years. To prevent such a catastrophe, therefore,
we put the surplus puppies in an old sack and threw
them into the creek. The presumption is that they
were drowned.

I have eaten almost everything that swims, flies or
walks—that is covered with hair, fur, feathers, scales or
skin. Of birds, I have never knowingly eaten an owl,
a hawk, a crow or a buzzard. Of animals, I have always drawn the line firmly at dogs and pole cats. I
have eaten mules, frogs, rats, 'coons and cats. I ate a
cat once by mistake, and have several times wished I
had eaten the whole feline tribe, when some of the
meanest specimens of that species came caterwauling
around my peaceful home at midnight's sacred hour.

The circumstances under which I ate a cat by mistake, richly deserve notice here, as showing a little
negro's ingenuity and a white man's gullibility.

I bought from a negro boy, in the days of slavery, at
Jackson, Mississippi, what he said were two 'possums.
Many masters allowed their slaves large liberty, and
even encouraged them, in such trafficing, on their own
account. One of the so-called 'possums was very large,
the other quite small. The smaller one had been cut
off at both ends—head and tail. I asked the "nigger"
why he had thus shorn it of its fair proportions, and he
said:

"Well boss, I had ter cut off 'is head, 'cause I squashed it up monst'us bad w'en I kil' 'im, an' mos' folks don't like 'possum tail much anyhow, an' I cut dat off too so de 'possum'd look sorter squar' like."

"SORTER SQUAR' LIKE."

Satisfied with this plausible lie, I paid the price and took the 'possums. I always knew that an experienced and well-trained negro could lie as adroitly as a white man, but I confess that I was not expecting to find such originality and ingenuity in a mere child, of either race, as a liar, in an emergency like this.

By chance, Dr. Mitchell, a local scientist of some note, dined with us the day we ate the abridged animal. When we had completely demolished the thing, except one piece which still remained in the dish, I discovered some peculiarity about the bones on my plate, of which there were not a few. So I said:

"Doctor, these don't look like 'possum bones."

He looked attentively at the bones on his own plate for a moment, and then said:

"All of you please pass your bones to me."

He was evidently getting interested. We all watched him in breathless suspense. He placed the bones together, studied them attentively for several minutes, and reluctantly accepted the only conclusion that was consistent with his knowledge of "boneology" and the facts before his eyes. Finally he said:

"Parson this thing was a cat!"

Perhaps he stated it in even stronger terms than that. He probably used a vigorous adjective just before the word "thing," which it would be an offense to pious ears to repeat. But suppose he did, what of it? I need not give his exact language, if I but state clearly his conclusion, which I have done. Under the excitement of the moment he should be allowed more latitude, in the selection of adjectives, than I have a right to claim.

I have had many years in which to formulate suitable language to express an idea which burst upon his mind like a clap of thunder from a clear sky. And yet I cannot feel that I have really made any great improvement upon his language.

His conclusion created a panic at the table. Mrs. Caskey beat a hasty retreat, the children laughed, the doctor looked non-plussed, and I vowed vengeance upon the negro. After the first shock of surprise and mortification, the practical elements of my nature asserted themselves. It was plain to see that apologies were useless. The cat was all eaten but one piece, and there

"PARSON, THIS THING WAS A CAT."

could be no place found for repentance. Having set my hand to the plow, I was not the man to turn back. It was needless to hesitate or falter at that stage of the case. Procrastination is the thief of time. I wavered no longer, but boldly stuck my fork into the last re-

maining piece of the misrepresented animal, and quietly
finished my dinner.

Mast was abundant, and hogs gathered a bountiful living in the forest.  The branches of forest trees would
bend and break under their load of acorns and nuts,
and no man pretended to feed hogs at all.  Indeed, there
were large sections of country in which no one pretended to
claim any ownership of
hogs, more than deer.
Every man killed his
meat from the woods.
Hogs were always abun-
dant and, in autumn, they
were thoroughly fat.  In
sections of country where
each man had his own
hogs, we penned and fed
pigs just enough to tame
them and haunt them to
their home.  For the rest
of their living, they looked to the mast.  In the
fall, when hogs were fat
on acorns and nuts, we
killed our year's supply
of pork from the woods.

" A HASTY RETREAT."

The country was peculiarly well adapted to the raising of every variety of poultry.  All kinds of domestic
fowls supported themselves and raised their young by
scratching for bugs, and every family was abundantly
supplied with eggs and chickens the year round, practically without trouble or expense.  The greatest and
only difficulty in raising poultry was the trouble of pro-
tecting the fowls from the ravages of minks, foxes,

hawks, owls, hungry dogs and chicken snakes. With a little care in guarding them against such enemies, the poultry department of every household was self-sustaining and very profitable.

Coffee cost fifty cents a pound, and we only drank it for breakfast Sunday morning, except when the preacher or some other distinguished guest was present. It always tasted pretty strong of water, but made up in heat what it lacked in strength. Occasionally we had a taste of "store" tea, but not often. Those who craved a stronger beverage than milk, at regular meals, contented themselves with tea made from sassafras roots or an aromatic bush called spicewood, which grew in swamps and along the banks of mountain streams.

Persimmon beer was also a favorite drink at the table in every family. The ripe persimmons were put in a large cedar churn or keg, warm water was poured on them and left to ferment, when it was ready to be served. It was palatable, refreshing and slightly stimulating. When served with Johnny-cakes, ash cakes, Presbyterian bread or baked sweet potatoes, it made a nutritious and very strengthening diet.

Cows found abundant food "in the range" the year round. Cane-brakes furnished an inexhaustible supply of excellent provender for them during the winter, and grass grew luxuriantly all over the country during the spring, summer and fall. Every family was, therefore, abundantly supplied with milk, butter, beef and cheese, without any expense at all beyond the small amount of labor necessary to prepare such things for the table.

There was no such thing as cheese for sale in stores. Every woman manufactured a supply for her own use. A woman who did not know how to make cheese would have been pronounced a first-class ignoramus by the whole community.

Household furniture was all made by hand out of rough timber and with crude tools. An ax, a saw, a drawing-knife, and a few plain augers and chisels of different sizes, constituted the full kit of tools, of the best equipped workmen. With such tools we made all our chairs, stools, benches, tables and bedsteads. There was not a bureau, sideboard, washstand or wardrobe in the whole country. Such a thing as a piece of painted or varnished furniture of any kind was unheard of. There was not even a saw-mill in all the country. The timber out of which we made all our furniture was split from the logs with maul and wedge, hewed to the proper size and shape with an ax, dressed to a reasonably smooth surface with a drawing-knife, put together with chisels and augers and held in position by wooden pins. Common nails were not in use.

A furnished room contained, say, a bed, a few rough chairs and stools, a long bench, a dining table and a cupboard made of rough clapboards. The average residence had but one room, which served all the purposes of parlor, sitting room, library, family room, bed room, kitchen and dining room. A brief description of a fashionable bedstead will give an idea as to the general character of household furniture, and illustrate how it could all be made, from rough lumber, by awkward workmen, with the few crude tools already described.

A bedstead had but one leg, or post, which stood near one corner of the cabin. The distance from the lone post to the log walls of the cabin was about four feet in one direction and seven feet in another. These distances measured the width and length of the bed.

The leg, or post, was simply a stick of timber, about as large as a man's leg and as high as his waist, split from a tree, hewed square with an ax and smoothly dressed with a drawing-knife. Large auger holes were bored in two sides of the post, near the top, and similar holes were made in the logs in the walls of the cabin at the same height. Two pieces of timber, prepared after the same manner of the post, one four feet long and the other seven, served as rails of the bedstead. The ends of the rails were trimmed to fit the holes in post and walls, and one end of each rail was driven into a hole in the post and the other driven into a hole in the cabin wall. This made the frame-work of the bedstead. Rough clapboards were placed over this frame, after the manner of slats, and a dry cow hide, hair turned up, was spread over the clapboards, to complete the ground-work of the bed.

There was nothing particularly ornamental about this piece of primitive furniture, but it is difficult, even now, to see how it could have been improved upon with the rough material, crude implements and awkward work-men we had to depend on in its construction. Economy, utility and durability were the strong points of those old-time bedsteads.

The first piece of furniture not made by our own hands in the manner described, which ever came into our house, was a big chest, with lock and key, made by a neighborhood carpenter, who, about that time, began to devise various improvements in household furniture. He possessed extraordinary skill as a workman, and in devising improved articles of furniture, both useful and ornamental, he seemed gifted almost to inspiration. In some way, which is a profound mystery to my mind even to this day, he gathered sufficient information con-

cerning the progress the world was making beyond the
limits of our little neighborhood, to provide himself
with many new and strange tools, which were eminently useful to him in his trade, but marvelous in our eyes.
His designs in ornamental and useful articles of furniture were unique and original, and all his work was ex-
ecuted with a neatness and taste which, to us, seemed
little short of witch-craft. It is easy enough to look
back now and see that he was but a pioneer in the manufacture of ornamental household furniture, but the
wisest men of earth then had no conceptions at all as to
what developments lay along the line of his humble
work.

Before we bought our large chest from the ingenious
workman, my mother kept her coffee, sugar and other
valuables in large gourds under the bed. We called
them fat-gourds, either because they were fat and plump
in shape, or because they were extensively used to hold
lard. Such gourds grew to enormous size. Many of
them would hold as much as a bushel.

Our large new chest had two apartments, in one of
which we kept coffee; in the other, sugar. There was
no such thing as locking a fat-gourd. Under the old
order of things, therefore, my wayward hand would occasionally find its way into the gourd which contained the
sugar, but that detestable new chest was always locked,
and the key I could never find. On this ground alone
I based many an argument against the abominable innovation which, to my boyish mind, seemed absolutely
unanswerable. It is worthy of note, even now, that
with that first improvement in articles of household furniture, came the lock and key, which are emblems of
distrust, suspicion and selfishness. And every step along
every line of so-called improvement from that day to

this has seemingly increased man's greed for gain and weakened his confidence in his fellowmen.

In early days we had no locks for anything. The first lock that ever came into our community was bought by a farmer and attached to the door of his corn crib. It aroused the indignation of the whole neighborhood, and the people, in mass meeting assembled, compelled him to remove it. They held that it was a reflection upon the honesty of the neighborhood and an insult to the whole community. They freely granted that he had a perfect right to lock things from his own children in his own house, if he felt so disposed, but to turn a key in the face of the whole community was a public insult they would not submit to.

The people of that age had faults, of course, but *avarice* was not one of them. No man seemed to be making any special effort to accumulate a fortune. Everybody was content to enjoy the blessings of a land which literally flowed with milk and honey, without a desire to monopolize the world or heap to himself riches he could never expect to need in providing himself either food or raiment.

Men occupied government land for years without a shadow of a legal title to it. Everybody knew that the only right they had to it was, that they had selected it and built a house and cleared a farm on it. It was generally understood that anybody could file a legal claim upon such tracts of land, at the government land office, and take them from the claimants with all the improvements belonging to them, and yet such settlers were never molested. The fact that land was more plentiful and less valuable then than now does not entirely explain it. Men valued such tracts of land then high enough to *buy* them when they could have taken them by law for nothing by simply filing claims on them.

There was simply less greed for gain then than now. People had not yet learned to make a display of wealth. The richest could only use what they could eat and wear, and the poorest could easily gather that much from bountiful nature by a little labor.

That was an age of sociability, equality, hospitality and general neighborliness. Our dependence upon each other drew us close together. Many things in our work required the combined strength and general co-operation of the whole neighborhood, and such occasions were always enjoyable social gatherings, as well as important business combinations.

House - raisings, log - rollings and corn - shuckings, among the men, and quiltings and picking-bees, among the women, often called the entire neighborhood together for a day of work and social pleasure. Usually there was an agreement between the maternal and paternal heads of the household, which brought the men and women all together in those co-operative workings at the same place on the same day. That is to say, the wife would invite her lady friends to a quilting the same day the husband called his neighbor men to assist at a log-rolling. While men and boys rolled logs, women and girls cooked and quilted, and we all united in a kissing frolic or a hoe-down at night.

The style in which a bridal couple, in good society, begin life on leaving the hymeneal altar, is, in all ages and countries, an exponent of the customs of the people. This fact gives point to the following story, in this connection:

Matthew Thomison married in our neighborhood when I was a boy. He and his bride were members of respectable families, and fair specimens of as good society as the country could boast.

Before the celebration of the marriage, he "leased" a piece of land, which he agreed to clear and fence for the privilege of cultivating it three years. He built a log cabin, in which he proposed to go to "keeping house," with the help of his prospective bride. When their fortunes were united by the holy bonds of matrimony, their available assets consisted of an old blind horse, a slide and a few articles of household and kitchen furniture which the bride received as bridal presents from her parents, friends, relatives and well-wishers. As the bride was both a beauty and a belle, her presents were numerous, and hence the future looked bright to the happy pair.

The next day after the wedding, the old blind horse was harnessed, and the bride's goods were packed into the slide. The bulk was not large, the load not heavy.

A bed, an oven, a skillet, a bucket, part of a side of meat, a gourd of lard and part of a gourd of sugar completed the inventory. The bride and groom took a seat on top of the load, and, with a cluck to the horse and a hearty good-by to the crowd, started on a short bridal tour to the cabin in the woods.

The country was mountainous and the road was rough. About the middle of the journey, as they were going down a steep hill, with a considerable slant to the leftward, the husband leaned over to give his young wife a re-assuring kiss, and just at that critical moment the slide ran over a stump on the upper side of the road and turned upside down.

Out they all tumbled, bridal couple on the bottom, and bed, sugar, oven, skillet, meat, bucket and slide on top. The gourds were smashed, the skillet was broken and bucket, lard, meat and sugar were considerably scattered. The old horse would have completed the wreck by running away with the slide, if he could have seen which way to run.

There was nothing unusual about this bridal tour then, and whatever amusement it may excite now serves only to emphasize the changes that have taken place in the customs of the country since the days of my boyhood.

# CHAPTER VIII.

### CLEARING LAND.

Log-rollings, in which main strength and awkwardness were essential elements, were thoroughly characteristic features of pioneer days. It does seem that, if men had anything like genius in those days, they must have employed it to think out the hardest way to do everything.

In clearing land, all trees over twelve inches in diameter were "deadened," all under that size were cut down. The deadening process was simply to cut around the tree, with an ax about three feet above the ground, a notch from two to three inches deep. Trees thus girdled, or "deadened," would decay at the "deadening" and fall down about the third or fourth year. They were then cut in pieces, piled in heaps and burned. All logs on the ground when the land was cleared had to be disposed of in the same way. Piling logs into heaps to be burned was called "log-rolling," and such work required the combined strength of the whole neighborhood.

The principal implement used at a log-rolling was a "hand-spike," which was simply a stick cut from a small sapling, usually dog wood, and dressed to proper shape with a drawing-knife. It required one "hand-spike" to every two men, with a good supply of extras, to cover accidents of breakage and other emergencies. Such "spikes" were about six feet long and from three to four inches in diameter at the middle. The "spike"

"LOG-ROLLING."

tapered gradually from the middle toward each end, and at the ends, it measured about an inch in diameter.

The logs to be "rolled" were from ten to fourteen feet long, and many of them from three to four feet in diameter. The "hand-spikes" were put under the log and the men were arranged on opposite sides of it, a man to each end of every "hand-spike;" and they simply lifted it by main strength and carried it to the "log-heap." We often carried logs so large that a man could not see his partner, at the opposite end of his "hand-spike," over the log, when it was lifted up. The "hand-spikes" had to be put so close together, to make room for men enough to carry the largest logs, that we could not step over twelve inches at a time without getting on the heels of the man immediately in front of us.

Such lifting strained every muscle and fiber in the body. If any man in the crowd gave down under his load, or made an awkward step and stumbled, his failure increased the burdens of all the others and literally crushed them to the earth. Sometimes the log would roll on the sticks as it was lifted, and in such cases the men on the side to which it rolled would be compelled to give down. When each man had every pound he could carry, the merest trifles sometimes produced serious results. If a man accidentally stepped into a hole, or placed his foot upon a soft spot of ground, his misfortune brought disaster upon the whole crowd. When he sunk down his load fell upon the others, each one of whom already had every ounce he could carry. Many a time have I seen a dozen strong men straighten up with a log which was heavier than they could carry, and for several seconds stand under the fearful strain, unable to take a single step. To come up steadily with such a log, hold it a few breathless seconds, and again

9

lower it steadily to the ground, required *nerve* as well as *muscle.* If any man had become frightened and suddenly dropped his load, the whole crowd would have been instantly crushed to the earth and some one, perhaps, caught under the log and fatally injured. When one of those immense logs rolled on the sticks, every man on the side toward which it turned would put his shoulder bravely under it, brace himself for a powerful effort, and, putting forth his utmost strength, stand like a martyr by his comrades in distress, quivering in every muscle and fiber of his body, till the word could be given and the log steadily lowered to the ground. It was a rare thing for a man to fail in courage or lose his presence of mind in such emergencies.

The Spring was the log-rolling season. Such work usually began in February and continued till about the middle of March. As soon as the logs were all rolled on one farm, we went to another, and so on, from day to day, till all the logs in the neighborhood were rolled. We often put in every day in succession, Sundays excepted, for a whole month, at such work.

It was hard work, but it developed some as fine specimens of physical manhood as the world has ever produced. Their grasp of hand, strength of muscle and powers of endurance were as far superior to anything in this effeminate age, as giants to dwarfs.

Why it was called log *rolling* is not easy to understand. Perhaps the original idea was that the logs could be *rolled* together and burned, but if so, that theory was abandoned before the days of my earliest recollection. It was always *log-lifting*, as far back as I can remember. True, we occasionally *rolled* a log into position, but such cases were the exception and not the rule.

Houses were all built of logs. When the logs were cut and hauled to the place where the house was wanted, the neighbors were requested to come together on a set day and put up the building. This was called a house-raising.

In some places the forest was so dense that logs enough to build a house could be cut within a few rods of the building site. In such cases we would carry the logs with " hand-spikes," after the manner just described in log-rollings, on the day of the house-raising. Some of us would carry logs while others raised the building.

When logs were cut too far from the building site to be carried, they were usually dragged to the place with a yoke of oxen, hitched by means of a log chain, one end of which was tied to the log and the other to the ox-yoke.

We always built a house in a day. That is, we would raise the walls, lay the floor and put on the roof. The finishing touches of stopping the cracks, building the chimney and putting down the hearth were left for the owner to attend to in his own way, and at such times as suited his convenience.

The popular size of a house was eighteen feet wide and twenty feet long. To begin at the foundation of a house, the first things in order were two side sills, placed on blocks of wood or pillars of stone. The sills were twenty feet long and usually eighteen inches square. Sometimes the size was reduced to twelve or fourteen inches square, but it was generally considered unsafe to use a smaller sill than eighteen inches. Just why it was considered necessary to have such ponderous pieces of timber for sills in order to make the house secure, I am not able to explain.

The sleepers, which rested on the sills and supported the floor, were round logs about twelve inches in diameter. They were hewed to a line on top, with a face from three to five inches wide, and made to fit the sills by a flat notch at each end.

Floors were all made of either puncheons or dirt. It was no unusual thing to leave out the sleepers and use the ground for a floor. In fact, when a man was able to have two houses, the one used for a kitchen and dining room almost invariably had a dirt floor.

Puncheons were broad pieces of timber, split from pine or poplar trees, with maul and wedge, and hewed to a smooth surface on one side, with a broad-ax. They were usually about six feet long, from three to four inches thick, and from ten to twenty inches wide. They were trimmed at each end with an ax till they fit down neatly and solidly on the sleepers, smooth side up, and were heavy enough to remain in position, when once properly put down, without being fastened in any way.

Those old puncheon floors were neither air tight nor ornamental. The edges of each puncheon were hewed to a line with a broad-ax, and when the cracks between them did not measure over an inch in width at any place, the floor was considered "well-jointed."

Hens usually made their nests under the cabin floor, possibly to be safe with their eggs and little chicks from hawks, owls, minks, foxes and other enemies, and the ease with which a puncheon could be "raised" was a great convenience in getting eggs or looking after the newly-hatched brood.

Before nails came into general use, the cracks betweeen the logs in the walls of the cabin were "chinked" with small blocks of wood split for the purpose, and "daubed" with mud made from red clay and plastered by hand. The process of "daubing" a house was very simple. A man stood near the crack and threw the soft mud against the "chink," by handfuls, with suf-ficent force to make it stick fast. When a crack was thus "daubed," the full length of the house, he would press the ends of his fingers against the "daubing," after the manner of a brick-layer's trowel, and walk rapidly along the house so as to draw his fingers over the full length of the crack, thus smoothing down the "daubing." It should be explained that the words "chink" and "daub" were both used in a local technical sense not given them in the dictionaries. To "chink" a house was to put blocks of wood, called "chinking," in the cracks, and to "daub" it was to put the mud on the "chinking" in the manner described.

The prints of the fingers were always indelibly stamped upon the "daubing" in every crack in the house. After nails came into use the cracks in houses were stopped by nailing clapboards over them. The roof of every house was made of clap-boards. A clapboard was simply a piece of riven tim-ber, usually oak, four feet long, from four to six inches wide and about a half an inch thick. At a later day, clap-boards were made three feet long, and, in some cases, as short as two feet. Before nails came into use, the boards were put on the roof by means of "ribs," "but-ting-poles," "knees," "end-stuff" and "weight-poles. Each of these words had a technical meaning in the architecture of that day which cannot be well under-stood without some knowledge of the construction of log cabins.

When the walls of the cabin reached the proper height, a longer log was put on at each end, which extended about eighteen 'inches beyond the sides of the house at each of the four corners. On the outer ends of these long logs were placed two logs extending the full length of the house. These logs were called "butting-poles," and they marked the limit of the eaves. On the end-logs the next "round" above the "butting-poles," side-logs were placed about two feet out of the perpendicular of the side-walls, toward the center of the cabin. These logs were called the first "ribs." On the first "ribs" rested the next two end-logs, which, of course, were shorter than those that had gone before, by as much as the first "ribs" were drawn within the perpendicular of the side-walls. These shorter end-logs were called "end-stuff." On them rested two more "ribs," which were placed about two feet further out of the perpendicular wall, on each side, toward the center of the cabin. These were called the second "ribs." Then came more "end-stuff," then more "ribs," and so on till the frame of the cabin ended with a "ridge-pole," or "center rib," at the cone.

The first course of clapboards was placed on the first "rib" and the top log of the wall of the cabin. The ends of the boards extended over the wall about eighteen inches and "butted" against the "butting pole," which was fastened to the long end-log, on which it rested, by wooden pins driven into augur holes. This made the eaves.

When the first course of boards was laid down, sticks of wood, split for the purpose, about two feet long and five or six inches square, called "knees," were placed at intervals along the course of boards, with one end resting, at right angles, against the "butting-pole." A log, called a "weight-pole," was next laid the full length of the house, on this first course of boards, just above the upper ends of the "knees." This "weight-pole" held the boards in position and served as a "butting-pole" for the next course of boards and row of "knees," and was itself held in position by the row of "knees" against which it rested. In like manner came course after course of boards, with "knees" and "weight-poles," as just described, till the roof was finished with a cone at the "ridge-pole," or top "rib." The gable ends were closed up with "end-stuff," which was a necessary part of the frame-work of the roof. When nails came into use, "knees," "weight-poles" and "butting-poles" were dispensed with, and the boards nailed to the "ribs." In a few years more even the "ribs" were supplanted by the more "stylish" rafters and lathing.

The heating apparatus was a large open fire-place in one end of the cabin. Ordinarily such a fire-place was about five feet long, two feet deep and five feet high. The chimney was built of wood and lined with mud, made of red clay. When the mud got thoroughly dry it was as hard as brick. The fire-place was lined—bottom, back and sides—with large flat rocks. The top of the fire-place, in front, was simply the first log of the cabin wall, above the opening cut for the fire-place. This log had to be high enough not to catch fire, and hence was fully five feet above the level of the hearth, or bottom of the fire-place. The fire was simply an immense heap of wood, or rather logs, as long as the fire-place and as large as a man could carry. A log of unusual size was always put in the back of the fire-place, and the rest of the wood was piled about it in front. Those back-logs were often too large to be carried, and were *rolled* into the cabin and to their place at the back of the fire-place. A good back-log would last a day and a night. When the nights were very cold, we supplemented our scant supply of bed-covering by keeping up a roaring log fire all night.

The idea of a carpet of any kind had not entered into the mind of the most far-seeing inhabitant of the country, and the cold wind gushed up through the numerous cracks in those old puncheon floors with a vigor that kept up a continual coolness in the family circle. Above our heads there was nothing but the thin clapboard roof between us and the freezing elements, and through innumerable crevices in it the cold snow and chilling winds sifted down on us practically without hindrance. Many a time I found fully two inches of snow on my bed, at the back end of the cabin, when I awoke in the morning, even when a booming log fire had been kept up in the fire-place, at the other end of the house, all night.

A cabin usually had one door and one window, the shutter to each of which was made of rough clapboards fastened together with wooden pins driven into auger holes. There was not an ordinary pane of glass in the whole country. In the shutters of door and window were more crevices through which the cold found easy access to the shivering, suffering, defenseless household. In fact there seemed to be just warmth enough inside of those thoroughly ventilated huts to attract all the cold blasts in the country for miles around. The inside of every cabin was, therefore, nothing but a huge mass of concentrated winter weather and suffering humanity.

In building the immense log fires, we would occasionally jar portions of the mud lining out of the old stick chimney, leaving the bare wood exposed to the fire. The heat and sparks would often fire the thoroughly dry and highly combustible timber thus exposed, and hence the fire department of the household was liable to be called out at any hour of the day or night, especially in very cold weather.

Those old-time log cabins were always supplied with water from a living spring, which, from some inexplicable reason, was always at least two hundred yards away and invariably at the foot of a steep and rugged hill from one hundred to three hundred feet below the level of the cabin floor. We had to pack every drop of water we used up those long, steep and rugged hills, in heavy, home-made, wooden buckets. Why every body *would* insist on building a house on the very top of the highest, steepest and roughest hill in the country, from two hundred yards to a quarter of a mile from the spring that was depended upon for every drop of water needed about the house, is, with me, one of the unsolved mysteries of that wooden-headed age, to this good day. Or why we never took advantage of the elementary principles of common sense which were accepted by Solomon and Jacob, and indeed by many benighted heathen nations, when they dug wells and built cisterns, centuries before our day, is a profound mystery to me yet.

The chimney was sure to catch on fire the coldest night of the season. We always built a big fire in severe weather, and a big fire was usually what burned a chimney.

To be aroused from sweet dreams by the shrill scream of a female fire alarm, at midnight, in mid-winter, when the ground was covered with snow and the path to the spring, paved with a solid sheet of ice, was an experience far more frequent than pleasant in the days of my boyhood. Of course there was never a drop of water nearer than the spring in such an emergency, for in extremely cold weather we always emptied the water buckets when we retired at night, lest the water should

freeze in them and burst them to staves. To hastily
jump out of a warm bed, jerk on a few articles of clothing, seize a water bucket, plunge into the middle of a
night as dark as the bottomless pit and as cold as the
North pole, and grope your way down the rugged hill,
over a continuous sheet of slippery ice, after a bucket
of water, to check the mad fury of destructive flames,
was not calculated to develop piety or encourage religion
in a boy of my temperament. The boy who could,
under such circumstances, run himself completely out
of breath, with a heavy load of water, up a steep hill,
slip on the ice just as he reached the top of the hill,
turn his bucket up-side down and convert his improvised fire engine into a shower bath, without pulling the
stop-cock of his profanity wide open, was a living contra-
diction of the dogma of original sin and a walking specimen of the doctrine of the final perseverance of the
saints.

The funnel of a wooden chimney was simply a pen
about two feet square, built of small sticks. Sometimes
the sticks were round poles with a flat notch at each
end, so that they would fit together steadily, but oftener
they were narrow, riven slats, about an inch thick by
two inches wide. When all other efforts failed to stop
a fire in a chimney, the last resort was to climb up the
wall of the hut and push the chimney down. The
strength of a boy was sufficient to push off the whole
top of a chimney, but such heroic measures were
always the dernier resort.

The first improvement we made upon those rude log
huts, in the architecture of our homes, was to build
hewed-log houses. We used whip-sawed lumber for
floors and put on clapboard roofs with rafters, lathing
and nails. We made doors of whip-sawed lumber, hung

them with iron hinges made in the blacksmith shop and

"WE BUILT HEWED-LOG HOUSES."

put "store-bought" locks and brass knobs on them.

We put joists in the house, and laid a loft, and built stairs of whip-sawed lumber. We daubed the cracks with mortar, made of lime and sand, smoothed them over with a trowel, while the mortar was soft, and neatly white-washed them when thoroughly dry. We built stone chimneys, put in glass windows, talked about the great and rapid improvements the world was making, and began to look for the dawn of the millennium.

But such improvements only increased our labors. To prepare logs enough to build a hewed-log house was the work of many days. And harder work no man has ever done than to fell trees and hew house-logs. A broad-ax is an ugly looking tool, and the man who has used it properly and industriously will not say that it looks any uglier than it really is. It is heavy, unwieldy and dangerous. It requires much strength and considerable practice to handle it successfully and with safety. Many a poor man has gashed his foot, knee or shin most dreadfully, and made himself a cripple for life, in trying to learn to use a broad-ax.

In the days of hewed-log houses, we had to hew every sill, every log, every sleeper, every plate and every joist that went into a building. There was not a saw-mill in the country. We hewed everything, except the small amount of lumber sawed by hand with a whip-saw.

We would fell a tree, "scalp" it, "line" it, "score it in," and then "hew to the line and let the chips fall where they would." To prepare the logs, saw the flooring and build a hewed-log house was not the work of a few days. Such an enterprise often occupied months. We could not neglect the crop or fall behind with the clearing, to build fine houses. We only devoted such time as we could spare from the many other duties that daily pressed upon us, to improving our.homes. Often the very hottest days of summer, when we were not engaged in the crop or pushed with a piece of clearing, would be devoted to the heavy work of hewing logs in the forest. In such work we were, fortunately, protected from the heat of the sun by the shade of the forest trees, but often the impenetrable thickets completely shut out every particle of refreshing breeze. Many a day have I seen men wield a broad-ax under such circumstances till every thread of clothing on them would be as wet with perspiration as if they had swum a river. Scores of times have I seen them strip themselves and wring quarts of perspiration out of their clothing. I have seen them hang their perspiration-soaked shirts in the sun to dry while they toiled on without them for hours in succession. I have known their clothing to sour, mildew and be fly-blown under such circumstances. And all this òf white men too. There were but few slaves in the country then.

But why say I have *seen* all this? Why say they were *white* men? Have I not *experienced* it? Was I not there? Did I not wield a broad-ax? Was I not one of them in every sense? Ah, those days of arduous toil and pioneer hardships! How can I ever forget them? My work is well-nigh done; my race is nearly run; my course is almost finished; my journey is about to end. But, with labor and suffering no pen can describe, I cheerfully contributed what I could, along with the now rapidly perishing generation of pioneers, towards laying the foundation of the wealth and greatness of the best country this world has ever known, and I am profoundly thankful that it was my privilege to bear an humble part in such noble work.

The first real sawed lumber we ever had was manufactured by hand with a whip-saw. It took two men to operate those primitive machines for the manufacture of lumber. A hole was dug in the ground, over which a crude scaffold was built. The saw-log was

"A PRIMITIVE SAW MILL."

put on the scaffold, and one man stood in the pit below the log while the other one stood on the scaffold. The log was first hewed to a square with a broad-ax, and then "lined" on the upper and lower sides at every place where it was to be sawed. The men then drew the saw up and down through the log along the line, sawing off one plank, or board, about every hour. Two first-class men would saw as much as two hundred feet of lumber in a day.

# CHAPTER IX.

Hitherto no mention has been made of some of the hardest work that women had to do. To wash and iron the clothing in which men did such work as has been described, was a weekly task, for the women of every household, of no ordinary magnitude. There were no steam-laundries then. There was not even a washing machine or a wringer of any kind. The combined inventive genius of the whole country had not so much as conceived the idea of a simple scrub-board.

The washing-place for our whole neighborhood was a well-shaded spot on the bank of a living stream of clear, soft water, in a grove of mammoth beech trees. The trunks of those aged trees were thickly carved with names, dates and awkward rhymes. By such inscriptions every love-sick swain in the country had, for many years, declared the state of his affections and given a specimen of awkward writing, bad spelling and bungling grammar. It was the ambition of every lover to carve, on those old beech trees, his name, the date, and a ridiculous rhyme which set forth the fact that he was desperately in love, but did not reveal the name of his heart's idol. Such inscriptions were carved mornings, evenings and Sundays. At all other times, the place was occupied by women and girls engaged in the week's washing, and those melancholy lovers always carved their tender inscriptions in solitude.

It is not difficult to understand why lovers delighted

(144)

to put such inscriptions there. Every girl in the whole neighborhood spent at least one day in each week at the washing place, and there was comfort to the heart of every true but modest lover in the thought that *she* will see *my* name and read *my* rhyme and know whom *I* love.

The boys who were too small to work in the field had to help the girls with the washing. I look back to the days I spent with my sisters under those old beech trees in balmy Spring, sultry Summer and melancholy Autumn, as among the happiest of my life at the old homestead. My duties were not hard, my surroundings were pleasant and my sisters were indulgent.

The washing process was very simple. The clothes were first well smeared with soft soap and then thoroughly boiled in a large washing-kettle. They were then taken out of the boiling water, laid on a bench and vigorously pounded with a heavy paddle. This was called "battling," which is another instance of a word misused. The pounding, or "battling," could be heard fully a quarter of a mile. When the clothes were thoroughly beaten, they were put into a tub of hot water, and again smeared with soft soap. The washer-woman then rubbed them vigorously between her bare knuckles, after which they were put into another kettle of clear water and thoroughly boiled again. When taken out of boiling water the second time they were put into a tub of clear, cold water and all the soap was thoroughly washed out of them. The water was then wrung out of them, and they were hung in the sun to dry.

It was the work of the small boy to keep the kettles filled with water, carry wood, keep up the fires, and do all the "battling," while his sisters stood over the tub

10

and did the rubbing. But my sisters were never exacting. The brook was well supplied with mountain trout and speckled perch, and I knew well the art of making "pin-hooks" with a pebble for a "sinker." I half suspect, now, that they were willing enough at times to do my work while I fished, in order that they might have the better chance to read the latest inscriptions on those old beech trees, unobserved. I doubt not but that they often bent over the wash-tub with a new joy at their hearts, a flush on their cheeks, a quiver in their breath and unshed tears of delight in their eyes, because of some new names and awkward rhymes they found on the old beech trees while I sat on the mossy bank of the babbling brook, under the honey-suckle bushes, lazily dipping my bare feet into the water, softly singing an accompaniment to the music of the bees among the flowers above me, and patiently holding my little pin-hook for a "bite."

Ah, well! It is all gone by forever now, but as I sit here by my desk in the midst of a crowded city to-night, hundreds of miles from the old homestead, and look back over the dreary stretch of weary years to the time when I fished with a pin-hook in the little brook under the old beech trees at the neighborhood washing-place, I wish, with all the fervency of a lonely heart, that I could once more see the old place, just as it was then, and enjoy a few hours of sweet companionship with the old-time friends and acquaintances, surrounded by the scenery familiar to my boyhood, before I go to my long home.

But I look back to some other experiences of boyhood life at the old homestead, with far less pleasure. I have no desire to dwell upon them. It is with no feelings of pleasure that I recall them now, and I fain would leave them in the oblivion to which they were long since cheerfully consigned, but for a feeling of obligation to the reader, to give a faithful description of life in this country, just as it was in the years long gone by.

There was not even so much as an ounce of soap in the whole country, except that which the women made. Every home had a miniature soap factory in which the women of the household made soap enough every Spring to answer all the purposes of the family during the year.

The essential ingredients of soft soap were alkali and grease. All the bones from the bacon, beef and pork used by the family during the year, and all the refuse scraps of meat of every kind, were carefully saved for soap-grease. Even the entrails of hogs and beeves were often cleaned, cooked and preserved, for the same purpose. All this made more work and menial drudgery for women and small boys.

Those who consider " a hog killing time " simply a feast of fat things and a season of unalloyed pleasure, certainly do not base their opinion upon a small boy's experience, on such occasions, in this country, more than half a century ago. It requires a more brilliant imagination than I possess, to extract a high order of enjoyment from the drudgery of converting the internal improvements of a score of hogs into soap-grease, in the open air, exposed to wind and weather, when the thermometer was crawling down towards zero, and sleet, rain and snow were alternately pelting my shivering, poorly-clad little body.

We first had to tediously cut from the mass all the fat we could, with knives, to make lard, and then the entrails had to be cut into small pieces, emptied of their contents, put into old buckets, carried to the creek, thoroughly washed and packed back home, to be cooked for soap-grease. This was my work in "a hog-killing time," during the days of my far-away boyhood. In such work I had to hunch myself and shiver over the nauseating heap on the ground for hours at a time. And then I had to take an old bucket, heavily loaded with such stuff, on my shoulder, plod my weary way, through wind and cold, to the far-off spring branch under the hill, and there sit and dabble in the freezing water till the mass was thoroughly cleaned. I leave the reader to imagine my opinion of a "hog killing time" when, on my way to the spring branch, with such a load, I would stumble, as occasionally I did, capsize my vessel and pour its offensive contents on my head and over every part of my body. Nothing but the leper's cry of "Unclean, unclean, unclean" will express *my* idea of a small boy's part in an old-fashioned "hog-killing time!"

The alkali used in making soft soap was obtained from the ashes which accumulated in those large, old-fashioned fire-places during the cold season. An ash-hopper was an indispensable article of out-door furniture in every home. Imagine four sticks cut from saplings, forked at the top, driven into the ground, about four feet apart, in the form of a square, and about three and a half feet high. Such sticks were about as large as a man's ankle. Other sticks, about the same size, were laid in the forks of these posts, forming a square frame. Half of a hollow log, making a trough, was placed on the ground across the middle of the square frame, and inclined, by a rock under one end, sufficiently to cause water to flow down it with considerable alacrity. Clapboards were then set in the square frame, one end in the trough and the other supported by the frame, so as to make a sort of triangular box, of which the trough formed an acute angle and the clapboards, two sides. Each side of the hopper inclined at an angle of about forty-five degrees. The top of this box, or hopper, was either left open entirely, or covered with loose boards, and the ends, each of which was triangular in shape, were closed up with clapboards. Such was the old-time ash-hopper which stood in the yard near every cabin. .

The ashes were put into this hopper as they accumulated in the fire-place during the cold season. When the time came to make soap, in early Spring, we had to carry water—from the spring of course—and pour into the hopper till it soaked down through the ashes and ran out at the lower end of the trough, strongly tinctured with alkali. To carry all that water for the ash-hopper, was more work for the women and boys of the household. It took about one hundred buckets of water to soak all the alkali out of a hopper of ashes.

The alkali was put into a pot, or kettle, and boiled down to a very strong solution. Grease was then added, and the mixture was boiled down to the consistency of thick paste, when the soap was ready for use.

The corn-shuckings of those days were occasions of neighborhood gatherings of no ordinary importance. We always shucked every ear of corn before putting it into the crib. We hauled it and threw it in a heap, on the ground beside the crib, and then called the neighbors together for a corn-shucking.

We usually began the shucking in the afternoon, and continued, till toward the middle of the night. This was necessary, as a matter of economy in time. At that season of the year, we were always greatly pressed with work, and could ill-afford to spare day-light for such co-operative workings.

When the nights were dark, we built scaffolds around

CORN-SHUCKING.

the corn-heap, covered them with dirt or a flat rock, and built lights on them, of pine knots. Three or four scaffolds well supplied and frequently replenished with good fat pine knots, would light up the grounds for several rods around the corn-heap, almost as bright as day. A small boy would keep up the blazing fires on the scaffolds, which would furnish all the light the workers needed.

The corn was thrown into the crib as it was shucked, and the shucks were stowed away in rail pens, built for them, by the small boys, to be fed to the cows during the winter.

The crowd was always divided, at a corn-shucking, by two men, who threw for " heads or tails," with a silver coin, for first choice of shuckers. The corn-heap was also divided into two parts, as nearly equal as could be determined by guess and measurement, and the " captains " of the two squads of shuckers again threw for " heads or tails," for choice of sides. The work then began, and from start to finish the shucks flew in every direction and the clean ears of corn fairly rained into the crib. The rivalry between the two squads of shuckers would grow more interesting and exciting as the divided heap of corn gradually melted away, and sometimes the intense determination of both parties to win in the race, would lead to charges of unfairness, angry recriminations and a general fisticuff. When it came to a general row and a free fight, every fellow stood to his post and fought for his party. Such fights were fierce, but short, and when they ended every man resumed his place at the corn-heap and proceeded with his work, with renewed energy, without any feeling of malice or fear of an enemy in his heart.

Corn-shucking was dusty work, and the shuckers required much water, as well as a liberal supply of a stronger beverage, to allay their oft-recurring thirst. But we lost no time in drinking.

One man was always appointed to carry the beverage to the men around the corn-heap. He took them in regular order, and handed the drink to each man, as he came to them, in a small tin cup. When the race was close and the excitement was very high, a man would not even stop shucking long enough to swallow the drink, but would gulp down the beverage, without the loss of a second, while the waiter held the cup to his mouth.

Whenever a boy or a young man found a red ear of corn, he put it into his pocket, and when he went to the house, after the shucking was over, he presented it to the girl of his choice, and for this simple act of gallantry he was permitted to kiss her publicly. I took a solemn vow, then, that, if I ever lived to be a man, I would farm for a living, raise nothing but corn, plant only red seed and shuck every ear of it myself! But alas! Times have changed and red corn has lost its charm!

The quiltings of the long ago deserve a place in these reminiscences. They were simply feminine accompaniments of log-rollings, house-raisings and corn-shuckings. Wheresoever the men and boys were gathered together, to roll logs, raise a house or shuck corn, there would the women and girls be also, engaged in a quilting.

When the corn was shucked and the quilting was done, the lads and lasses joined in a midnight revel in kissing plays or a lively hoe-down, older women related their experiences with ghosts and discussed the signs which, to them, betokened the near approach of the end of the world, and men who had

long since past the courting period of joyous youth,
watched the winsome maidens and gallant beaux, with
longing eyes, and loudly applauded the kissing climax
of every play.

Quilting was a tedious business. The whole quilt had
to be closely stitched, by hand, with seams about an
inch apart. To arrange the quilt so that the women
could have the best
advantages in their
work, it was sewed to
frames, or four slats of
wood, and " hung," by

QUILTING.

means of four ropes, one end of each of which was tied
to a corner of the frame and the other to a "rib" at the
roof of the cabin. The women were then seated
around the quilt, on chairs, stools, or long benches, as
close together as they could comfortably sit, on all the
four sides of it.

The height of the quilt, above the floor, could be regulated by lengthening or shortening the ropes by which

it was "hung." It had to be on a level with the breasts of the quilters when they were seated around'it. Each woman passed one arm under the quilt and guided the point of her needle with her fingers beneath, while she extended the other arm as far as she could reach over the top of the quilt and manipulated the other end of the needle with her fingers above. She sat the first seam, or row of stitches, as far from the frame as she could reach, toward the center of the quilt, and each succeeding seam about an inch nearer the frame, till she finished the first "shell." When all the "shells" on the four sides of the frame were "quilted," they rolled the part thus finished around the frames and proceeded with the second row of "shells," and so on till the work was ended with the last "shells" in the middle of the quilt.

It was a hard day's work, for about ten women, to quilt one quilt. The quilts were all made of small pieces of cloth, of various colors, cut from remnants of goods, and worn-out garments, and stitched together on some uniform pattern, with an eye to beauty and regularity as well as comfort. The lining was home-made goods, and the padding between quilt and lining, which gave weight and warmth to the quilt, was cotton batting carded by hand.

For an average woman to make the lining, card the batting, cut and sew the pieces together and quilt the quilt, required at least two months close work. A comfort, which is far superior to such quilts in point of both beauty and warmth, can now be bought for about two dollars. Nothing of the kind could then be bought at any price.

We knew nothing of insurance companies, of the modern kind, but every heart glowed with a sympathy for misery and a fellowship for misfortune, which effectually guarded all of us against ill-luck and accidents, to the full extent of our united ability. We were neighbors, and the trouble of one was the sorrow of us all. When one suffered loss we all lamented, and a personal calamity was a neighborhood misfortune.

It goes without saying that our crude homes, with wooden chimneys and huge log fires, were frequently burned. But when a home was consumed by flames, the neighborhood came together as one man, and not a soul left the spot till another house was built and the unfortunate neighbor was comfortably settled in a new house as bountifully furnished as was the old one.

We could easily cut the logs, hew the puncheons, raise the house, rive the boards and build the chimney in a day and a night in such an emergency. And when we came together to build a house, in such a case, each man brought a gift in the way of furniture for the new home. One man would bring a gourd of lard, another, a side of meat, others would bring quilts, articles of clothing, cooking vessels, water buckets, chairs, stools, soap, cards and dining-table furniture.

The women and children of the unfortunate family would be taken to the home of the nearest neighbor, and there the women and girls of the whole neighborhood would assemble and work, and plan, and weep with and for, the sufferers, while the new home was being built by the men and boys of the neighborhood. A list of articles needed, to complete the furniture of the new home, would be made out, and such as the neighbors could not *give*, the women would *make*.

My father's house burned about the middle of one cold night in December. Notwithstanding the severity of the weather, by sun-down the second day after the fire, and before the place where the old house sat had cooled off or quit smoking, we were all comfortably housed in a new cabin, with as much furniture as we lost in the fire.

About fifteen miles from Nashville, Tennessee, on the Lebanon turnpike, stands an old-fashioned hewed-log house. It is built of cedar logs, two stories high, and is well preserved, notwithstanding its age.

The land on which it stands was deeded to Robert Mitchell, August 7, 1767, by the State of North Carolina. The number of the deed is 417. The land is now the property of C. C. H. Burton, a descendant of Mr. Mitchell, and it has been in the possession of his ancestors since the date of the original grant. Mr. Burton's mother is yet living, and is now in her ninety-second year.

Thomas Everett, another descendant of Robert Mitchell, has some of the receipts given to Mr. Mitchell by the State of North Carolina, which show that the land was paid for in cloth and corn. Mr. Mitchell came from Ireland to this country. He was a weaver by trade, and he and his wife are buried on the place. The first house which Mr. Mitchell built is now used by Mr. Burton for a kitchen. It was built before the land was paid for, and is therefore more than a hundred years old.

The two-story, hewed-log house in which Mr. Burton now lives, was built for a hotel, or stage stand, in the old staging days, and was used for that purpose until the railroad was built and the old stage line, between Knoxville and Nashville, was abandoned.

At this old hotel John A. Murrell, the celebrated robber, murderer and slave-trader, spent many nights. Here, too, Sam Houston, the distinguished Tennesseean who figured so conspicuously in Texas politics, and about whose early life there hangs a great domestic mystery, spent a night soon after he separated from his young bride, *en route* to Texas.

Andrew Jackson, Felix Grundy, James K. Polk, John Bell and many other men of national reputation and world-wide fame, spent many nights in this old tavern.

The indictment and trial of Aaron Burr, for treason, is one of the most celebrated cases in the judicial history of the United States. The connection of Andrew Jackson with this celebrated case has been severely criticised by some, satisfactorily explained by others and extensively discussed by all. But it is not known by many people that Mr. Burr spent two nights at the old log tavern, which still stands near the Lebanon and Nashville turnpike, about fifteen miles from Nashville, on his journey to and from the Hermitage, to consult Mr. Jackson about that celebrated case and other important matters connected with the lives of those two eminent men, and the early political history of the United States.

There lives to-day an aged woman, in that old log tavern, who was a sprightly little girl about seven years of age, when the distinguished Aaron Burr was a guest at the wayside inn.

The husband of this remarkable woman died a few years ago at the age of ninety-six years. She has one brother yet living, who is seventy-five years old, and two sisters, one of whom is seventy-one and the other seventy-eight years of age. They are all in good health and remarkably well preserved.

She still lives in the simple style of olden times, and takes no particular interest in modern progress and improvements. She has her cards and wheel, and she spends her time knitting as industriously as if the comfort of a whole family depended upon her labor.

The day she was ninety-one years old, she brought out her cards and wheel, and spent much of the day in carding and spinning. She is simply a petrified specimen of life as it was in this country seventy or eighty years ago.

Her son is a well-to-do stock farmer, and, withal, a man of considerable general information. He has traveled extensively in America and Europe, and he converses intelligently on all the leading topics of public interest. He has remodeled the old hewed-log house, and furnished it in modern style, except the one room of his revered mother. He values the original old hewed-log walls very highly as sacred family relics, but he has so changed their appearance, by modern improvements, as to make his home both convenient and comfortable, and, at the same time, effectually protect the historic walls against decay.

In this old country home, surrounded by an excellent farm in a high state of cultivation, and amply provided with everything essential to her comfort, it is interesting to see this aged woman working away at her knitting as if her labor was the mainstay of the whole plantation. Her crude furniture, simple habits, untiring industry and rigid economy, in the midst of all the comforts and conveniences of an ordinary Tennessee country home of these modern times, clearly display the striking contrast between the old and the new order of things. She lives more in the past than in the present. The roar of the rushing train, the clatter of patent binders and the shrill whistle of steam engines are noticed only because they disturb her reveries about the howl of wolves, the scream of panthers or the hum of wheels, in the long ago, when she helped to lay and execute the plans of great industrial enterprises.

She was a contemporary of the Indians, and she remembers where they marked certain trees on the place, for purposes of their own, by hacking them with their tomahawks. A few years ago, some men on the place chopped into those old marked trees and found the hacks of the tomahawks fully four inches under the bark. The bark on the trees had grown over those old Indian marks, and all outward traces of them had long since disappeared.

In the days of her girlhood there was scarcely a house nearer the old tavern than Nashville, and hardly more than a country village there. The old two-story hewed-log tavern was a famous building throughout the country, and its erection was a business enterprise which distinguished her ancestor as a capitalist and a man of big schemes and reckless expenditures. The building, when completed, was leased in turn to Ramsey Y. Mason, John I. Hooper and Robert Hallum. These men all distinguished themselves as capable managers of immense business schemes, by leasing and successfully running the celebrated, two-story hewed-log tavern on the Nashville and Knoxville stage line. It was no ordinary enterprise to manage a hotel in which Presidents and Vice-Presidents lodged in those days. It is true that a common commercial traveler would protest against such hotel fare now as Aaron Burr considered first-class then, but the landlord of to-day has facilities, at slight expense, for making his guests comfortable, such as money could not buy at any price eighty years ago.

It is difficult to imagine the President or Vice-President of the United States putting up at a wayside tav-

ern, built of logs, only two low stories high, with only
six rooms to answer all purposes of kitchen, dining
room, landlord's family room, guest chambers, sitting
room, parlor, office and bar-room. Fortunately, the
rooms were all large, though low, and well supplied
with beds. Four beds in a room and two guests in a
bed was an economical arrangement well calculated to
encourage sociability among travelers and strangers, as
well as to make a remarkably small number of rooms
accommodate a suprisingly large number of guests. It
would be a sample of democratic familiarity inconsist-
ent with our ideas of propriety now-a-days, to put the
President of the United States in a room, at a public
hotel, with seven other men who were entire strangers
to him; but that only shows how far we have drifted
from our original moorings of primitive simplicty. It
seems almost sacrilegious to think of a common traveler and utter stranger sleeping with the President, or
even the Vice-President of the United States at a country tavern now, but this only illustrates the wide difference between old styles and modern customs. To my
mind, there is something really fascinating in the old
order of things. There is a novelty, which is really refreshing, in the idea of a common clodhopper and
rank stranger jamming his knees against the small of
His Excellency's back, in the middle of a cold night, as
he gave the cover a vigorous yank and said: Hello, Mr.
President, can't you let the cover come this way a few
inches?

A few weeks ago I visited that old house and conversed for several hours with the family who occupy it,
about its remarkable history. There is not a doubt in
my mind as to the accuracy of every statement of fact
here given concerning it.

There are many old people now living in the vicinity of this old house, who know its history as a popular tavern on the Nashville and Knoxville stage line before the days of railroads. This was the route mostly traveled from all the country West and Southwest to Virginia and the Carolinas. It was also the principal stage line connecting all this western country with the seat of government, and distinguished lawyers, politicians, government officials and military commanders were, therefore, frequent guests at the old wayside inn. From this tavern to Virginia, the whole country was called "the wilderness," in those days, and old negroes who made the journey with their masters seventy years ago evidently think there is still a vast stretch of dense forests and unbroken cane-brakes, inhabited by hostile Indians and ferocious wild beasts, between them and their old Virginia homes.

11

# CHAPTER X.

In preparing newly-cleared land for the plow, we first piled the large brush in heaps, and then carefully raked the whole face of the earth with little wooden hand-rakes, such as we used in gardening, till all the small twigs, and even the leaves, were gathered in piles, to be burned.

Of course all such trash ought to have been plowed under, to enrich the land, but it required more sense than the whole population of the country possessed, to master such a self-evident proposition as that.

We had but one kind of plow and that was called a bar-share. It was a profanity-provoking old fraud, with a long iron share and a wooden moldboard. When it struck a rock, stump or other solid substance, the handles would fly up with a quick jerk, and drop back with a vigorous punch. As they went up, they would almost invariably catch you under the chin and snap your teeth together like a rat trap; and as they came down, they rarely failed to give you a dig in the stomach which would knock the last prop from under your tottering piety and leave you gasping for breath and lamenting the poverty of your vocabulary. When it came to a root, it gave you no warning at all, but slowly sneaked under the thing so far that you had to back your team into the snow-banks of last winter, to get it out. When it found a root that was weak and yielding enough to serve its impious purpose, it would creep cautiously under it, stretching it to its utmost tension, till the team perceptibly slackened speed. You would then strike your horses with the whip, they would make an extra surge, the root would snap, the old bar-share would slip through the rent, and both ends of the broken root would come back at your defenseless shins with force enough to bark them from ankles to knees.

When we planted corn, we covered it with a hoe. We had not sense enough to see that it could be covered with a plow more rapidly and with far less work, and to think about a corn-planter was a mental feat which the brighest intellect in the whole mutton-headed lot of us could not attempt without a stimulant.

We plowed corn four or five times and then laid it by with a hoe by drawing a heap of dirt as large as an old-fashioned potato hill around every stalk. So great was the fertility of the soil that, after we quit working corn, late in summer, cockle burs and spanish needles would cover the whole face of the earth and grow as tall as a man's head on horse-back. We had to hitch a horse to a brush and drag between the corn rows, in the Fall, to break down the burs and weeds, so that we could gather the corn. We made from fifty to seventy-five bushels of corn per acre.

Cotton first began to be planted in our neighborhood when I was a boy. Each farmer planted a small patch for home use, and whenever it began to thunder, in the Fall, we would stop all other work, and all hands would rush to the cotton patch and pick every boll that was open, before it rained. We thought it would ruin cotton to get wet.

We planted cotton in drills, and put seed enough in one row to plant ten. Hoeing cotton was hard, tedious work. We first scraped each side of the drill with a hoe, leaving a narrow strip of cotton and weeds in the middle of the row. We then cut through this narrow drill with a hoe, leaving the cotton, weeds and grass in bunches two or three inches square and from eighteen to twenty inches apart. We then stooped down and pulled out all the weeds and grass in each bunch, and all the cotton but one stalk, with our fingers. I thought I had hoe skill enough to do some of this finger work with my hoe, but the first time I tried it I was soundly thrashed for my bold experiment. 'Twas ever thus with me in boyhood days. Every effort of suppressed genius to exert itself, brought me to grief.

We did a vast amount of unnecessary work, and in the very hardest possible way, as usual, in preparing land for the plow, in Spring, on which cotton grew the previous year. We simply pulled up the old cotton stalks, one by one, with our hands, piled them in heaps and burned them. For a boy eight or ten years old to pull up cotton stalks from seven to ten feet high, which had roots like young trees, was an industry well calculated to develop every muscle in his little body. Such work could be done only when the ground was thoroughly soaked with heavy rains, in early Spring, after the hard freezes of inclement Winter. I have pulled cotton stalks many a day through an incessant drizzle of cold rain, all the time wading mud and slush ankle deep with not a shoe on my foot or a dry thread in my clothing. The cold mud, chilling rain and raw wind would chap my hands, feet and face, and the continual strain on my muscles would set my back to aching in every joint of my spinal column. Long before night my hands, would be blistered and bleeding, and my appetite as voracious as a buzz-saw. Many a night, after working hard from daylight till dark, I have rolled on the floor before the fire, in our cabin home, and cried, in a perfect paroxysm of misery, with my aching back, blistered hands and bleeding face and feet, till exhausted nature found partial relief in troublous dreams. As I think of those days of misery and nights of suffering, there comes to my memory a vision of loveliness indescribable in the tear-bathed faces of loving, sympathizing sisters and mother, bending over me with simple salves and ointments of their own make, in tireless efforts to relieve my misery, and sooth me to sleep. For another sight of those blessed faces, another touch of those loving hands and another sound of those sweeter voices, to me, than angels' harps, I would cheerfully put my frail body to such a rack again. Mine was a hard lot, but I had sympathy in my suffering. Many a time would a pale-faced, over-worked, poorly-clad, frail-bodied mother or sister tenderly lift me from the cabin floor, where I had fallen asleep, and carry me to my humble couch rather than awake me to misery again. Many a time have I felt myself tenderly pressed to the loving heart of mother or sister, and, half waking, half dreaming, heard the whispers of pity and love, and the prayers of faith and hope, fresh from the loving heart, for me, as hot tears fell upon my scarcely more than baby face, and a loving kiss passionately pressed my childish lips. We were poor and illiterate, but not without the finer feelings of true love and keen sympathy one for another in our misery. The God of the poor was our God. The eye that never sleeps was over us; the arm that never fails, around us. He who sees the sparrows when they fall, and hears the softest murmur of sorrow from the lips of the humblest little one, in all the universe, who believes on him, continually hovered over us, and through all our troubles and sorrows safely guided us with his eye.

My work on the farm and in the clearing began when I was about seven years old, and before I was out of frocks. In preparing land for the plow, in early Spring, on which corn grew the previous year, my father cut the old corn-stalks with a hoe, and I picked them up

" REAP-HOOK."

with my hand, and piled them in heaps to be burned. This was my first work in the field. There was not inventive genius enough in the whole country, to conceive the idea of as simple a thing as a horse-rake, to gather corn-stalks in piles to be burned.

We cut our wheat with reap-hooks and threshed it with flails. As a harvesting machine a reap-hook was as simple as it was slow. It was simply a long, crooked knife. The operator held a bunch of wheat in his left hand and cut it with the reap-hook, which he manipulated with his right hand. We had to stoop down and cut the wheat off but a few inches above the ground. It was hard work, and tediously slow. A man could not harvest more than half an acre of wheat in a day, and there was more hard labor in one day of such work than in a whole week of harvesting with a patent binder.

A flail is aptly described by Webster as " an instrument for threshing or beating grain from the ear by hand consisting of a wooden handle, at the end of which a stouter and shorter pole, or club is so hung as to swing freely." The simplest method of making a flail was to cut a hickory sapling long enough for both the handle and the shorter pole, or club. At the place where the handle was to end and the club to begin, we beat a section of the sapling, a few inches long, with a hammer or the back of an ax, till it was a mere withe and perfectly flexible. Ordinarily, the handle of a flail was about five feet long, and the club about two feet in length. We laid the wheat on the floor of the barn, or on a covered pen of rails, and pounded it to a mass of chaff, broken straw and wheat. This work was always done in the hottest days of summer.

When the wheat was threshed, we sifted it through a sieve, or riddle, made for the purpose, to separate the wheat from the straw and coarse particles of chaff. Such sieves were home-made, of course. They were simply large boxes, with perforated bottoms woven of hickory-bark, white-oak splits or raw-hide strips. The holes in the bottom were about one-fourth of an inch square. In sifting the wheat, all the finer chaff that was small enough to go through the holes in the home-made sieve, would remain with the wheat, of course.

To separate it from the wheat, one man would pour wheat and chaff together, in a small stream, from a vessel held high above his head, while two other men fanned vigorously, with a sheet or bed quilt, as it fell. This fanning process was an art that required "skilled labor." The fanners would take hold of opposite ends of the sheet or quilt, stretch it tight, and fan, by a peculiar motion of their arms, with all their might, in the direction the wind was blowing, as the wheat and chaff fell.

In course of time the reap-hook was supplanted by the cradle, and the tramping of horses and oxen took the place of the flail. We thought the millennium was surely at hand then. The great progress of the world and the astounding inventions of men, were, to us, unanswerable arguments in support of the theory that the end of the world was rapidly approaching. How Gabriel could sit calmly by and see one man cut three acres of wheat, with a cradle, in a day, and tramp it out with an old blind horse, in a few hours, and not give his horn a toot, was more than we could understand.

The first cradles we ever used were crude and unwieldy. They little resembled the more perfect implements of the same name which are still in use in some parts of the country.

Why we did not, from the first, adopt the process of threshing wheat by tramping it with horses and oxen, is another inexplicable mystery. That is by no means a modern idea. It was generally practiced in Palestine in Bible times. But then many things in matters of religion that were practiced in Palestine more than eighteen hundred years ago have not been generally adopted by the churches in this country yet.

In preparing a threshing-floor, we sometimes swept

the ground clean, wet it thoroughly to free it from dust
and pounded it hard, with mauls, to make it firm.

CUTTING WHEAT WITH A CRADLE.

Sometimes we used the puncheon floors of barns for
threshing-floors, sometimes we used the smooth surface
of large, flat rocks for that purpose. The process was

simply to spread the wheat, in the sheaf, on the threshing-floor, and ride or drive the horses or oxen, over it at
a brisk trot, in a circle, like circus horses, till the wheat-
straw was thoroughly tramped to pieces and the wheat
was completely thrashed. We then cleaned the wheat
by hand in the manner described in connection with
flailing.

| Is it any wonder that, with our lack of both tools and
sense, in the midst of a howling wilderness, we had a
hard struggle to keep soul and body from parting com-
pany? | The economy we practiced and the hard work
we did, with the improved methods we now have of
doing things, would put any family in independent circumstances in a few years.

I remember that, when my father had eleven in family, his store account, for a whole year, was only sixty-
seven dollars. When he settled with his merchant and
paid off his year's account, he came home and gave us
all a long lecture upon our extravagance, and declared
that such reckless expenditures would bankrupt him. It
sounds more like fiction than history to say the entire
store account, for a whole year, of a family of eleven, five
of whom were young ladies in fashionable society, was
only sixty-seven dollars. When my father was eighty
years old, the store account for himself and his wife
only, for a year, was one hundred and fifty dollars. By
chance, I was at his house when he settled with his
merchant and paid his account for the year. I reminded him of the time when he lectured us for extravagance when the year's account for all eleven of us was
only sixty-seven dollars. But the dear old man merely
said :

" Yes, my son! But times have changed greatly
since then! "

Well, he was right. Times have changed since then sure enough.

A queer old man was my father. He always raised horses for his own use, and a few for sale; but he never would raise a mule or own any negroes, beyond a few trusty old domestic servants which he treated very much as he treated his own children. He had an inexpressible aversion for both mules and negroes, and always said:

"If there had never been a negro in the world, there never would have been any demand for mules. He never owned an acre of land till late in the evening of life. Why, I do not know. Land cost nothing but the clearing of it, yet he was content to "*lease*" every acre he needed. That is to say, he would clear land owned by other men, for the privilege of cultivating it three years. Many hard-working, but improvident men of his age, did the same. From my earliest recollection to the time I left home, to engage in business for myself, we put in our time closely every day in the year that we were not engaged in cultivating the crop, clearing, building houses, making rails and fencing land, for other men, on a "lease." We built houses and cleared land enough for a dozen good homes, and yet we were homeless. When we cleared a field, our "lease" would hold it just long enough to get it clear of roots and in a good state of cultivation, when we had to turn it over to the rightful owner and take another "lease" in the woods. By going a few miles out of the neighborhood, we could have selected a homestead of as fine land as the country afforded, but we had not enterprise enough to do it.

I made the first important rise in the world when I bought, with the price of my own labor, a very high, home-made, "stove-pipe" hat. It was not *called* a "stove-pipe" hat then, because there was no such thing as a stove pipe, to suggest such a name, but that is really what it was. It was made of 'coon's fur. In *color* it was unique; in *shape*, variable and uncertain. When new, it was, in shape, the express image of the hatter's "*block*" on which it was modeled, but as it grew older, day by day, it gradually lost its beauty of form. It seemed that it could never make up its mind as to what shape it really preferred, and, though it changed its form every day and every hour, it never improved its original appearance. Each new form was less comely than its predecessor, and the changes followed each other with ever increasing rapidity as the moments flitted by. Finally, it got soaking wet in a hard rain one day, and, to hold it on my head, against the pressure of a brisk wind, I took hold of what, up to that time, I had understood was the brim of the thing, and yanked it down with more vigor than discretion. *Presto change!* It was without form and void! The brim was gone, the crown was no more! It was simply a long, conical bag, as large as my head at the bottom and as sharp as an acorn at the top. I calmly looked upon its shapeless ruins and thought of its departed glory for a few brief but bitter seconds, and then threw it into the ash-hopper with a feeling of disgust for all the glory of the world akin to that expressed by Solomon, the wise, in his ever memorable words: "Vanity of vanities, saith the preacher. All is vanity and vexation of spirit?"

We raised no hay, but pulled fodder as a substitute. The season for fodder pulling was in the month of August, and about the first of October we began to gather corn, pick cotton and sow wheat. We rarely finished working the crop before the middle of July.

When I was fifteen years of age I went to school six months in succession. Up to that time my education had been in homeopathic doses, about a month at a time, between fodder-pulling and cotton-picking. My six months term at school finished my collegiate education, except a post-graduate course at the anvil in a blacksmith shop.

The only kinds of gambling we ever engaged in were horse races and shooting matches. Strange to say, those things were not then considered gambling, even by preachers and other church dignitaries.

A shooting match was simply a trial of skill in rifle-shooting, with beef as the stake gambled for. A man who had a beef for market would appoint a time and place for a shooting match, bring his beef to the ground and sell it out in "*chances,*" in the shooting match. Each chance entitled the purchaser to one shot in the "match." By common consent and tacit agreement, the beef was divided into five parts as follows: Two hind quarters, two fore quarters and the hide and tallow, and lead shot into the tree against which the mark was set. The best shot took first choice of the five parts, second best, second choice, and so on till the beef was all divided among the marksmen.

So great was their skill in rifle shooting that, at sixty yards, off-hand, a man who failed to break the small circle around the center of the mark was severely ridiculed and openly disgraced. When I was but ten years old, if I brought home a squirrel, from one of my hunts, shot anywhere except in the head, my father sharply rebuked me for my lack of skill as a marksman and threatened to take my rifle from me and get me a shot gun.

It is strange that no one ever detected any gambling in

CLEARING LAND AT NIGHT.

a shooting match. My father was an elder in the Presbyterian church, and would have scorned the idea of gambling in anything, and yet he won all the beef our whole family needed, at shooting matches. His reputation as a marksman was so well established that the neighbors would frequently give him first choice of the the five parts in the beef, not to shoot at all. If he bought as many as five "chances," he rarely failed to get the whole beef with his five shots.

We did much work at night in clearing land. The small boys would gather brush and pile them on fires to make light for the hands to work by and to get the brush out of the way, while the larger boys and men cut saplings, felled trees and deadened timber in the clearing. We often worked at night in this way, for hours.

# CHAPTER XI.

Drinking was as common as eating. Still-houses were more numerous than school-houses. Whisky, apple brandy, and peach brandy were almost as generally used as water, and nearly as cheap. Every man could make his own beverage without paying even an occupation tax. Those who did not feel inclined to make it themselves, hauled their grain or fruit to the nearest still-house, which was never very far, and had it made " on the shares." Every householder laid in his yearly supply of "sperits" as regularly as his bread-stuff. No man could maintain a good character as a church member without keeping constantly on hand enough "sperits" to stimulate "the parson" at his regular monthly visits.

It is perhaps not expedient to use names or specify time and place, but a story of two prominent church members will illustrate the spirit of the age. They had been to market to lay in supplies for the annual revival at their church. They talked thus with each other as they journeyed homeward :

"How much 'sperits' did you git?"

"Ten gallons."

"Jest sech stinginess as that will sp'ile the meetin' an' kill the church. I got twenty gallons, myself, an' you are jest as able to support the gospil as I am, if you wuz n't so dog stingy."

(176)

Fifty cents would buy a gallon of the best whisky in the market. One no more thought of entertaining guests without drinks than without regular meals and lodging. Drinking was not restricted by law, opposed by temperance organizations or discouraged by churches. Preachers drank habitually, but not to drunkenness, and openly took their stimulants at public bars.

In later years temperance organizations and churches began to discourage drinking, and the more progressive preachers in all churches became total abstainers and earnest temperance advocates. The conservative preachers and church members held out firmly against such unwarranted innovations and interference with personal rights. This led to wide-spread discussion, general disputation and continual wrangles in churches throughout the country. Some churches prohibited their members from joining temperance societies on pain of excommunication. In many places churches divided on this issue. Paul's admonition to Timothy: "Drink no longer water, but take a little wine for thy stomach's sake, and thine often infirmities" was well thumbed in every Bible. From the prominence given that text in the pulpits of all the churches, one might have supposed the country was suffering from a sweeping epidemic of stomach troubles and infirmities of one sort and another, for which strong drink was the only remedy.

I deem it unwise to give names, date, or locality, but I had the following story from the lips of the preacher in the case:

A total abstinence preacher and a strong advocate of the cause of temperance conducted a revival in a neighborhood near a saloon. Many souls were converted, and, among the number, the saloon-keeper himself. The

12

converts not only professed religion, but, under the good man's preaching, they were also converted on the temperance question. The saloon-keeper was in trouble. He did not want to sell any more whisky, but everything he had in the world was invested in the stuff. To pour it out was in accordance with his feelings, but that meant financial ruin. The welfare of his family was not the only thing to be considered. He had bought much of his liquor on a credit, and the rights of his creditors were clearly involved. To pour it out would leave his family without a penny and himself without ability to pay his honest debts. He was greatly troubled, but finally decided to state the case to the preacher and ask for advice. The preacher was in doubt what to advise him to do, and decided to lay the case before the brethren. They all thought and prayed over it in great seriousness. The revival grew in interest. A deep religious feeling pervaded the entire community. Sinners repented, saints rejoiced, scoffers wondered and wags grew serious. The preacher inveighed against sin in general, explained to all the way of life, and denounced drunkenness and the liquor traffic as a sin against God and a crime against mankind. The saloon-keeper groaned in spirit, but no one could solve his difficulty or suggest any way to lighten his burden.

Finally, under the excitement of the revival, the zealous new converts and the happy old brethren decided to buy the whole stock of liquor and pour it out. The preacher seized the idea with delight and urged them to carry out the good resolution.

Accordingly they started a subscription, to make up the money, and appointed a day considerably in the future to meet at the saloon and consummate the business. Unfortunately, the revival closed and the religious excitement collapsed before the day arrived when the faithful were to meet at the saloon, to purchase and pour out the condemned beverage.

The pilgrims gathered promptly, but each one had a sort of I-didn't-know-it-was-loaded and wish-I-hadn't-done-it expression on his countenance. But no one had the nerve to back down. The money was promptly handed over and counted down to the ex-saloon-keeper and late convert. The whisky now belonged to the church, but no one offered to pour it out. Evidently

"THE MONEY WAS COUNTED."

they all felt the sacrifice they were about to make. Truly, the spirit was willing, but the flesh was weak.

It is interesting to study the work of grace in the heart, the re-action from intense religious fervor and excitement, the strength of temptation, the weakness of human nature and the deplorable victory of sin over the saints, as illustrated in this remarkable case. But a few days ago every man in this little band of brethren was all aglow with religious zeal, and not one in the number but would have been indignant had any man accused him of the weakness they all now felt. The way to heaven seems plain enough, and easy enough too, to the religious enthusiast in the midst of a revival. Many a man can "bid farewell to every fear" and "face a frowning world" during a protracted meeting, who will not walk two squares to a prayer-meeting three weeks after the revival has closed. It is no unusual thing to see a man "bound for the promised land" one week, during a revival, and bound for the nearest saloon the next week, every morning before breakfast. There are scores of church members who will "bear the toil, endure the pain, supported by his word," right through a rousing revival, and break down under the re-action and go to pieces morally, supported by a keg of Milwaukee beer, in less than a month after the revival closes. I have no objection to the doctrine of final perseverance of the saints. It is a good doctrine. I like it. As a theory, it has my unanimous endorsement. What I want to find is a congregation of Christians which, as one man, will give the world a practical illustration of it.

The saints who met at the old-fashioned country saloon, a short time after the revival closed, to buy the whisky and pour it out, were all right in theory. It was in *practice* they so signally failed. For several moments after the whisky was bought and paid for, they sat in solemn silence and deep meditation. Finally one old brother said :

"My old 'oman's out'n camphor."

Of course that was a "feeler" only. For several seconds no one responded to it. The silence seemed almost dense. The devil was clearly at work on the new converts. By and by another old brother said :

"My old 'oman was a telling of me t' other day as how she needed some sperits to make bitters."

Another period of painful silence. Every man was fighting a mighty battle in himself against the world, the flesh and the devil. Two souls in that faithful little band had already showed signs of alarming weak-

"THE OLD 'OMAN'S OUT'N CAMPHOR."

ness. Evidently they were hard pressed in the struggle. Possibly they had already surrendered. Who would be the next to fall? The silence was broken again by the faltering voice of another weak brother. He said:

"It's good fur snake bites."

The pilgrims now began to get interested. They crowded around the three brethren who had spoken so signifi-

cantly of "camphor," "snake bites" and "bitters."
The crisis was passed.    The battle was lost to the saints.
The devil's guns had swept the field.

The talking now became general.    They all said it
looked like foolishness to throw away several gallons of
good "sperits" which they had paid for, when they all
had to buy such stuff, much as they detested it as a
beverage, for camphor, snake bites, bitters and other
medical purposes.    The ex-saloon-keeper and late convert had a full supply of jugs, bottles and kegs.    Why
not buy all the vessels he had on hand and divide the
"sperits" among the brethren in proportion to the
amount of money each one had paid?    Of course that
was the only wise thing to do under the circumstances,
when it was suggested.    It was commendable economy
against shameful waste.    It was also a part of their
duty to the ex-saloon-keeper and late convert, to buy
his stock of jugs, bottles, barrels and kegs, as well as
his stock of liquor.    What use could he have for such
vessels after his saloon was closed?    He could not sell
them ; he was not able to lose them.

The jugs, bottles and kegs were promptly bought, and
the liquor was equitably divided among the brethren.
Then came another pause in the proceedings.    The convention again needed a leader, and for lack of one it
collapsed.    The silence of a Quaker meeting settled
down upon the little band of halting pilgrims.    What
they needed now was a man to cry "make way for liberty," and throw himself upon the altar of his country,
so to speak.    That man was not present.    There was
not even one to say "give me liberty or give me death."
They stood like sheep for the slaughter, and like lambs
before the shearer, they were dumb.    By this time it
was night.    Clearly, something must be done.    It was

time to adjourn, and yet the main business of the convention, as they all understood it now, had scarcely been touched. Finally, the camphor man said:

"My old 'oman's mighty partic'lar about the kind of sperits she uses to make camphor out'n."

"THE SECOND BALLOT."

No one else spoke. The silence was painful. The pilgrims groaned in spirit. By and by the snake-bite man said:

"I would be afeared to resk anything but the best o' sperits fur a snake bite."

Only a sigh from the rest of the pilgrims. For several seconds no one else spoke. Everybody seemed embarrassed. The last speaker was clearly endorsed by the whole convention, but no one seemed disposed to put the question squarely before the house. At last the bitters man said:

"My old 'oman always tells me to be shore'n' *taste* liquor before I bring it home fur bitters. It takes mighty good sperits to make bitters that's wo'th a cent."

This sounded like business. The pilgrims became interested again. They crowded around the speakers. The suggestion about tasting the "sperits" fairly electrified the crowd. Clearly that was the proper thing to do under the circumstances. The bitters man tasted the liquor in one of the jugs. He was somewhat doubtful as to the quality of the stuff. He wanted to know whether the other jugs contained a better quality of "sperits." He tried another jug and pronounced it better. One of the other brethren present openly expressed doubt as to this taster's judgment. The doubter tasted both jugs. They at once got into an animated argument and both men tasted both jugs again. They were further apart on the second ballot than the first. They put the question again, including other jugs. Result, a "dead lock" on the third ballot and neither of the tasters could remember which jug he said was the best on the second ballot. Clearly they were both too drunk by this time, to know anything about it. Each one of them appealed the question to the house. This made it necessary for every body to taste the contents of all the jugs in dispute, and in less than an hour that little band of loving brothers was a howling mob of drunken backsliders. They whooped, they yelled, they embraced each other with maudlin affection and sang sketches of revival hymns. They preached, they exhorted, they prayed, they shouted, they quarreled, and finally they ended the carousal in a free fight and a general fisticuff.

Scarcely an incident in this story is exaggerated in

"WE'R ON OUR JOURNEY HOME."

the slightest particular. I had the story from the old preacher who figured so conspicuously in the matter, and whose flock it was which thus publicly disgraced itself *en masse*. The church is to-day intact, as a religious organization, and one of the most solid and substantial country churches in the South. Actually a score or more of the leading members of that church, years ago, not many days after the close of a very successful revival, met at the saloon of their newly-adopted brother in the church, bought the whole stock of liquor on hand, divided it among themselves, all got as drunk as lords and ended the meeting with a general row, just as I have related.

Preachers and church members who drank regularly were not bad people. They simply drank in all good conscience. They did not consider it wrong to drink. In the matter of unyielding and uncompromising fidelity to what they believed to be their duty, the people of that age were not inferior to this generation. The change in public sentiment, since those days, on the drinking question, shows encouraging progress in the moral education of the world.

All reformations must needs move slowly. It is not easy for middle-aged men to conform their conduct to new theories. The work of reforming a people has scarcely begun when they are brought to see the necessity of reformation. Indeed it is but a small part of the work of reformation to bring them to acknowledge the error of their way and resolve to change their course of life. Even after all this has been done for them, there must needs be a long and tedious stumbling over old habits and acquired appetites before the work of reformation is perfected. When the preachers and church members of olden times, who were habitual drinkers, undertook to conform their lives to newly-acquired ideas and convictions touching the drinking habit, they were not unlike their brethren of the present generation in that they often fell into temptations and for a season gave way to an ill-trained appetite.

# CHAPTER XII.

An old-time country funeral was an occasion of no ordinary importance. A simple service of song and prayer was usually held at the grave, but the regular funeral sermon was preached at a place and time duly appointed and widely advertised, weeks, and often months after the burial. When a man's wife died, the accepted code of etiquette prohibited him from showing any signs of a disposition to make other matrimonial arrangements for the future, till after the funeral of his lamented companion. When a woman lost her husband, she disgraced herself if she received any attentions at all from the sterner sex, before the funeral. The period between the burial and the funeral was a season of mourning, and society would not tolerate anything remotely resembling a courtship in either widows or widowers during that time. On this account, there were probably cases in which precocious relicts lamented the customary delay of such memorial services quite as much as the original bereavement. To lose one life-partner by death was scarcely a greater calamity, in the estimation of some widows and widowers, than to miss a good chance to get another, through respect to an exacting public sentiment. Such perplexities, however, tended to increase the causes of sorrow during the weary period of mourning between the burial and the funeral. Those who did not mourn for the dead, pined for the living. With the grave between them and their

lost love behind, and the funeral between them and
their heart's idol before, they were hopelessly shut in between the memory of the past and their anxiety for the
future, with no source of consolation for the present.
Yet no widow or widower, who had any regard at all
for the respect of the best people of the country, would
venture to engage in anything like courtship before the
funeral of the late lamented.

Many people selected the preacher to preach their
funerals before they died. This was frequently done by
very old people, and by those who died of lingering, in-
curable diseases. In some instances persons arranged
all the details of their own funerals years before they
died, even to the designation of the place where it
should be preached, the text of Scripture it should be
preached from, the songs that should be sung and the
singers who should sing them.

Men often revealed life-secrets to preachers whom
they selected to preach their funerals, to be made public
in their funeral sermons. The people, therefore, took
great interest in the funeral of every man, about whose
life hung a mystery of any kind. It was no unusual
thing for a funeral sermon to throw a flood of historic
light upon the past life, as well as a halo of prophetic
illumination around the future destiny, of its subject.

In communicating to his chosen preacher the leading
points of his own funeral, a man always remembered
his friends, relatives and enemies. He left a message
for each, in the form of a piece of brotherly advice, a
gentle rebuke or a word of exhortation. All such messages, advice and admonitions were adroitly worked into
the sermon. Those who were of "the same faith and
order" of the deceased, touching religious convictions, and
"in good standing and full fellowship," were commend-

ed for their soundness in the faith and exhorted to continue steadfast in the doctrine. Those who were members of some other denomination in religion were delicately but indirectly reminded of their heresy, and pointed to the true church. And finally, those who were without God and without hope in the world were lectured for their waywardness and warned of their danger.

. Skillfully and delicately managed, all this, in a funeral sermon, made a profound impression upon the community. When a preacher wisely manipulated his material in a funeral sermon, it was difficult for the hearers to rid themselves of the feeling that they were listening to a message from the unseen world. Of course the judicious preacher, in dealing with denominational differences, for instance, would never put the case with offensive bluntness. It was easy enough to give it the milder form of a lamentation from the grave over the loss of church fellowship, in this life, by reason of the denominational differences in question, and if the preacher stated the case strongly in this light, and backed it up by the most confident asseverations of the deceased, in his very last moments, that *his* faith was clear and *his* church undoubtedly right, the sermon rarely failed to raise grave apprehensions in the minds of members of other denominations, if nothing more.

Public sentiment required the preacher to state definitely what was the future and final destiny of the soul of the deceased. There was no evading this point. It was required of the preacher to tell not only where the departed spirit had gone, but to give his reasons for concluding that it had gone there. From his opinion in such cases, there was no appeal on this earth. People went to funerals to learn the final destiny of departed spirits with as much confidence as they examined an almanac to learn when the moon changed. This imparted to every funeral sermon something of the seriousness and solemnity of the last judgment.

Of course there were people who gravely doubted whether the judgment rendered in the funeral sermon would, in all cases, be confirmed· by the upper court, but such doubters were not very numerous or outspoken. The fact that the preacher was taken into the full confidence of the deceased in the manner already explained, gave his words great weight concerning the spirit's fate in the world to come. His opinion on this point, skillfully interwoven with messages from the dead to the living, seemed to partake of the nature of such messages, and we were all inclined to accept what he said as though it were a voice from the unseen world. I speak now from the recollection of the impressions funeral sermons made upon my mind in early childhood, rather than from any distinct remembrance of the exact words of the preacher on such occasions. I know I got things mixed in my childish mind along this line sometimes, but still my impressions were not entirely without foundation in the literal meaning of the plain words of the sermons. I remember well that my little head often became so confused between what the dead man *said* and the living preacher *imagined* and *inferred,* that I would almost regard the parson's vivid and glowing descriptions of heaven and hell as the testimony of the deceased, as an eye-witness of those things, sent back to us by the preacher.

There was still another ground for our faith in the preacher's knowledge as to the destiny of souls departed, apart from the fact that he was the full confidant and spiritual adviser of the deceased even down to the

very valley and shadow of death. In those days
preachers were called to the ministry, and qualified for
all ministerial functions, by direct and plenary revelations of the Spirit of God. At least they so claimed,
and the people so be-
lieved. They claimed,
and the people general-
ly believed, that they
were in communication
with God by the pres-
ence, power and revela-
tions of the Spirit in
their hearts. We under-
stood that what they
preached on any subject
was given them from
God by such spiritual
revelations.

To study a subject,
prepare a sermon or
even select a text be-
fore going to a regular
appointment for preach-
ing was a sin of pre-
sumption with some of
those old-time country
pulpit lights. It was
no unusual thing to
hear " book larnin' " of          " CLERGYMAN'S SUIT."
every kind publicly denounced from the pulpit as a
species of infidelity, in preachers, toward God, and a
sinful exaltation of human wisdom against divine power
and spiritual guidance in the ministry. Even ability
to read was, by some, considered *prima facie* evidence

of heresy, and a preacher not infrequently demonstrated his orthodoxy, to his own satisfaction, by boisterous asseverations of his ignorance in the pulpit.

Those old preachers were, nevertheless, men of great power and influence among the people. A slouch hat, hip trousers and a coarse shirt completed a fashionable clergyman's suit, and strong lungs, vigorous jestures and copious tears constituted the leading elements of strength in a popular sermon. Some people believed that preachers spake as the Spirit gave them utterance, as implicitly as they believed any other tenet of their religion. Many people and preachers had no other idea as to the use of the Bible than that of a suitable place to find texts for "sarmints" and to record an epitome of family history in the form of a condensed record of births, marriages and deaths. The idea that it was a book of practical instruction touching personal and religious duties, given by revelation of the Spirit of God through inspired men, to be read, understood and obeyed by ordinary men, seems never to have entered their minds. Beyond the knowledge of a few disconnected texts, which such preachers learned largely from each other, and which such people took for granted were somewhere in the Bible and meant anything, in a general way, that the preacher saw proper to *say* they meant, but which really meant nothing in particular to such wooden-headed audiences, the Bible was a sealed book. It was a rare thing for preachers of that class to know exactly where, in the Bible, their favorite texts could be found. They always quoted a text from memory at the beginning of their remarks, and never used any other portion of Scripture during the long harangue called a sermon. They rarely failed to misquote the texts that were in the Bible, and not infrequently based a sermon on a familiar adage, supposed to be Scripture, but really not in the Bible in any form. There are people yet living who have heard sermons on the texts: "Make hay while the sun shines," and "Every tub shall stand on its own bottom," and probably the preachers are not all dead yet who have based sermons on such texts, supposing that they were in the Bible. In citing a text the preacher gave himself the widest latitude by saying it will be found "somewhere betwixt the lids of the good book," and the people never looked to see whether it was there or not. If, after hearing a sermon, a man chanced to stumble on the text in his random reading in the Bible, and found that it read "jest adzactly as how the parson said it read," that was evidence abundantly satisfactory to him of the correctness of the whole sermon, no matter what it contained.

Errors of pronunciation sometimes twisted very plain texts so as to make them fit all sorts of sermons. A case in point was that of an old preacher who selected the familiar passage from the writings of Peter against those who "shall bring in damnable *heresies*," as a text against *gossiping*. It was a mistake in the pronunciation of the word "*heresies*" that suggested the appropriateness of the text as a foundation for the remarks the faithful old preacher wished to make against "*damnable hearsay*." Regardless of the real meaning of the text, the sermon was a timely rebuke against certain old women of the neighborhood whose busy tongues were continually stirring up strife in the community by repeating, with appropriate additions, subtractions and variations, everything they heard about other people.

In view of all the surroundings, it is not difficult to

13

understand why the people firmly believed the preacher knew exactly what was the destiny of every man whose funeral sermon he had occasion to deliver. Why should he not know? Was he not called of God to the minis-

"DAMNABLE HEARSAY."

try? Was he not in constant communion with God by the Spirit? Could not and did not the same Spirit which suggested his texts, arranged his sermons and guided his delivery, reveal to him the secrets of the un-

seen world when his preaching was of necessity along
the line of such deep mysteries? And besides all this,
did not the man whose funeral he was preaching plainly
*tell* him, in strictest confidence, where he was going at
the very last moment before he took his departure to
the land of disembodied spirits?

The idea that a preacher could make a mistake, in a
funeral sermon, as to the destiny of the deceased, was
preposterous, to that class of believers and reasoners.

Though everybody understood that the preachers had
only to make known, in the funeral sermon, the final
destiny of the deceased, whatever that might be, the
people were disposed, with strange inconsistency, to
hold him responsible for the fate of the dead. Hence
they talked about *preaching* folks to heaven or to hell,
in discussing funeral sermons, as flippantly as if it were
merely optional with the preacher as to what disposition
should be made of the souls of the dead. To preach a
man to hell invariably aroused the indignation of
his friends; to preach him to heaven invited the silent
contempt, if not the open ridicule, of his enemies.
Thus the poor preacher was beset with formidable difficulties on the right hand and on the left. He could
only state what he knew as to the destiny of departed
souls. For that destiny, whatever it might be, the funeral preacher was in no way responsible, but the people
declined to see it in that light. They would not even
allow him to escape the dilemma by omitting from the
funeral sermon any reference at all to the destiny of
the deceased. He was compelled to preach the man to
heaven or hell one, in words of no uncertain import,
and accept the consequences.

It is impossible to describe the intense interest of the
whole country in those long-appointed funeral sermons.

Everybody wanted to hear the dying confessions and last messages of the deceased, and to learn for certain what was the fate of his soul. It may be said, to the credit of those old-time preachers, that the story lost nothing in the telling. They were men of fertile imaginations as well as retentive memories, and the material furnished by both memory and imagination was used to the best advantage, by the help of vigorous gesticulation and stentorian voices.

The whole country for miles in every direction, would come together to hear those set funeral sermons. Many a woman walked and carried an infant in her arms from two to four miles, to a funeral.

In case a man died without arranging for his own funeral beforehand, his friends and relatives had to settle all the details of the memorial services among themselves. To do this without differences and unpleasant disagreements, was next to impossi-

GOING TO THE FUNERAL.

ble. Those interested in the funeral were often scattered over a wide scope of country; they not infrequently belonged to different churches: they had all the sectional prejudices peculiar to their respective neighborhoods; each family had its favorite preacher; and every delegation had its choice as to where the funeral should be preached. These differences often produced unpleasant discord in efforts to settle the details of the funeral services. Sometimes they led to alienations in

families, wrangles between different neighborhoods, factions in society and open schisms in churches. When the arrangements were all settled, due announcements were made of the time, place and preacher of the funeral, in all the country churches for miles around, several weeks in advance of the day set for the services.

Funeral congregations were always large, and men of business soon learned to take advantage of them for purely selfish interests. Members of churches and even preachers of the gospel looked upon funerals as favorable opportunities to push various business enterprises of a purely personal nature. Jockeys went to funerals to sell or swap horses; candidates, to electioneer; road overseers, to "warn hands;" school teachers, to circulate their "articles" and make up schools; sheriffs, to serve warrants, subpœna witnesses and summon jurors; creditors, to collect debts; and farmers in general, to "lease" land, buy mules, sell bee-trees and ask hands to log-rollings, house-raisings and corn-shuckings. In a word, everybody in the country went, if for no other purpose, because everybody else would be there—men, women, boys, girls, babies and dogs.

The preacher who was to deliver the sermon always extended the ministerial courtesy of an invitation to a seat in the pulpit, to other preachers present, especially to those of "the same faith and order." For the preacher in charge of ceremonies to allow another preacher to occupy a seat in the audience, was an open declaration of "non-fellowship," and for a preacher in the audience to decline to take a seat in the pulpit, was to declare the preacher in charge of the services unsound in the faith. When the pulpit was too small to accommodate all the preachers present with seats, as was frequently the case at such large gatherings, "the preacher in charge" of the ceremonies designated a reserved seat on a long bench in the amen corner for such ministerial brethren as he deemed sound in the faith and worthy of recognition as preachers. It was cus-

GOING TO THE FUNERAL, TO SWAP HORSES.

tomary for one of the brethren invited to a seat in the pulpit to "open meetin'" with reading, singing and prayer.

On one of those great funeral occasions, a blessed old preacher, who had walked a long distance through dust

and heat, was invited to a seat in the pulpit, and asked
to "open meetin'." He wore red, cow-hide shoes and
home-spun clothes, and his face was all covered with
dust and streaked with great drops of perspiration

"A HUNTIN' SEED PEAS."

which literally rained down his whole anatomy. He
arose, hymn book in hand, looked over the vast audience and said:

"Breethering, as bein' as I'm here, I'll open the meetin' fur brother Buncomb, an' then he'll preach the fun-

eral sarmint accordin' to previous a-p'intment. But while I'm before you, I want to say as how my main business over here is a huntin' of some seed peas, an' if any body here has got any to spar', I'd like to know it after meetin'!'"

A man moved from Tennessee to Texas. It was a long journey, in an ox wagon, through a dangerous country. Post-offices were few, mail routes were slow and uncertain, a postage stamp cost twenty-five cents and there were practically no such things as newspapers, and no facilities at all for gathering news. The emigrant was not heard from by his friends and relatives in Tennessee for several months after his departure, but finally a letter came, bearing the sad news that he was dangerously sick. Nothing further was heard from him, and finally his friends and relatives concluded, perhaps correctly, that he was dead. They therefore selected a preacher and appointed a time and place to preach his funeral. An immense congregation assembled, as usual on such occasions, and the preacher introduced the sermon by saying:

"The last time we hearn from him he was very sick, an' seein' as how he's never writ any more, the breethering, friends and relatives consider it onsafe to wait any longer about the funeral, an' so the time has ariv, a-cordin' to previous a-p'intment, to preach the funeral."

Just why the "breethering" considered it "onsafe" to wait any longer, he did not explain. The case illustrates, however, the importance the people generally attached to funeral preaching. To lay the body of any man, woman or child to rest in the grave without a funeral sermon to follow at some future time, was uni-

versally considered "onsafe." If any man had suggested such a thing, he would have been considered wanting
in reverence for the dead, respect for the living or regard for civilized society. There was nothing more
strenuously enforced by public sentiment than the custom of preaching funerals. Even the custom of bury-
ing the dead, was scarcely more universally observed
than that of funeral preaching.

The prevailing theology of the particular time and
section of country now in mind, was Calvinism of the
most pronounced type. The people were taught from
all the pulpits, except on funeral occasions, that a certain number of men and angels was predestined to
eternal damnation before the world was made, and that
the number to be saved and the number to be damned,
were both so very definitely fixed that neither of them
could be increased or diminished. It was also clearly
explained and generally understood that but few souls
were elected to salvation, or could, by any means, be saved.
Every body firmly believed that a vast majority of the inhabitants of the world would go to hell when they died,
and the people would have died at the stake rather than
renounce publicly that fundamental tenet of their religious faith. And yet, according to the funeral sermons,
nearly every body went to heaven, and every body but
the bitterest enemies of the deceased raised a howl
of indignation at the funeral preachers the few times
any of them dared to express an opinion that the devil
had captured a soul. A few of the meanest and most
unpopular men of the country were preached to hell, as
I am reliably informed, at a very early day, but I never
heard such a funeral. The non-elect must have all died
before I was born. I have heard scores of funerals, but
never a soul did the devil get, out of the whole lot of

them. Even when the doctrine of predestination began to give place to that of man's free agency, the funeral preachers kept hell as vacant and as hot as ever. While men lived, the preachers told them they were going straight to the devil, but when they were dead, the funeral sermon never failed. to land them in heaven. The fact is, preachers did not have the courage of their convictions. They honestly believed in hell, and predestination, and damnation, but when they came to make a personal application of the doctrine, they lacked the courage to say the man's soul is in hell, beyond hope or help.

And yet, strange to say, the people saw nothing ridiculous in all those old funeral ceremonies and sermons. The funerals of those days surpassed anything we ever see in modern times, in the matter of deep and universal sorrow for the dead, and warm, loving sympathy for the living.

I remember one case, when I was a boy, in which a very old man in our neighborhood selected me for tenor in the choir at his prospective funeral. He chose about a dozen other young people in the neighborhood to complete the choir, and gave us a list of the songs he wanted us to sing. We practiced the pieces diligently for several years, and rehearsed before the old man scores of times, Sunday afternoons. He was something of a songster himself, and he took great pains to explain to us how to render the difficult passages in the music. He criticised us freely, and offered numerous suggestions as to the peculiar attitude we should assume, and the various accents, tremors, pauses, swells and inflections we should observe, in order to bring out the sentiment of the poetry and give solemnity to the music.

I have no recollection of anything in all my life as a

boy or young man, in which I took a deeper interest than in those rehearsals of that old man's prospective funeral. I say, as a boy or young man advisedly, for I had well-nigh past the period in life when even the latter title could be consistently applied to me, before the old man died.

I cannot think he so far over-rated my humble gifts as to select me as one of the singers in his prospective funeral on account of any talents I possessed as a vocalist, either natural or acquired. I cannot claim more than a third-rate reputation as a singer even now, after life-long and diligent application to the science and art of song, to say nothing of what I must have been then. I have an idea that the dear old man selected me from feelings of pure friendship, lest he should offend me by denying me the pleasure of chanting a dirge over his grave. Why he designated me as a tenor in the funeral choir, it would be interesting to know. However, his motives would have been equally obscure if he had selected me for any of the other parts in the music. Probably he named me for tenor at random because he knew I could sing that as well as any other part, and understood that I would wabble over the whole compass of the human voice and sing abstract sketches of all the parts in the piece as I meandered through the performance, anyhow, no matter what part he might assign me. My social qualities and handsome looks were doubtless stronger points in my favor than my musical accomplishments, as indicating to the old man my peculiar fitness for the part of leading tenor in his funeral choir. He had a keen appreciation of good humor, a soul for the sentimental and an eye for the beautiful. He really seemed to desire that a ripple of smiles and a vision of youthful beauty and loveliness should encircle his grave as his soul went marching on to judgment, even if such an arrangement in the selection of his funeral choir should compel him to sacrifice the harmony of his dirge for the sake of those other, and, to him, more desirable qualities in the singers.

If anything could surpass the anticipated pleasure we all—including the old man himself—felt in the prospective funeral, it was the enjoyment we found in the Sunday afternoon rehearsals. We met at his home, rehearsed the performance, ate peaches and watermelons in summer and nuts and apples in winter, and courted the girls at all seasons of the year. Still, the old man failed to perform his part in the final act. *We* were all growing older and uglier; *he* seemed to grow younger and stouter. Some of the most beautiful girls and handsome boys in the funeral choir had married and started together on the journey to their own funerals, replenishing the earth as they went, while their places in the circle of chosen singers had been filled by society favorites from a younger generation, and still the old man declined to furnish the corpse for the funeral. I began to think we would have to bury him alive, or else take him "on the wing" and work off his funeral as a piece of light comedy, to end the farce!

But the old man died at last. And a sadder day our little neighborhood never knew. Tears flowed freely from eyes unused to weep, and a deep gloom settled down upon the whole community. With a few simple tools we made a crude coffin, which we painted, or rather dyed, with ooze boiled from the roots and bark of herbs and forest trees gathered by loving hands. With sad faces and heavy hearts the women of the neighborhood met at his home and made his grave-clothes and winding-sheet. With picks and spades we dug his grave at the place he had selected, under his favorite old oak, near his humble home. As we worked, we talked of his many deeds of love and words of wisdom, and each heart felt an indescribable loneliness to think of life in the neighborhood without him through the dreary years to come. Tenderly and solemnly we looked through our tears upon his benevolent, smiling face for the last time, and with anguish indescribable we lowered him into his narrow vault. With uncovered heads we listened to the old preacher, who was also a life-long friend of the deceased, as he read, through sobs and sighs, the passage of Scripture selected for the occasion so many years ago, by the loved one now in the grave before us. We had all read it, at his request, many times before. We had heard him read it scores of times himself. We all knew it almost by heart. And yet it burst upon us like a new revelation in that last solemn reading. We had never heard it on that wise before. The reading ended, we all reverently kneeled down on the ground while the faithful old preacher offered up prayer to God. Women freely wept, old men and hardened sinners drew the sleeves of their begrimed shirts significantly across their eyes, and sobs and sighs burst from sorrow-burdened souls in all parts of the assembly. We tried to sing the song he had selected for the occasion, but failed. After years of patient practice and scores of thorough rehearsals, every singer broke down completely, and we all fell into each other's arms and sobbed as if our hearts would break. Tenderly we covered him up, and sorrowfully we turned our faces homeward. The patriarch of the neighborhood was dead. Henceforth we were as a family without a father. We were orphans in the world, and well-nigh penniless.

Why attempt to describe the funeral proper, which came several months later? The scene at the grave was re-enacted there. We had no magnificent funeral procession, but that was a genuine, heartfelt funeral none the less on that account.

# CHAPTER XIII.

## CALLED TO PREACH.

Country preachers were, in the main, illiterate men of strong, practical, common sense, full of faith, zeal and deep-toned piety. As a class, they labored hard all the week and preached on Sunday, without remuneration for their pulpit services. Preachers and church members, with few exceptions, held that it was wrong to pay a preacher anything at all for preaching. Methodists and Presbyterians were the first to advocate the doctrine that preachers should be supported by their flocks, so that they might devote all their time to the work of the ministry. This question was earnestly discussed throughout the country, and preachers and churches which contended that the ministry merited a support and ought to receive it, arrayed against themselves strong opposition and bitter prejudice in many communities. Nobody looked upon preaching as a mere profession, and for any man to have entered the ministry with a view simply to make a respectable living at the business, without a feeling of personal obligation to save souls and a strong assurance that God had called him to preach the gospel, would have been to act the part of a hypocrite in the estimation of the whole world. The gifts of prayer, preaching and exhortation, in public, were more generally distributed and universally exercised among church members then than now. Those who were not called by the Lord and ordained by the church, to preach the gospel, frequently took an humbler part in the public work and worship of the church, in prayer, exhortation, song service, experience meetings and altar exercises.

It was, indeed, a rare thing to find a church member who did not take some part in the public work and worship of the church. In fact, no one could have any part at all in church work without rendering some personal service. There were no calls for money, and hence no chance for any man to satisfy his conscience with the thought that he had paid his part and therefore discharged his duty. It was not the province of some to furnish the money and of others to do the work necessary to convert the world and run the church. Every soul had to *work* its way to heaven, so to speak.

It is all well enough to cultivate the grace of giving in church work, but the idea that money can supplant personal service in religious matters is mischievous and ruinous. Munificent giving in a church is a blessed thing if coupled with zealous, personal service, but many churches give liberally and yet die daily. It is a fact worthy the most serious consideration, that many of the religious denominations which to-day give most liberally to home and foreign missions make the slowest increase in membership. It is also a fact that some of the religious denominations which increase most rapidly in membership are not large givers to home or foreign missions. This is no argument against giving money to church work, but it demonstrates the folly of substituting money for personal service and individual effort and consecration in matters of religion. It is a question whether liberal giving, extravagant expenditures, and large schemes which require immense sums of money for carrying forward church work, really indicate a healthy spiritual condition in any religious body. The ecclesiastic history of the world, as well as the plain words of the Savior, seems to indicate rather that the kingdom of heaven " cometh not with observation." The ages of spiritual decadence in the history of the church have, I believe, always been characterized by immense revenues, large endowments, costly houses of worship and glittering paraphernalia. All reformations in religion have succeeded by the personal zeal of penniless advocates against the plethoric purses of richly endowed organizations. When religious people depend more upon money than morality, collections than consecration, policy than prayer, vanity than virtue, looks than love, and fine houses than firm faith and pure hearts, the time of their dissolution as a religious body is at hand. Strong organizations, fine houses and plenty of money—all these things may be very well in their way, but without *charity* they are but "sounding brass or a tinkling cymbal."

Religion was far more universally respected then than now. In fact, every body believed in it, and tried hard to get it. I knew not an infidel or a skeptic in the whole country when I was a boy. Every body who could get religion was a member of some church, and those who could not get it rarely ceased to try, and never seemed to doubt the reality of heaven and hell, the existence of God and the inspiration of the Bible.

The preacher who could get the longest sermon out of the shortest text, by guessing at what it might or might not mean, without the remotest idea as to what it really did mean, was considered the biggest preacher in the country. Monthly preaching was the order of the day in all churches, and no church pretended to meet at all except when the preacher came to his regular monthly appointment. Preachers frequently walked long distances, to their appointments, and, in warm weather,

14

rarely wore any coats. When the weather was cool enough for coats out of the pulpit, it was customary for a preacher to pull off his coat and hang it on a peg driven in an auger hole in the wall behind the pulpit, for his convenience, when he arose to begin his sermon. It was, indeed, a cold day when a parson wore his coat throughout his sermon. In many cases the brother would begin his remarks with his coat on, when the weather was very cold, and pull it off in the middle of his discourse, as he warmed to his work, without pausing a moment or losing a word in his vehement harangue. And as he approached the grand climax of earnestness and eloquence in his rousing exhortation, he not infrequently unbuttoned the collar of his coarse, home-spun shirt. Throughout his exhortation he perspired profusely, wildly gesticulated, frothed at the mouth, poured forth a mighty torrent of bad grammar, yelled at the full strength of his powerful voice, took frequent and copious draughts of water from a gourd, out of a home-made cedar bucket on the pulpit before him, and blew a perfect snow-storm of froth over the audience in every direction.

The people formed their opinions of a sermon, not so much from what the preacher *said*, as the way he *acted*. They felt no particular interest in a message that was delivered without all those external evidences of earnestness. Why should they? It was the common faith of the country that the preacher knew what he was about, and if he did not act as though he thought the people were in danger and that he had the means with which to deliver them from their peril, why should they feel alarmed about it? Would a mother whose daughter is in a burning building calmly read the indifferent girl a short essay, sing the doxology, pronounce the benediction and go away without any manifestations of earnestness or alarm? Those old-time preachers believed in hell, and they believed that many people were in imminent danger. Their sermons were neither very logical nor very grammatical, it is true, and their deportment in the pulpit was never very dignified, but they were always deeply in earnest. And as for dignity, and grammar, and logic, and all that, they had quite as much of it as a modern pastor would display in making his escape, or in helping his children to make their escape, from a sinking vessel or a burning house. I have seen some very dignified men and women, in these modern times, slide down a ladder from a third-story window of a burning building, in the middle of the night, in a very undignified manner. There are probably two extremes touching this question of pulpit mannerism, and if we admit that those old-time preachers were on one extreme, it may be well, at the same time, to ask how far modern pastors are from the other?

The effect of such vehement eloquence, intense earnestness and unwavering faith, in the pulpit, was manifest in the devotion and activity, in the pews, and the universal respect for religion among those without the pale of all churches.

The sturdy integrity of that generation is in strong contrast with the business trickery of modern times. Those old-time people rarely attempted to evade the payment of debts by taking advantage of legal exemptions and technicalities. Seduction was very rare and divorce unknown. For one man to have eloped with another's wife would have shocked the whole community. Business failures were rare, and creditors never pressed their claims against debtors in embarrassed circumstances. I never knew of a case of embezzlement, breach of trust or suicide in those days.

It was a mark of cowardice, and a disgrace, to carry concealed weapons. To have used a knife or a stick in a fight would have excited the contempt of the whole community. For a large man to attack a small one was an offense as grave as to insult a woman. If no man offered to defend a man too old, too feeble or too drunk to defend himself, when attacked, it was a disgrace to the whole community.

I remember well the first murder that was ever committed in our neighborhood. It spread consternation over the whole country. Farmers left their plows in the middle of the field, and all business stopped as suddenly as if the angel of doom had sounded the knell of time. The whole neighborhood turned out and scoured the country day and night for days in succession in search of the murderer.

In early days, Hard-shell Baptists, as they were called, were the dominant religious party in our neighborhood. In fact, they had almost a monopoly of religion among us. A little later, however, the voice of the ubiquitous Methodist circuit rider was heard in the land, and in his wake came the Cumberland Presbyterian pastors and evangelists. Their coming inaugurated a war of words touching man's free agency and God's predestination, and stirred up no little contention and strife among the people on the questions of temperance, revivals, support of the ministry and education of preachers. Preachers began to wear their coats in the pulpit and to give the book, chapter and verse where their texts could be found.

When we finally began to pay preachers anything at all, we arranged a schedule of prices on a decidedly low scale. A Methodist circuit rider, if unmarried, received one hundred dollars per annum. If married, he received one hundred and fifty dollars a year, and fifty dollars extra for each baby he had under ten years of age. This liberal premium upon Methodist babies, in fixing the wages of the ministry, was soon abandoned.

Cumberland Presbyterian preachers and resident ministers had no market value. Each one got what he could and managed to live on what he got. Primitive Baptist preachers never would accept any remuneration at all, and to the very last they protested and argued against the principle of paying preachers anything for their services.

The figures named, now seem to be a very low price for gospel work, but a preacher came out about as well financially then as now. If married, his wife made his clothes and the neighborhood cobbler gave him his shoes. If single, the women of the church made his clothes, and the people gave him his board and washing. Preachers passed ferries, bridges and toll-gates free, and blacksmiths charged them nothing for shoeing their horses. They really had but little use for money. They feasted on the very fat of the land free of charge, whereever they went.

We had no Sunday-schools, but singing-schools flourished in every neighborhood. Ten days was the usual length of such schools, and it was customary to teach them only two days in each week. This stretched a school of ten days over five weeks, which just about covered the time between fodder-pulling and cotton-picking. The singing teacher usually had three schools under headway at a time, so that he could give two days in the week to each school and throw in Sunday for good count. The schools were in different neighborhoods, of course, and as the country was sparsely settled and neighborhoods were few and far between, a singing-school teacher would often have to ride on horse-back from sixty to seventy-five miles a week, to complete the circuit and visit all of his schools. Those who paid tuition in one school were permitted to attend any other schools the teacher had on hand at the time, free. Those who owned horses to ride, and who could spare the time, usually went the whole round with the teacher. It was no unusual thing therefore, for a cavalcade of from twenty to thirty young people—boys and girls, young men and young women—to put in the whole summer riding the circuit with the singing teacher. Members of the two visiting schools were always the welcome guests of the school visited. The long rides between schools, as well as the recesses in class exercises and the evenings and mornings, at the homes of the people, were highly appreciated and carefully improved by the young people as favorable opportunities for courtship.

We met at eight o'clock in the morning, brought our dinners with us, and sang till five o'clock in the evening—nine hours a day, hard singing, every day in the week for five weeks on a stretch, right through the hottest part of the summer! That's the way I learned to sing!

We learned nothing at all about the principles of music. Indeed our teachers knew nothing about either the science or art of music. They knew a few simple tunes, which they had learned by ear, and which they taught us to sing, very erroneously, the same way. The books we used had seven different shapes, for notes, to represent the seven degrees of the scale, and no teacher I ever knew in those days would have recognized his favorite and best known song if he had seen it in

" round notes." I had been to several singing schools,
and, in fact, had about finished my musical education,
before I ever heard of such a thing as "round notes,"
and the question was discussed throughout the country
as to whether any man could possibly learn a new piece
of music written in "round notes."

In our books, the four parts of music were called
treble, tenor, counter and bass. The treble, in those
old books, corresponds to our tenor in modern books,
the tenor corresponds to our soprano, and counter to
our alto. I have just examined Webster on these
points, and, as usual, he seems to differ from us in those
days as to the meaning of words. I am quite sure,
however, that my memory is not at fault as to what we
called treble, tenor and counter, for many living witnesses confirm me. Women invariably sang treble,
which corresponds to tenor in modern books.

The class in a singing-school sat on four long benches
in a hollow square, and the teacher stood, or rather ran
at large, in the middle of the square. He "beat time"
vigorously with long sweeps of his right hand and arm,
up and down, right and left, and every singer in the
class was required to closely imitate his every movement. His chief accomplishment was the ability to sing
any part in the music, and whenever bass, tenor, counter
or treble lagged behind or broke down in the performance he would run across the house to the support of
the broken or wavering line and bring up the strag-
gling forces. When any one of the parts got ahead of
the others in the performance, he would rush at the
foremost man or woman in the squad that was singing
too rapidly, stamp the floor, burst into the unruly part
of the song at the full power of his stentorian voice and
swing his long right arm more vigorously than ever, to

check the break-neck speed of the refractory warblers. By thus galloping around the square, he managed to keep all parts going, and rarely failed to bring us all in on the home stretch within a few measures of the same time! Such were the duties and accomplishments of the old-time singing-school teacher.

When the five-weeks term closed, the three schools met at some central point and closed the summer's work with a big, union, competitive singing. After the schools disbanded, the class in each neighborhood kept up regular singings every Sunday during the Fall, Winter and early Spring, and the next Summer went through a five-weeks' training again, in another regular singing-school. Such trained classes were in great demand during revivals and in camp-meetings. Good singers ranked next to good preachers and eloquent exhorters in working for mourners in the altar during a revival.

The annual camp-meetings were the harvest time for souls with all churches. Nine-tenths of all those who professed religion were converted in such meetings.

A camp-meeting, as the name itself indicates, was a meeting of ten days or two weeks, during which those in attendance camped on the ground and kept up the exercises almost day and night. The congregations assembled, for public services, under an immense brush arbor or long, open shed covered with clapboards. The ground under the arbor, or shed, was covered with wheat straw. To arrange seats, we placed large logs under the arbor, about ten feet apart, and laid on them rough slabs, split from poplar logs with maul and wedge, about three feet apart, in tiers the full length of the arbor.

At night we lighted up the grounds about the arbor

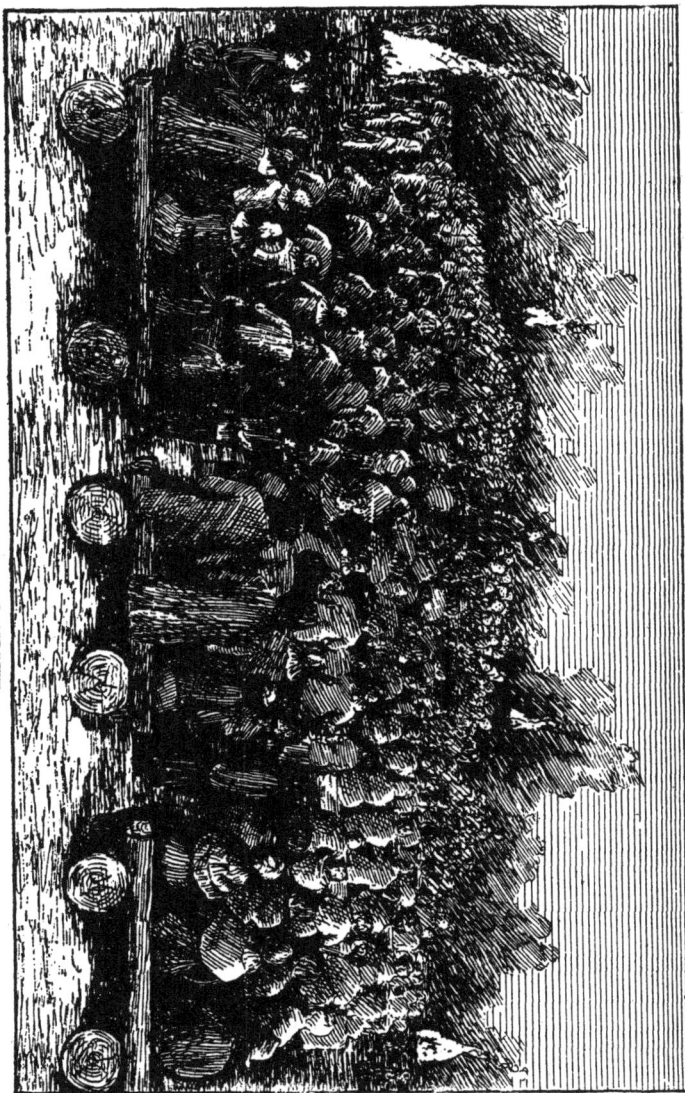

CAMP-MEETING AT NIGHT.

with pine-knot fires built on scaffolds of clapboards covered with dirt or flat rocks.

The campers either built pens of small poles, cut from saplings, and covered them with clapboards, for sleeping apartments, or improvised tents for that purpose by stretching quilts, sheets and counterpanes around and over crude frames made of small poles. The women cooked in skillets, pots and ovens around fires in the open air, and served the repasts on long clapboard scaffolds. Such meetings were held in warm weather, and hence the people slept comfortably on the ground in pole pens or crude tents with but little covering.

During a camp-meeting we met at the stand under the brush arbor or clapboard shed for prayers every morning before breakfast. After breakfast we spent about an hour in secret prayer in the woods. At ten o'clock we assembled at the stand again for preaching, which continued till noon or a little after. From noon till two o'clock we took dinner. At two o'clock we assembled at the stand again for preaching, which lasted till four o'clock, after which we spent another hour at secret prayer in the woods. We took supper at five o'clock, and assembled at the stand again for preaching and altar exercises at seven o'clock. From seven o'clock till we adjourned, which was often not till after midnight and sometimes not till daylight the next morning, the exercises consisted of preaching, exhorting, praying, singing, calling mourners, shouting and work in the altar.

In camp-meetings, Arminians preached, in almost every sermon, that salvation is free and that all are free to accept or reject it. Calvinists spent most of their time in the pulpit explaining the doctrine of predestination in such a way as to put it beyond the power of the elect angels themselves to make heads or tails of the explanation. But when it came to exhortations, Arminians and Calvinists all put themselves out to their full powers in vivid and blood-curdling descriptions of the lake which burns with fire and brimstone, and in soul-moving word-pictures of heaven and immortal glory. Their descriptions of hell and the intense agony of the damned, were perfectly appalling. They represented the breath of an angry God as continually blowing the fiery waves of the sea of torment over the writhing souls of the damned. Billows of flame rose mountain high and o'er each other rolled, until they almost scorched the angels of pity and mercy which leaned over the battlements of heaven and lamented their lack of power to help the condemned and tortured souls of their earthly friends and relatives. Amidst this awful sea of flame and fury, the writhing souls of sinners damned lifted their fruitless wail of misery in hearing of the joyful shouts and songs of the redeemed of all ages and countries, who are forever rejoicing in the paradise of God.

The preachers firmly believed it all, and the people never for a moment doubted it. The effect of such rugged eloquence and unquestioning faith was wonderful. Everybody was religious, or wanted to be, and those who doubted their acceptance with God were excited almost to frenzy by such preaching and exhortations. Immense audiences were thrown into the wildest confusion, and hundreds of people completely lost all self-control and shrieked like maniacs. Scores of sinners under conviction would fall prostrate in the dust, and lie perfectly helpless for hours at a time, trembling and wailing as if they were already doomed to endless torture. In some cases the nervous system

.was wrecked and reason dethroned for all time by the intensity of the excitement.

During the day and early part of the night some respect was paid to order and propriety in the exercises, but as the night advanced and the excitement increased, everything resembling order was forgotten or ignored. Seekers of religion no longer came quietly and kneeled separately at the altar of prayer. They came in droves and threw themselves literally in heaps in the straw which covered the ground in the altar. Some would be kneeling, some reclining on the rude benches about the altar, while scores would be lying prostrate on the ground, all agonizing and shrieking for mercy in an earnestness perfectly distressing to see.

The friends and relatives of the mourners, as well as the whole congregation of religious people, did all they could to help on the work of grace and keep up the excitement and confusion. Some pounded the mourners on the back with their hands and fists, some talked to them about their dead friends and relatives, and some embraced them, while every body seemed to weep and shout at the same time. Some in the audience would be praying aloud, some singing, some rejoicing and some mourning. Above all the confusion, the preachers, with voices like fog horns, kept up a continual exhortation about the beauties and glories of heaven, and the awful destiny of the damned in a horrible hell.

In their intense excitement, the people would jump, dance, clap their hands, swing their bodies and jerk their heads forward and backward, throwing hats, bonnets, and combs in every direction. The nervous excitement frequently produced muscular contortions, called "the jerks," which caused the long hair of women to crack like coach-whips as their bodies and heads jerked back and forth. During such periods of intense excitement the whole congregation, by some inexplicable nervous action, would sometimes be thrown into side-splitting convulsions of laughter. This was called the "holy laugh," and when it started in an audience no power could check or control it, till it ran its course. It would often last for hours at a time, and everybody in the audience, who was in sympathy with the excitement, would be seized with hearty convulsions of perfectly natural laughter.

At other times, the nervous excitement set the muscles to twitching and jerking at a fearful rate, and some of the leaders thus affected would begin to skip, hop and jump, and finally settle down to regular, steady, straight-forward dancing. When the leaders got thoroughly straightened out in a regular dance, all who were under the influence of the mental and nervous excitement would feel their muscles mysteriously twitching and jerking in harmony with the movements of the leaders, and the next moment they would involuntarily join in the wild dance. This was called the "holy dance," and like the "holy laugh," it was simply ungovernable till it ran its course.

At other times the mental and nervous excitement would take the form of "the jerks," as already described, in the leaders, and all who were in sympathy with the excitement would involuntarily fall into the uniform muscular movements of the leaders. When a man once started in a holy exercise of any kind, whether shouting, laughing, dancing or jerking, it was impossible for him to stop till exhausted nature broke down in a death-like swoon.

The groaning, shouting, shrieking, singing, exhorting, laughing, dancing, jerking and swooning made a medley of sights and sounds no pen can describe. When they swooned, they would often lie, for hours at a time, as unconscious as the dead, and physicians would sometimes have to be called, to restore them to consciousness again. In a few instances they died in that comatose state, in spite of all restoratives.

One scene which I witnessed in early boyhood will illustrate the character of preaching and religion peculiar to that age and country.

A preacher of rare gifts in word-painting delivered a sermon to an audience of fully three thousand people one Sunday night at a camp-meeting. The interest had been unusually deep during the afternoon, and the vast audience was at the highest tension of excitement when the services began at night. The preacher closed an unusually earnest sermon with a powerful exhortation, and asked every one in the audience who wanted to escape hell and meet him in heaven to signify it, at a given signal, by a clap of the hands and a shout of "glory." When the signal was given, that vast audience, as one man, gave a clap of hands which sounded like a thunderbolt and a yell of "glory" almost loud enough to wake the dead. The effect was almost electrical. Scores of sinners shrieked for mercy in all parts of the vast audience, hundreds of happy Christians raised wild shouts of joy and the rest of the surging crowd united their voices in a familiar song. The negro slaves were coming from all parts of the country to the meeting, and were scattered all over the woods for a mile around the camp-ground, when the storm of fuss and excitement burst under the arbor. The noise frightened them and they began to shriek for mercy and to pray aloud all over the woods, in the darkness, as though the devil himself were at their heels. There were hundreds of dogs in the camp, as usual, and, excited by the unusual noise and confusion, they rushed into the woods and the darkness in every direction, yelping as if a whole menagerie of wild beasts had been suddenly let loose among them. In a few moments they raised a free fight and a general row among themselves, and every dog on the grounds rushed into the fray. When the canine forces were all mustered, there was probably a square acre of yelping, snapping, fighting dogs within a few rods of the arbor. There were several hundred horses, mules, oxen and wagons on the grounds, and the unusual confusion, fuss and excitement stampeded the animals. The scene beggars description. Three thousand people in an uproar, hundreds of dogs yelping and fighting, negroes screaming and praying in every direction and a thousand frightened mules, horses and oxen dashing madly through the woods in the darkness—it was worse than bedlam let loose.

If a camp-meeting was not " a feast of reason, and a flow of soul," it was at least a feast of the best things the country could afford. It was a happy time for all except the toiling wives, mothers and sisters of the campers. The labors of such women began a week before the meeting—preparing for it—and continued a week or ten days after it, straightening up the confusion it caused.

During the meeting, we rose at early dawn every morning, and after a hasty breakfast assembled, at the tooting of a cow's horn, for morning prayers at the arbor. The women had to remain in the camps to " clean up " and prepare dinner.

The season of camp-meetings lasted about two

months in the hottest part of the summer. Such meetings were grand institutions for a worthless, thriftless set of poverty-stricken dead-beats, such as cursed every community. Such people always attended camp-meetings for the loaves and the fishes.

# CHAPTER XIV.

It was the common faith of the country that the excitement and capers of the people at camp-meetings were manifestations of the operation of the Holy Ghost on their hearts. Whether a man "shouted," "danced," "jerked" or "laughed," as a religious exercise, it was the work of the great Spirit in him.

Those who engaged in such exercises were conscious that their actions were involuntary. Whatever explanation may be given of those peculiar exercises, the fact that they were involuntary can not be denied. It is not the province of this book to explain the religious phenomena of those days. It seems pertinent to describe the religious exercises which characterized that queer generation, but beyond a statement of the facts of history it is not deemed prudent to venture in these pages.

The earnestness of preachers and people in matters of religion, as evidenced in such preaching and exercises as have been but imperfectly described, is worthy of special note. Whatever may be said as to the Scripturalness of their performances, there is no reason to doubt the sincerity of their motives or the vigor of their faith. Preachers and people evidently believed in the reality of heaven and hell, and showed their faith by their works. There was no such thing as playing at religion with them.

I remember well when first a few religious teachers

15                                                    (225)

began openly to express doubt as to whether the Holy Ghost caused all the excitement and absurd antics which usually attended a successful revival. Such doubters boldly expressed the opinion that "the jerks," "the holy laugh," "the holy dance," the vociferous "shouting" and the death-like swooning indulged in by religious people were all caused by mental and nervous excitement. This stirred up no little strife, contention and prejudice in religious circles.

Those who believed that such excitement was the work of the Holy Ghost, publicly and bitterly denounced all those who referred it to other causes as enemies of spiritual religion and teachers of dangerous doctrine. Such teachers were denounced from all the orthodox pulpits as unsound in the faith and excluded from the churches for heresy. Excitement ran high and prejudice was intense against them. Parents would not suffer their children to hear them preach, and all churches were closed against them. Preachers even refused to announce appointments for them, and the people were publicly warned, from all orthodox pulpits, of the danger of hearing their doctrine.

They were publicly charged with having committed the unpardonable sin against the Holy Ghost, and severely abused as rebels against God and enemies of all mankind. To say "the jerks," "the holy laugh" and "the holy dance" were caused by mental and nervous excitement was considered a personal insult by all who engaged in such things. That such things were the work of the Holy Ghost was a proposition which every man, who had taken part in them, thought he could establish by his own consciousness. It did not occur to the believers in such things, nor could they be made to understand, that they might be wrong themselves in attributing emotions of which they were conscious, to the Holy Ghost. They were conscious of certain emotions, and they knew they "laughed," "danced" and "jerked," as religious exercises, involuntarily. Beyond this they seemed utterly incapable of reasoning on the subject. They would not for a moment consider the idea that something entirely different from the Holy Ghost may have caused their peculiar emotions and involuntary actions. The man who doubted that such things were caused by the Holy Spirit, simply disputed their veracity as they understood it.

In many cases those who opposed such excessive excitement and peculiar demonstrations in religion were children of fathers and mothers who had served God after that manner all their lives and died in the belief that such things were the work of the Holy Spirit. Their doubts, therefore, were openly construed as reflections upon the veracity of their deceased parents. Of all men, such doubters were the most cordially hated by orthodox preachers and church members throughout the country. They were excluded from churches, ostracised from society, abused by the preachers and bitterly persecuted by the whole country. Nevertheless, they boldly proclaimed their views, and their heresy spread rapidly among the people.

The rise and progress of those new and unpopular doctrines touching the work of the Holy Spirit and the excitement of the people in religious revivals, changed the whole order of religious exercises and inaugurated a new era in preaching and Bible study. The people began to give closer attention to what preachers *said* and to care less about how they *acted* in the pulpit. Audiences demanded less *sound* and more *sense* in sermons. Preachers began to use more *mind* and less *muscle* in the pulpit. Exhorters quit drawing upon their imaginations for blood-curdling descriptions of hell, and began to set forth "the whole duty of man," as taught in the Bible, to move people to accept salvation. Scripture texts were no longer misquoted, from memory, and vaguely cited as "somewhere betwixt the lids of the good Book," with but little regard for their real meaning; but carefully hunted up, closely studied, accurately read, and correctly expounded to the people. The world ceased to regard the Bible as good for nothing but to supply boisterous preachers with disconnected texts for meaningless sermons, and began to study it closely, and prize it highly, as an inspired volume which reveals to all men the will of God, touching matters of personal purity and individual duty. Men began to lose respect for the authority of the church, and listen to the voice of God addressing them through the Bible. The doctrine of equal rights to all and special privileges to none, found a new application and many advocates in the matter of studying, understanding, and expounding the Scriptures. The people boldly denied the right of church or clergy to stand between them and the Bible, in the form of authoritative creeds, confessions of faith or books of discipline. The point was strongly urged, that, in the Bible, God has spoken, not to preachers, churches, councils, or conventions of ecclesiastical dignitaries, but to every creature in every nation. It was insisted that God is competent to speak, and that he has spoken, to the world, in the Bible, without an interpreter. It is not the province of learned leaders in religion, the people argued, to sit in solemn council and inform the world, in authoritative creeds, confessions of faith, books of discipline, or other doctrinal standards, what the Bible means and teaches on different subjects. The Bible was declared to be its own interpreter. The point was boldly made that no man has a right to make his understanding of the Bible the rule of another man's faith. This was a vigorous blow at the very foundation of the whole superstructure of denominational bigotry, among Protestants, and Ecclesiastical authority and infallibility among Catholics. It was the beginning of the end of bigotry in religion in this country. Denominational intolerance in religion rests, not upon the Bible, but upon what the fathers, founders and leaders of the denominations think the Bible teaches. To deny to any man the right to make his understanding of the Bible the rule of another man's faith, and to guarantee to every man the right to study, understand and obey the Bible for himself, unhampered by what other men think the Bible teaches, as expressed in doctrinal standards, was to at once lay the ax to the very root of the tree of religious bigotry and denominational intolerance.

Under the new order of things in religion, superstitious regard for a divinely called and specially qualified ministry gradually gave way before an intelligent faith in the teachings of the Scriptures. The ministry lost prestige, but the Bible gained power with the people. Preachers were no longer considered the particular pets and favorites of God, called and qualified by special revelations of the Holy Ghost, to lead the people in matters of religion. The idea that God, in the Bible, speaks directly to each individual soul, without the intervention or mediation of a divinely called and qualified ministry, grew in favor with the people daily.

The chosen priesthood, or divinely called and qualified ministry, was finally attacked boldly in its stronghold. The people began to openly doubt whether God specially called and qualified men to preach the gospel by particular revelations and manifestations of the Holy Ghost. They began to argue that all ideas of special calls to the ministry originated, like "the jerks," the "holy laugh," and the "holy dance," in excitement. anxiety, ignorance, tradition and superstition. The preachers who claimed that God had called them to preach, met all such arguments by their own direct testimony, and indignantly resented all such theories as impeachments of their sincerity and veracity. They held that their divine call and special qualification, by the Holy Ghost, to preach the gospel, was simply a question of fact which could be as clearly attested, by their own consciousness, as a pain in the back. The people met this argument of the preachers in ways which were often as amusing as they were damaging to the claims of the Lord's specially called and qualified preachers.

Those who desired to be preachers had to wait until the Lord called them. Sometimes a man would wait and pray for a call for weeks, months, and even years. When he finally received what he considered evidence that God had called him to preach, he had to appear before the church and state his case. If the church approved his evidence of a call, the proper authorities ordained him to the ministry; otherwise they advised him to wait for other and clearer evidence of his call. It was no unusual thing for the church to decide that what the preacher himself considered indubitable evidence of a call to the ministry, was really no evidence at all. This put an argument into the mouths of those who did not believe in such things, which those who did believe in them found it difficult to answer. When the church was continually deciding that men could be deceived, and often had been deceived,

as to their call to the ministry, the doubters
did not have far to look in order to find an answer
to the claim of the preachers, that a call to the ministry
was simply a question of fact which could be as satisfactorily attested, by a man's consciousness, as a
physical pain.

The doubters still further worried the saints by ob-
jecting to the idea that the church had a right to a veto
power against the Lord in the matter of calling preachers. The call of the Lord without the approval and license of the church, was not operative. This seemed
to be putting the Lord below the church, in point of
authority. The church really sat in judgment upon the
Lord's work. It was argued by the doubters, that, as
preachers were called to preach the gospel, not to the
church, but to the world, unbelievers were the proper
ones to pass upon the evidence of a preacher's call to
the ministry. Such arguments tended to make churches more lenient to those who desired to preach, and in
a few years they got so they would accept, as good, any
evidence which an applicant for license to preach might
give of his call to the ministry. Such laxity, however,
suggested to the doubters another plan to vex the
saints and demonstrate the fallacy of the doctrine of
divine calls to the ministry.

A man who was known to be waiting and praying for a call to preach, was plowing corn one hot day
in June. One of the doubters climbed a tree and concealed himself among its leafy branches, in the forest
near the field. In a solemn, sepulchral voice, the man
in the tree called the plowman and would-be parson
by name, and told him to go preach the gospel. Several witnesses of undoubted veracity, who could be relied
upon for secrecy, were stationed in the woods near

the field to hear the call and observe the result. The plowman, without investigation, raised a great shout of rejoicing, unharnessed his horse in much haste, and ran at once to bear the joyful news of his call to preach, to some of the leading members of his church. At the next meeting of the church the evidence of his call was heard and approved, and he was ordained to the ministry. This case was cited by the doubters throughout the country as an absolute demonstration that both preacher and church could be deceived as to a call to the ministry.

No one doubted the sincerity or veracity of those who claimed that God had called and qualified them to preach, or of those who took part in "the jerks," the "holy laugh," and the "holy dance." Of course believers, as well as unbelievers, admitted that there were some hypocrites among them, but everybody admitted the sincerity and honesty of the great majority of such zealots. The main argument against such things was, that those who believed in them were simply deceived. The clear issue on these questions greatly stimulated and encouraged public interest in religion and led to a more general study of the Bible.

The people argued, studied, preached, and contended about the doctrine of the Bible on all these questions continually. Even little children took a deep interest in such questions, and read the Bible daily to see what it taught concerning them. In a very few years everybody was well informed as to the teachings of the Bible. Many people committed much of the Holy Scriptures to memory, and carried Bibles in their pockets constantly. It was a rare thing to find half a dozen men together without two or three Bibles in the crowd, or to hear a conversation of a few hours without a religious discussion. It was no unusual thing to hear a man quote verse after verse, or even whole chapters, of Scripture from memory, in an argument, and tell the exact place in the Bible where it could be found.

The people seemed to understand the teachings of the Bible better than the divinely called and specially quali- fied preachers. While the latter depended upon their di- vine calls and qualifications, the former relied upon the Bible, and studied it night and day for information on religious subjects. It was nothing uncommon to see a plain clod-hopper, with open Bible, pointing out the errors in a sermon of one of God's specially called and qualified preachers, before the audience left the house.

The doctrines and practices of the whole religious world were closely compared with the exact words and plain meaning of the Bible, and at every point of con- flict, the Scriptures steadily gained ground against the traditions, prejudices, and superstitions of illiterate re- ligious bigots.

In the very beginning of the revolution in religious faith and practice, the adherents of the Bible, against tradition and superstition, planted themselves upon the proposition, that God, by revelations of the Holy Ghost, has clearly stated the whole duty of man in the Bible. All parties to the discussions admitted that the Scriptures of the Old and New Testaments were given by the Holy Spirit through inspired men, and those who stood for the Bible against tradition, excitement and superstition, stoutly argued that the Holy Ghost, oper- ating directly upon the heart of a man, would not lead him to do things which the same Holy Ghost, speaking through inspired men in the Bible, had not taught him to do. From these premises it was confidently argued that the Holy Ghost could not possibly be the author of any emotion in any man's heart, which would prompt him to do what the Bible teaches no one to do. To say the Holy Ghost has not fully taught man's whole duty in the Bible, was to question the completeness and fullness of God's revelations of his will in the Bible. To admit that the Bible does teach man's whole duty, was to admit that the Holy Ghost does not, in any case, move people to do things which are not taught at all in the Bible. This was a hard dilemma for those who believed that the Holy Ghost was the author of emotions in their hearts, which prompted them to do many things they could not find the least authority for in the Scriptures. Before such reasoning, the " holy laugh," the "holy dance," "the jerks," "shouting," "altar exercises," "divine calls to the ministry," and everything else in religious faith and practice not taught in the Bible, gradually gave way. The people were thoroughly aroused on religious questions, and they ' had the courage of their convictions. The changes came slowly in some places, but they came steadily and surely. Men threw tradition and superstition to the winds, and walked by faith, which came by hearing the word ot God, in all matters pertaining to religion. Every inch of ground was hotly contested, and every question of religious faith and practice was carefully investigated and thoroughly discussed in the change from the old to the new order of things in religion. Whenever a man, who had set his heart upon adhering to the Bible in all matters pertaining to religion, decided that he was holding any doctrine, or following any practice through superstition, tradition, or prejudice, without Scripture authority, he at once changed his course.

In the midst of a great revival, when the altar was crowded with mourners, and the whole congregation was " shouting," "jerking," " laughing," and " dancing," the leading preacher in the revival became convinced from his study of the Bible, that there was no Scriptural authority for such things, and while the congregation was taking dinner and recreation, at noon, he tore down the " altar," carried off the "mourners' benches," scattered the "straw," and pronounced the benediction upon that department of the exercises of the meeting. He then called the congregation together and asked the people and " the mourners " to be quiet the rest of the meeting, to listen to the reading of the Scriptures and to sober words of instruction and exhortation, and to give themselves in prayer, humility, earnestness and faith, to the service of God as taught in the Bible.

In this chapter I have described the change from the old to the new order of things in rural districts, within the bounds of my own acquaintance. While there was a similar change in religious circles about that time all over the South, it may not have been brought about in every locality in exactly the same way. I only describe what I saw, heard, and took an active part in myself, in the rather limited circle of my acquaintance. Whether the things I have described prevailed over the South generally, or only in certain localities, I presume not to say. If the reader is in doubt on that point, he must look to other sources for information.

# CHAPTER XV.

Those who believed in an excess of excitement, and who took part in "shouting," "jerking," "dancing," and "laughing," in religious exercises, relied largely upon experience meetings to start a revival. In such meetings each one told his own experience of the work of grace in his heart, in turning him from darkness to light, and from the power and dominion of satan unto the worship and service of God.

In one of these experience meetings, a miserable old sinner and noted backslider, told how he was first checked in his wild career of sin, by the death of his lovely and beloved little girl. For a time he was faithful to the Lord and zealous in the good cause, but, by and by, he longed for the flesh-pots of sin, and turned back in his heart and life to the weak and beggarly elements of the world. Again God arrested him, in his downward course to ruin, by the death of another beloved little daughter. He lived a consistent Christian life for a few months after the death of his second child, but in an evil hour again yielded to temptation, and was led captive by the devil at his will. God came to his rescue again, in the death of his third and last little one. He lived righteously before God for a few weeks, and then went over the line into the devil's dominions again. Once more, and but a few weeks ago, God again snatched him as a brand from the burning, and called him to repentance by the death of his beloved wife. And now he stood alone in the world, bereft of wife and all his children, whom he was hoping and striving to meet in the Christian's home in glory.

It was a good experience, well told, and not without a good effect upon all who believed in such things. It started quite a revival in the meeting. But a man who did not believe in such things, threw a damper over the excitement aroused by the story, by saying, in the hearing of many people in the congregation: "Well, I must say, the Lord has managed this case very badly. He has killed one good woman and three innocent little children trying to save this old back-slider, and the chances are that the devil will get the old humbug yet. The next time he gets drunk and goes to pieces generally, there will be no wife or beloved little children to kill, and how will God ever get him straight any more? If I had been managing this case, when I had to kill that first child to get the old fraud straight, I would have broken his neck with a stroke of lightening, and sent him on to glory just as soon as I got him on the right track."

In traveling through the hill country of the South a few years ago, I fell in company with a superannuated deacon, whose memory of men and movements extended back to the first years of the present century. He talked freely about the changes I have been trying to describe in religious faith and practice, and his story was full of interest to me. Following a custom of several years standing, I took down some of the most interesting parts of the ex-deacon's reminiscences, and here give a transcript of a few pages of my note book, with slight changes and emendations:

"Yes, sir! I'm a quar sort uv a bein', stranger, any

way you take me.  I never seen a book uv any kind on surveyin', fur instance, an' yit, I'm a nat'ral born surveyor.  I k'n foller a line any d'rection, over any kind uv country, and through all sorts uv weather, jest as easy as a houn' can foller a fox.  My wife l'arnt me how to read, an' 'er uncle l'arnt me how to write, an' I l'arnt everything else myself.

"When I fust moved to this country I settled in the Mississippi bottoms, jest over on the Arkansaw side uv the river, because thar were oodles of b'ar an' other game in the canebrakes, an' I guess I'd a bin thar yit, a bossin' niggers, an' a-drivin' mules, an' a-raisin' cotton, if I hadn't a hearn Josh Atkinson preach.  Josh wuz a rattlin' good preacher them days, an' he changed my idees consider'ble.  I got my fust stock uv religion frum Josh, an' hit wuz this shoutin', happy sort o' reg'lar old-fashioned, camp-meetin', fire 'n' brimstone religion, too.  In them days Josh Atkinson could put more rousement into a meetin' with one pra'r an' five minutes zortin' than folks ever hearn uv in these times.

"I quit the bottoms, an' Josh he went into partnership with a real edicated preacher in camp-meetin' work.  The edicated parson could preach fust rate, but he couldn't pray nor zort wuth a cent.  But let me tell you, him an' Josh made a whole team when they went into partnership.  The main thing in a meetin' them days wuz good zortin' an' pra'r, but you had to have a little preachin' fur fillin', uv course.  Well, Josh, he never could preach wuth shucks, but the other feller could preach from the word go, an' Josh, he knowed how to put in the rousement.  Folks these days don't know nothin' 'bout rousin' times in a meetin'.  I come o' that sort o' stock myself.  My folks has always bin good at rousin' things up at meetin' or any where else they go, as fur back as I ever hearn tell on 'em. We used to make it mighty interestin' fur the other side in a fist fight, before any uv us j'ined the church. When we fust settled in Arkansaw we jest had to fight almost day an' night to keep up the morals uv the country. I didn't care a cent fur religion in them days, but I always did stand squar' up for good morals. So did all my folks, an' we jest would have good morality where-ever we lived, if we had to lick the whole country ever' day to git it. Arkansaw wuz a awful place in them days, an' I recon me'n' my folks did more to keep up the morals uv the neighborhoods we lived in, even before any uv us j'ined the church, than anybody else an' his folks in the whole country.

"My father wuz always a law-abin' citizen, but he'd fight ever' time when a man tried to run over the morality uv the country. He fit Uncle Sam Dangrum in North Car'liny, before any uv us ever seen this country, an' bit off his nose—bit the thing clean off up to his head an' swallered it! Uncle Sam Dangrum wuz a tryin' to run over the morals uv the country, an' my father jest couldn't stan' that, an' so they fit, an' off come Uncle Sammy's nose. We all called him Uncle Sam, an' so did everybody else, but he won't no nat'ral kin to us. Well, that wuz about the biggest bite any uv my folks ever took, an' it come mighty nigh a bein' more'n we all could chaw! You see, it wuz ag'in the law to bite off a man's nose in them days, an' so we all had to light out fur Arkansaw. My mother run away frum her folks an' married my father when she wuz fourteen years old, an' she had eighteen children, an' so we made a right smart settlement when we got to Arkansaw."

At this point I ventured to remind him that he

started out to tell me something about his recollection of the days when religious excitement ran high all over the country, and preachers and church members put in the "rousement" at revival meetings. He said:

"Oh, yes; I quit the bottoms and follered Josh an' his partner around to all their camp-meetin's, jest to enjoy the rousement. Well, sir, that edicated preachin' partner what Josh went in cahoot with in the camp-meetin' business, soon turned ag'in Josh's pra'rs, an' zortin', an' rousement. Hit wuz a sight to hear 'em argy. At fust, I thought the edicated chap wuz ag'in Josh jest because the folks all liked Josh's rousement better 'n his highfaloot'n sarmints, an' I wuz as mad as blazes an' right in fur lickin' 'im. I felt ag'in 'im jest adzackly like I use ter feel ag'in a man as tried to run over the morals uv the country in my fightin' days, before I j'ined the church, but the more I studied 'bout it, the stronger his p'ints looked.

"He said it wuz all excitement, an' folks would git jest as shoutin' happy when they wuz wrong as they would when they wuz right, providin' they *believed* they wuz right. He said the main thing in religion wuz to love God with all your heart and to love your neighbor as yourself, anyhow, an' he couldn't see why folks should make such stark fools uv theirselves a-lovin' God an' their neighbors. He said he thought it would be better to put in the time we spent a-yellin' an' a-cavortin' all over keration, in doin' the will uv God as it wuz laid down in the Bible, an' a-carryin' food an' clothin' to our neighbors as wuz needy. He said a young man never went crazy with 'the jerks,' an' the 'holy laugh,' an' the 'holy dance,' an' the 'shoutin'' when he wuz a-lovin' his sweetheart, an' a man never cut sich capers a-lovin' his wife, an' a child never took on so a-lovin' its mother, an' a mother never went into sich spells a-lovin' her children, an' he didn't see why folks should raise sich a rousement a-lovin' God an' their neighbors, which wuz the main thing in religion.

"Well, sir, the more he talked in this way, the plainer it all looked to me. Sich talk soon took all the rousement out'n Josh, pore feller, an' he drawed out 'n the firm an' quit the preachin' business He never took any hand in reg'lar gospil work after that. He wuzn't wuth a cent fur sich preachin' as is done these days nohow. He always said as how he loved God, an' he loved his neighbors, an' he always attended all the meetin's 'o the church, an' tried to do his dooty as a Christian, an' he took a hand in every good work, but after they quit the rousement in revivals he never tried to do no reg'lar gospil work in the pulpit. I have done the same way, an' I recon its right an' proper, but it don't look like religion alongside uv the way we use to carry on in camp-meetin s.

" I want to hire a han' to help me make a crap nex' year, an' I want one as don't drink nor cuss. I don't want sich wickedness about me, an' I won't have it neither. I had a good han' a-workin' with me fur ten dollars a month, but I found out he wuz a-drinkin' an' a-cussin' on the sly, and so I told him he must quit it or quit me one. I offered to raise his wages to twelve dollars a month if he would quit drinkin' an' cussin', but he said as how he wouldn't quit cussin' an' drinkin' fur two dollars a month fur no man, an' so I paid him off an' he quit.'

This old man was simply a piece of theological driftwood, left high and dry on the bank of the spiritual channel, by the great flood of religious excitement which swept over the entire country about the begin-

16

ning of the present century. He was a high-water mark of the clerical ignorance and religious "rousement" which prevailed throughout the country in rural districts less than a century ago.

Those who were excluded from the various religious denominations as heretics for opposing religious fanaticism, clerical ignorance, divine calls to the ministry and all other forms of superstition, prejudice and bigotry, went right on with such religious work and worship as they understood the Bible to teach, independent of all denominations and without any written creed or doctrinal standard but the Bible. They insisted that a man could be a Christian and go to heaven by doing the will of God as taught in the Bible, without formal connection with any denomination in religion. Each man among them studied the Bible for himself, formulated his own faith and engineered his own religion. They argued questions earnestly among themselves, and on many points differed widely in their convictions, but each man held firmly to his Bible and contended for his right to formulate his own faith without dictation from others. They never settled upon any fixed system of doctrine, or subscribed to any statement of their faith, except the Bible. They refused to organize themselves into a general denomination, or to yield any of their individual liberties in religious faith and practice to denominational authority. Their doctrines spread, their numbers multiplied and their wealth increased, year by year. Gradually their heresy seemed to evaporate, and their orthodoxy began to appear. In course of time they were considered orthodox by all denominations in religion, and those people who excluded them from churches for heresy a few decades before, were universally regarded as fanatical, ignorant, superstitious, over-zealous religious bigots.

Verily, orthodoxy and heresy are strange things in religion. It is doubtful whether orthodoxy really means anything but the big side in a doctrinal argument in religion, and heresy is probably but another name for the minority in a division of a church on questions of doctrine. Orthodoxy with one generation is ignorance and superstition with the next, and the heresy of the father is often the orthodoxy of the son.

# CHAPTER XVI.

## THE BEGINNING OF MACHINERY.

The cotton gin was invented in 1793, but people picked the seeds out of cotton with their fingers in some parts of the South more than a third of a century after that date. This shows how slow they were to adopt new improvements in those days. Several reasons may be assigned for such tardiness. A cotton gin by itself is worth but little in manufacturing cotton goods. Without other machinery to fully equip a factory, it is a matter of little consequence whether the seeds be removed from the lint by a gin or with the fingers. If we must card, spin, warp and weave by hand, we may as well pick the seeds out of the cotton the same way.

Improved machinery for doing things is all well enough if you have enough of it. But one piece of machinery is of no great consequence in the process, when nearly all the work must be done slowly and tediously by hand. When the cotton gin was invented, therefore, it had to sit in idleness nearly fifty years, till other machinery could be invented, in order to make the manufacture of cotton goods an industry of some consequence.

It takes considerable capital and no little ingenuity to establish and operate a factory of any kind. There were not money and skilled labor enough in the United States to manufacture cotton goods, or anything else, on a very large scale seventy years ago. It took more than half a century to accumulate the wealth, develop the ingenuity and educate the labor necessary to manufacture anything of much consequence, even after the public mind was turned in that direction.

The demand for goods of all kinds was hardly large enough to make manufacturing a business of much importance. It would not pay to buy machinery, build a factory and train a full crew of hands, in order to make one suit of clothes. When the country was sparsely settled and the habits of life were simple and inexpensive, it was cheaper to make such things as the people needed, by hand, than to try to build factories for that purpose.

There was no way to get manufactured goods to the people, in those days, even if there had been the best of facilities for manufacturing everything that was needed. There was not a railroad in the world, and not even a respectable wagon road in. this country. General Jackson had to cut a road through an almost unbroken forest from Tennessee to Louisiana when he marched his army to the famous battle of New Orleans. There were no boats on any of the rivers in the South but flat-boats, and they would not run up stream.

The fastest mails in the country were carried on horse-back or in stages, between important points, at the rate of about six miles an hour. It took twenty-five cents to pay the postage on a letter, and such other packages as now pass through the mails could not then be sent at all.

There were few banks, no express companies and no post-office money orders. The only way to send freight was by wagons or on pack horses, and the only way to send money was to go and take it. It would have been an expensive business for a factory in Michigan to have tried to sell goods in Alabama.

The first railroad ever built in the South, so far as I

FAST, THROUGH FREIGHT.

am informed, was in Alabama, between Decatur and Tuscumbia. The track was simply flat bars of iron, such as we now use for wagon tires, nailed to pieces of wood, called stringers. The stringers were hewed square, with broad-axes, and placed upon cross-timbers, such as are now used for cross-ties on railroads. The motive power of the train was an old mule, and the entire length of the road was forty-five miles. The track was fastened to the stringers by short nails driven through holes, in the ends of the iron, into the wood. The cross-timbers were wide apart, and the stringers would spring downward in the middle under a heavy load. This would bend the track and pull the nails, which held it down, out of the wood. When thus loosed from the stringers, the ends of the iron bars would bend upwards and stand up several inches high. When these bent ends rose up high enough to strike the car wheels above the center, they would plunge up through the bottom of the car, as the wheels ran under them, and do much damage. The elevated ends of bent track were called "snake-heads," and the railroad management stood in great terror of them. They were considered so dangerous that passengers were not allowed to travel on the cars at all.

The road was used for freight business only. It was very serviceable in transporting river freight, for flat-boats, past the celebrated shoals on the Tennessee river. Decatur is above and Tuscumbia below the shoals.

There was not even a coal oil lamp in all the country. An ordinary match would have been a miracle to us.

Mr. Harris was a country post-master in Wilson county, Tennessee. Some one sent a letter to his office addressed to a man who had moved out of the settlement. He kept it till the time prescribed by law for its delivery elapsed, and then forwarded it to the dead-

letter office at Washington City. At the dead-letter
office it was opened and found to contain a bill of
money. It was returned to Mr. Harris, with a letter of

FAST MAIL.

instruction from the dead-letter office, apprising him of
its valuable contents and directing him to make diligent enquiry for the man to whom it was addressed,

and, if possible, deliver it to its rightful owner. Mr. Harris kept it several months, failed to find the owner, and again forwarded it to the dead-letter office. I know Mr. Harris well. He still lives near Lebanon, Tennessee. I went to his house, spent several hours in conversation with him, and verified every fact in this strange story to my entire satisfaction. Why he did not burn the letter and keep the money is a problem I shall not stop to discuss. The United States civil service of those days evidently differed widely from that of modern times in more than one respect.

The best informed people of those days seriously argued that improved machinery would never pay. And it never would have paid if the people had not changed their manner of living.

Our present intricate system of railroads, telephones, express companies, telegraph lines, mail service, stock companies, bank exchanges, insurance companies, money orders, newspapers and vast manufacturing industries was not designed or foreseen by anybody. It has grown up in the last seventy years as if by chance. It is an evolution. It has organized itself without consultation, unity of purpose or harmony of design in its originators, so far as human minds have originated and developed it. For myself, I cannot doubt but that all the finite minds engaged upon this wonderful structure have but performed the part assigned them by the infinite Intelligence who framed the system of worlds, and who guides the progress of the universe.

It is hardly proper to speak of labor-saving machinery. It perhaps takes as much labor to run the world now, with all our machinery, as it took in the days of our forefathers.

So far as I can see, it takes as much labor to make a

dress, for instance, on a sewing machine as it took to make one by hand fifty years ago. There are tucks, and gores, and ruffles, and hems, and flutes and flounces on a dress now that our grandmothers never dreamed of in all their dress-making philosophy. The introduction of machinery has wrought a great revolution in the world, but, so far as I can see, it has done far more to increase the expense of living than to save labor. In the way of a labor-saving institution, I know nothing superior to the dense ignorance and serene contentment of the lowest grade of barbarism.

The simple customs of our fathers began gradually to pass away with the introduction of modern machinery. When the manufacture of cotton goods began to attract attention as an important industry, the production of the fleecy staple loomed up as a profitable branch of agriculture. This turned attention to the low bottoms and fertile valleys of the South, which hitherto had been considered almost worthless, and in a few years such lands commanded a higher price than any other in the country. They were peculiarly well adapted to the production of cotton.

Up to this time African slave labor had not been very profitable in the United States, and there was no great demand for it. But when the production of cotton developed into an important and profitable branch of agriculture, and when the low, malarial regions of the South began to be opened up for cotton plantations, African slave labor seemed almost indispensable to the occupancy and cultivation of the richest part of the Southern States. It is interesting to note that the slave population and cotton production of the United States increased rapidly, and at something near the same rate, from the beginning of the present century to 1860. In

1776, for instance, there were only about 300,000 negroes in the United States. In 1790 there were 697,-
897; in 1800, 893,041; in 1810, 1,191,364; in 1820,
1,538,022; in 1830, 2,009,043; in 1840, 2,487,455; in

BOUND FOR THE LAND OF COTTON.

1850, 3,204,313; in 1860, 3,953,760.

In 1770 the entire cotton crop of the United States,
exported, was three bags from New York, four bags
from Maryland and Virginia and three barrels from North

Carolina. A bag of cotton then did not mean a bale of
modern size and weight. That was before the days of
modern cotton presses, and cotton was packed in bags
by hand. As late as 1791 the entire cotton crop of the
United States amounted to only 2,000,000 pounds, or
about 4,000 bales of modern size and weight. In 1830
the crop was 976,845 bales; in 1850, 2,096,706; in 1860,
4,669,770.

In point of climate, negroes are perfectly at home in
the low, malarial regions of the South, where cotton
grows to greatest perfection, and where other people
could scarcely live at all when the forests were first
cleared away and the country opened for cultivation.

When slave owners and capitalists from all parts of
the United States began to rush down in the low bottoms of West Tennessee, Arkansas, Mississippi and Alabama, to open cotton plantations, I was a boy not yet
out of my teens. The excitement was intense, and
movers were continually passing through our neighborhood in Middle Tennessee from Virginia and the Carolinas, bound for the land of cotton. Many of our
neighbors were leaving every year, and, as might have
been expected, I caught the fever too, and determined
to try my fortune with the rest of them. So I tied up
my scant supply of clothing in a little bundle, swung
it over my shoulder on a stick, bid a tearful good-bye to
the friends and scenes of my boyhood, tenderly kissed
father, step-mother, sisters and brothers, and started on
my weary tramp to Mississippi.

# CHAPTER XVII.

Slavery, as an important factor in the development of the South, was short-lived. It began properly when the production of cotton first attracted attention as an important and profitable branch of agriculture, and lasted but a few decades. Thirty years compassed the principal part of its existence, and a much shorter period than that covered all of its worst features. It never amounted to much before 1830 in the main part of the cotton belt, and not till about 1840 did it develop into very gigantic proportions or manifest its ugliest features. During the decade from 1850 to 1860 it attained its greatest proportions and developed its worst abuses.

When I tramped from Tennessee to Mississippi with a small bundle of clothes on my back, while yet a boy in my teens, I invaded the land of cotton with the advance guard of slavery proper, and from that time till the emancipation proclamation was issued, I was familiar with every phase of life and of slavery in the very heart of the cotton belt. Though I was at one time the owner and proprietor of a large cotton plantation, completely stocked and equipped with mules, negroes and the best agricultural implements of that age, I took but little interest in it and it soon passed into other hands. I was not a brilliant success as a cotton planter. The plantation came to me partly through the generosity of a personal friend and theological admirer, and from me

(253)

passed to shrewder financiers than I ever hope to be, on strictly business principles, unencumbered by any bonds of carnal affection or spiritual affinity, between me and my successors in proprietorship, save such as I owe to all of Adam's race. Howbeit, I bear them no ill will. What once was mine became rightfully theirs without fraud or unfairness on their part, and with more of feelings of relief than of loss on my own part. The wreck of my fortune and loss of my property, as a cotton planter, sufficiently attest the mildness of my reign and leniency of my administration as a slave owner.

During many years of my life among cotton planters and slave owners in the South, I was a' Christian in faith and a preacher of the gospel by profession. The intimate and confident relationship of a pastor to his flock gave me the best of oppportunities to know the true inwardness of the whole system of slavery. It was my duty to seek out the secret sources of sin and rebuke the outward forms of iniquity. As a preacher of the gospel I have not been without faults, but never have I been accused of a lack of diligence in acquainting myself with the secret sins, or of a want of courage in rebuking the open vices of the people where I have labored. It seems pertinent to say this much by way of showing my qualifications to describe the uses and abuses of the system of slavery in the South.

The treatment slaves received at the hands of their masters differed widely in different cases. It was as varied as the treatment which horses or other dumb animals receive at the hands of their owners. In fact, different slaves of the same master received different treatment. Everything depended on the temper of the master and the disposition of the slave. No description of the system of slavery as it existed on cotton plantations is perfect, therefore, that does not tell the full story of the life of every master and of every slave. I cannot attempt such a description in a volume of this size. The most I can hope to do is to briefly sketch the general outlines ot slavery, in all of its phases, as I saw it on the great cotton plantations of the Mississippi bottoms. I shall try to give the worst abuses as well as the best advantages the negroes received, during the days of slavery, and leave the imagination of the reader to fill out the nicer shadings of the picture.

In moving slaves down into the low bottoms and rich valleys of the cotton belt, from older settlements in distant countries, the able-bodied, middle-aged men and robust young women were often sent forward in charge ot an over-seer, a few years in advance of the older and feebler men and women, and the young children, to open farms and build homes. In making up a crew of hands to send forward into the big bottoms, hard masters often disregarded family ties and parental feelings among the slaves. When it was deemed best, as a business policy, to send husbands and fathers to the bottoms, miles away, and keep wives, mothers and children at the old plantation, families were broken up without a moment's hesitation. When such separations were but temporary, and the members of divided families of slaves remained the property of the same master, with every assurance of an early reunion, the case was not so bad. But the great demand for able-bodied slaves in the cotton belt opened up a regular traffic in negroes between the old and new countries. Many slave owners in older states, who had more negroes than they needed, preferred to sell some of the most troublesome ones on their plantations rather than go to the trouble and expense of opening cotton farms in the bottoms, and many men went regularly into the business of buying negroes in the older states and selling them at a good profit in the new country. This led to many separations of families among slaves, which they all knew would be as lasting as life itself. Slave dealers often sold a young husband in Arkansas and his newly wedded bride in Mississippi or Alabama. In such cases the negroes could never hope to know anything of each other after they were separated. They could neither read nor write, and they were never allowed to travel beyond the bounds of the immediate vicinity of their respective masters' plantations.

In justice to Mr. Caskey, I should, perhaps, explain that I am mixing my own observations rather freely with his recollections in describing the various phases of slavery in the South, as well as in everything else I have tried to describe in this book. I am a much younger man than he, but all my early life was spent near the cotton belt of Alabama. My father was intimately associated with cotton planters and slave owners in the days of my childhood, and his friends of those days, who often visited our home and conversed freely in my presence, were familiar with every phase of plantation life and of the whole system of slavery. We had a cozy little home in the mountains, a few miles back from the broad valleys and rich bottoms where negroes and cotton principally flourished, but not too far away to be constantly associated with every phase of life on cotton plantations.

Possibly I over-rate the heart-troubles which slaves suffered in such family separations as I have tried to describe. I know negroes, with few exceptions, in those days, like some white folks now-a-days, were coarse-natured and unsentimental creatures, but it is hard to forget early impressions. A few old slaves whom I well knew and devotedly loved in the tender years of my childhood, had each a story to tell of loved ones left behind in the old "Ferginny" home. I dare say my childish interest in such stories often stimulated the imaginations of my dusky old friends, even to the stretching of their veracity, in dealing with the facts of history, but they told their tales of sorrow with a pathos and solemnity which deeply touched my baby heart and often opened the fountain of my childish tears. And when, with heavy heart and tear-bathed cheeks, I would steal away from their humble cabins in the lonely watches of the night, after listening for hours to their tales of sorrow, strains of pathetic song from a full chorus of negroes would often come sobbing after me like the wail of lost souls from a deserted grave yard. Such things greatly troubled my baby heart, and I cannot forget those early impressions even now, but since, in maturer years, I have learned more about negro character, and white folks' character too, I suspect that such family separations did not really trouble them as much as I then supposed. The old-fashioned plantation negroes did not take much trouble to themselves about anything. They were, by nature, rolicking, cheerful, fun-loving, care-defying and contented creatures. They would sing a doleful song or tell a sad story with a solemnity of countenance and pathos of voice never excelled even on the stage, and the next moment they would "pick de banjo," dance a jig or enjoy a joke with all the hilarity and abandon of a soul without a care. They never had the blues or gave way to despondency. All the world was, indeed, a stage, to them, and life was but a comic farce.

Many slave owners would not make themselves parties to the separation of negro families by buying any

17

member of a divided family. In many cases, masters of noble impulses and a large bank account, gathered up the fragments of broken families by purchases, from different parties, and gave the sorrowing hearts a glad

SOULS WITHOUT A CARE.

reunion and a happy home on their great plantations. The domestic and marital feelings were not very strong in the class of negroes ordinarily handled by slave dealers. As a rule, it was only the grossest, meanest class of slaves that masters in older states would sell to dealers, to be carried away and sold on the great plantations in the bottoms. Negroes of that class were not noted for their refinement of feelings, and hence they probably suffered less real heart-sorrow on account of such family separations than better specimens of their race would have felt. With them, families were not bound together, at best, by any very strong feelings of marital affection, parental love, filial devotion or fraternal relationship.

There were cases, however, in which the best of negroes suffered such family separations. They were all subject to the fortunes and misfortunes of their owners. In case of financial failure, the negroes on a plantation were sold at public auction to satisfy the claims of creditors, along with land, mules, agricultural implements and other property. But even in these extreme cases, the more humane buyers and sellers looked somewhat to the feelings of slaves by disposing of them in families.

It was in such a financial crash as this, that the good old servants I so devotedly loved in the days of my childhood were parted from their loved ones at the old "Ferginny" home. The old home and parts of their families were bought by one man while they themselves became the property of another.

And I now suspect that much of their trouble was a sort of patriotic sorrow for the downfall of the old plantation, quite as much as parental grief at their separation from their children.

It is a strange fact, that negroes, in the days of slavery, felt something of the same pride in their master's plantation that patriots feel in the land of their love. It was a great bereavement to those old-time negroes to be separated from family companions whom they loved, of course. It is also a great sorrow for a wife, a mother, a sister or a father, to see a tenderly-loved and manly soul, pass forever from earthly companionship in the midst of battle in defense of his country. But the ruin of the country, after all, is a deeper sorrow in many such cases, than the loss of the loved one.

This feeling of patriotism toward the old plantation, with slaves, was one of the strangest things in negro character. They seemed to forget all the toils and sufferings of their slavery, in their admiration of the magnificence of the plantation built up by their labors and their bondage.

Poor men who owned small farms and few slaves, treated their negroes much better, as a general rule, than slaves were treated by masters and over-seers on large plantations. In fact, a man who was able to own but eight or ten negroes and a small farm, treated the few slaves he did possess about as well as he treated his own boys. Master, master's sons and slaves, in such cases, all worked together in the same field, ate about the same kind of provisions and dressed pretty much in the same kind of every-day clothing. They took holidays together, and, all in all, enjoyed life, on a small scale, as well as poor folks in general. Negroes on large cotton plantations had almost an infinitely harder time. And yet, strange as it may seem, negroes in general looked with perfect contempt upon what they called " dese yere pore folks niggers." To belong to the richest man, and to labor on the biggest plantation in all the country was a distinction which all negroes coveted, and those who enjoyed such high honor found ample compensation for all the abuses they suffered, at the hands of hard overseers, in the wealth and magnificence of their master's plantation. Even now, it is difficult to find an old negro who will admit that he belonged to a poor man before the war. A negro who belonged to twenty different men before the war, nineteen of whom were poor but indulgent masters, while the other was wealthy but noted for the severity of his treatment of slaves, will invariably parade the fact that he belonged to the rich man and worked on the big plantation, but say nothing about the lenient treatment he received from his poor but indulgent masters.

This is a strange thing in negro character, but a latent vein of the same folly runs through the whole human race. It is this glorying in institutional splendor and magnificence regardless of personal comfort and convenience that causes religious people to want to belong to the biggest church and to worship in the finest house in the city. To maintain such magnificence in the ecclesiastic institution, people will submit to many personal and spiritual inconveniences and abuses. It is universally acknowledged that, as a rule, there is less brotherly love, spiritual fervor, personal consecration and social enjoyment in a big church and a magnificent house, than in an humbler, smaller institution. Besides, it costs money, which people of ordinary circumstances can ill afford, in justice to themselves and their families, to maintain such magnificence. Why should religious people burden themselves financially, despise the poor, contemn unostentatious worship, glory in a big church, rejoice in a costly house, run after ritualistic pomp and make a show of expensive paraphernalia in religion in general, rather than enjoy richer spiritual blessings in heavenly places in Christ Jesus, with less show and far lighter personal burdens? For the same reason that the poor ignorant negroes, before the war, would rather suffer ten fold more personal hardships, as slaves, and belong to a rich man on a big plantation, than to live with an humble master on a small farm.

The same innate disposition to court personal hardships for the worthless privilege of belonging to a magnificent institution, crops out in every political government on earth. And the admiration for the glory of the institution at the expense of the personal convenience and comfort of the people, has always been in proportion to the arrogance of the classes and the ignorance of the masses. The most burdensome forms of political government, and the most magnificent and expensive systems of church polity, have always been in ages and among people of the densest ignorance. All tendencies to glory in the magnificence of institutions to the neglect of the welfare of the people, whether in political or religious affairs, are sure signs of the decline of real intelligence in the people. The pomp and splendor of all forms of government, and the tame submission of the people to excessive personal burdens for the glory of their leaders and rulers, and for the establishment and support of gilded magnificence in public institutions to the oppression of the people, whether such things are in politics or religion, are but repetitions of the folly of the poor ignorant negroes who preferred the heaviest burdens of bondage to the mildest forms of slavery, for the empty honor of belonging to the richest man on the most magnificent plantation in the country.

Before we further consider the various forms and severity of the punishment slaves received, it should be remembered that the punishment of crime among them before the war was delegated by the State to their masters. It is not proper, therefore, to censure slave owners for the infliction of punishment upon criminals which is considered commendable in a government. Over-seers whipped negroes, before the war, it is true, and so did sheriffs whip white men in many States.

The slave population of the South numbered millions. Among the negroes of the South were many criminals, whose punishment passed from masters to courts by virtue of the emancipation proclamation. This was right. But it is not right to make no allowance for this punishment of crime in making out the indictment of wanton cruelty against slave owners, in the treatment of negroes.

Take the one item of breaking up families, for instance. I doubt whether a greater number of families were broken up among the negroes, by slave owners before the war, than are now broken up by courts in the punishment of crime. And with the few exceptions already mentioned, negro families were broken up before the war by way of punishing criminals, just as they are broken up now, by the courts, in sending criminals to work-houses, jails and penitentiaries. Slave owners sold negroes, mainly, because of the same disposition which now leads them into crime and to the penitentiary. There were exceptions to this general rule, of course, but it was a general rule none the less on that account. If all the punishment of crime, which is now inflicted by the courts, but which was then left to slave owners, be deducted from the count against slave owners in the matter of cruel treatment of negroes, the case against them will be greatly modified. This is not offered as a justification of slavery, but as a matter of simple justice to slave owners.

When a negro manifested the disposition of a criminal and repeatedly committed grave offences against the government he was under before the war, the master punished him for such lawlessness and, in extreme cases, separated him from his family and sold him. In such cases since the war, the courts have done the same, to vindicate the government and protect society. There were many slaves who were never punished before the war, just as there are many law-abiding negroes who have never been molested by the courts since the war.

# CHAPTER XVIII.

### AN OLD-FASHIONED BLACKSMITH.

Before I tramped from Tennessee to Mississippi, with my wardrobe on my back and all my earthly possessions on my person, I served an apprenticeship at the blacksmith trade. I was what the world would now consider a poor vagabond, but I was a white man and a good blacksmith, which was then considered a good inheritance. I had a good trade, a clear conscience, indomitable energy and a healthy constitution. Many boys of my age had less, few had more. I was in "the land of the free and the home of the brave," and the country was undeveloped and unoccupied around me. I did not feel at any great disadvantage in the race of life with landlords and slave owners. Negro property and cotton plantations were not rated high in estimating wealth in those days. It was yet an experiment as to whether such things could be made profitable at all. As to landed estates, they were as free as water and as boundless as the country around me. I had no land because I did not consider it worth claiming, and I coveted no slaves because I was not sure I could make them worth their food and raiment. Plantation aristocracy and wealth in this country were things no man had dreamed of up to that time. Slave owners were not yet able to live without work, and I considered it an even chance whether masters and slaves would not all starve to death in the bottoms before farms could be opened and homes built.

The trade of a blacksmith was a fortune in those days. Plows, axes, hoes, horse-shoes, knives—in fact everything

**MY TRADE WAS A FORTUNE.**

in the hardware line had to be made by hand in the blacksmith shop. There was not a hardware store in the whole country, and nothing in the way of manufactured hardware could be bought in the market.

When I reached Mississippi I opened a shop and had all the work I could do at my own prices. I worked almost day and night and charged liberally for my labor. I often worked till late into the night, and always began my days' labor before daylight in the morning. My shop was continually crowded and my customers were easy to please and prompt to pay. I accumulated wealth rapidly, and soon ranked with the rich people of the community.

I did not tramp my way to Mississippi from choice, but of necessity. There was no other way to get there, so far as I could see. I might have gone through on horseback or in a wagon, but, unfortunately, I had neither wagon nor horse. As well as I now remember I did not have even a night-mare on the whole trip!

There were no public conveyances of any kind in the country at that early day, and scarcely any roads. With great difficulty, slave owners carried their negroes, teams, provisions and tools through the country on foot with the help of a few wagons. Negroes usually walked, and each one carried a load, proportioned to his strength, of such things as would be most needed in the new country. Provisions and tools were carried in wagons, and in many places the negroes had to cut roads through the forest for the supply wagons. It was like an invading army moving into a hostile country, to subjugate it. In many cases, squads of negroes were driven from the Carolinas and Virginia, to the bottoms and valleys of Mississippi, Arkansas, Alabama and West Tennessee, hundreds of miles, on foot and loaded with packages of clothing, etc.

Large cotton plantations were managed by salaried over-seers. After slave owners got their business well established, they gave themselves largely to aristocratic society, and left their business almost entirely to their over-seers. The wages of an over-seer depended mainly

BOUND FOR THE BOTTOMS.

upon the net profits of his employer's business under his management. The man who could make the most cotton, at the least expense, with the fewest mules and negroes, commanded the best situation and the highest salary in the country, as an over-seer. This was a constant temptation to over-seers to impose excessive labor upon the slaves.

It has been supposed that the anxiety of the over-seer to save expenses often caused him to fail to provide for the negroes sufficient food and raiment. This I gravely doubt. Such cases never came under my observation. Indeed, I think the negroes of the Mississippi bottoms, as a general rule, had better food, raiment, lodging and medical attention before the war than they have had since. This is my observation, and it is also backed by a sound business policy. To raise no question as to the feelings and impulses of our common humanity, in slave owners and over-seers, business interests demanded that the negroes be supplied with wholesome food, comfortable clothing, good lodging, medical attention and sanitary advantages. These things were necessary to keep the negroes in condition to do the most work. The sickness of a negro meant the loss of his labor for the time, the trouble of nursing him and the expense of a doctor's bill. The death of a negro was a clear financial loss, equal to about ten good mules. Of course the better class of slave owners and over-seers would provide everything necessary to the best possible physical condition and general health of the negroes from higher motives than mere business interests, but the very meanest of them could easily be moved by a sound business policy, as apparent as this, to look to the health and comfort of their slaves.

There were doubtless times, in the early settlement of the country, when negroes suffered for both food and raiment simply because their masters did not have, and could not get, such things for them. There were times, in fact, when the master himself, as well as every member of his own family, suffered similar want from the same cause.

I have also known negroes to suffer slight inconveniences for want of food, a few days at a time, on account of their own wastefulness and improvidence. The overseer issued rations to the negroes once a week. The poor ignorant creatures seemed determined not to learn that a week's rations must last a week. They would waste their provisions the first part of the week, and then plead for more before distribution day. To teach them the importance of economy, they were sometimes allowed to run on short rations till general distribution day, when they thus wasted their allowance. But it was a lesson the poor creatures could never learn. They are, as a race, as improvident to-day as they were before the war. It is always a feast or a fast with them. They will give their last bite of meat or morsel of bread, when they are not hungry, to a hungry dog, tie an oyster cup to his tail when he has eaten it and fairly split their sides with laughter to see the poor, frightened brute run away. If they have a good square meal for supper, they will feast like lords and sleep as soundly as roaches without an idea or a care as to how they are to get their breakfast. These characteristics, of course, do not apply to the more intelligent specimens of the race.

The business of an over-seer was not calculated, particularly, to develop the finer feelings of humanity in him, and there were no business interests to restrain his haughty, over-bearing and abusive spirit in dealing with negroes. Human nature glories in authority. An abusive word, a vigorous kick, a lash with the whip or a lick with a club would very appropriately express the evil nature of a mean over-seer without at all damaging the working capacity or commercial value of the negroes. In these things, therefore, the poor slaves often suffered unnecessary and shameful abuses at the hands of little-souled over-seers.

Negroes are by nature peculiarly susceptible to kindness and flattery—fully as much so as white folks. Under the hardest over-seers, they received but little of either on the big cotton plantations. If they did their work well, it was accepted as the full measure of their duty, and they were dismissed without a word of praise or even an expression of satisfaction. The most they could ever expect, was to escape censure and save themselves from the lash. In my judgment, such treatment was one of the worst abuses they received. A gloomy life they must have had of it. Never a word of tenderness, of praise or of encouragement did they get under the meanest over-seers. Just here was a fine field for the introduction of the true spirit of Christianity, and I am glad to say that many masters and over-seers, under the benign and refining influence of the true spirit of the Christian religion, brought gladness and good cheer to many gloomy lives of poor, neglected slaves, by kindly words of merited praise. But the greed for gain too often choked the good seed of Christianity and prevented any such expression of kindly appreciation. On this point there are grievous sins upon the records of the courts above that must yet be accounted for by those who committed them. And sins of this class are by no means confined to slave owners and over-seers. There be those now living who are daily committing such sins against those with whom they associate.

On a large cotton plantation, negroes were whipped more or less every day—in many cases unjustly perhaps, and in not a few instances too severely no doubt. Still, the whipping was by no means general. Many negroes were never whipped at all. There were hundreds of masters and over-seers who never whipped a negro without a cause, and thousands of negroes who gave no cause for such punishment. Still, among the hundreds of slaves on a large plantation there were always a goodly number who called down upon themselves the lash of the most indulgent masters, by their own evil deeds, every day; and among the thousands of over seers in the South there were always some who occasionally would rashly whip the best of negroes without much cause. So, between the mean negroes and the bad over-seers, the sound of the lash and the voice of lamentations were heard in the land every day.

Ordinarily, the whipping was administered informally by the over-seer at the time the offense which called for it was committed. In such cases it was only a few lashes with a whip, a kick or a few licks with a sprout. But in the more aggravated cases of peculiarly obstinate, vicious, lazy and troublesome negroes in general, the punishment was administered with more formality and severity. Among the crimes for which the meanest class of negroes were whipped—apart from the general charge of laziness—may be mentioned such things as the abuse of a wife by a husband, abuse of children by parents, stealing, quarreling and fighting, disturbing religious exercises among the negroes, abusing mules, horses and other dumb brutes, etc., etc.

Over-seers sometimes organized a sort of court among the negroes to try such offenders, determine the guilt or innocence of the accused, fix the penalty and administer the punishment themselves. Mr. Garner, of Alabama, held regular courts of this kind on his plantation for years. Of course, all of the proceedings, in such cases, were under the jurisdiction and general supervis-

ADMINISTERED THE PUNISHMENT THEMSELVES.

ion of the master himself. And it is a strange fact, that

18

he nearly always had to interfere in behalf of the criminal and modify the severity of the punishment. Such proceedings, however, were very rare. With few exceptions, the over-seer took matters in his own hands, determined the guilt or innocence of the accused, fixed the penalty and administered the punishment himself without any unnecessary formality about it.

Africans had no very exalted ideas of honesty, morality or virtue when they came into bondage in the United States, and slavery did but little to improve them, as a race, in these respects. On some plantations virtue and the marriage relationship were scarcely more regarded among negroes than among horses and cattle. In such things the slaves themselves desired the widest liberty, and many masters gave them all the privileges consistent with business policy. There were many slave owners who encouraged chastity and fidelity in the marriage relationship, among their negroes, even in cases in which such a course seriously interfered with business interests and involved considerable financial sacrifice. All masters, however, were not of this kind. It must be confessed that on some plantations the restrictions of the master tended rather to increase licentiousness than to encourage virtue among the slaves. In very extreme cases, in fact, slave-raising seems to have been considered little more than a branch of stock-farming. On the plantations of the very worst masters, negroes had a form of marriage, but courtship and matrimony among them, in such cases, were subjected to the master's business interests. It is sufficient to say the negro men of the best disposition and the strongest physical constitutions had a plurality of wives, and that there were no old maids among the women, on the plantations of such masters. It is hardly proper to say the negroes, in such cases, were guilty of either polygamy or adultery. Their conduct was extremely unchaste, immoral and demoralizing, but I know not a word in any language to describe it.

# CHAPTER XIX.

Obstinate, determined and rebellious negroes often ran away from their masters or over-seers and hid themselves in the woods. They lived upon such food as they could gather in fields and forests or pilfer at night. In many instances they were secretly fed by other negroes. Sometimes they fled to the hill country adjacent to the great cotton plantations in the valleys and bottoms, and lived by stealing from the poor mountaineers at night. Occasionally they came upon women and children boldly in open day in the small homes in the mountains and demanded food. In some cases they killed domestic and wild animals, and cooked and ate them in their haunts in the woods. It was an easy matter for them to steal domestic fowls from barnyards, at night, and occasionally they would even pillage smoke-houses or country stores.

Over-seers and masters resorted to various schemes to catch runaway negroes. Certain men soon established reputations as experts in such business, and over-seers and masters employed them, whenever a negro ran away, to catch the fugitive. By devoting themselves mainly to such business, and by studying closely the geography and topography of the country as well as the peculiarities of negro character, they came to be remarkably proficient in their occupation.

The question of runaway negroes soon developed

into a serious problem with the white people of the
country. It indicated a spirit of insubordination which
caused grave apprehensions of a general insurrection
among the slaves. The fear was that if negroes were

RUNAWAY NEGRO STEALING CHICKENS.

allowed to remain too long in the woods they would
form bands of marauders and incite the slaves of
the whole country to a general insurrection. To
defy the authority of an over-seer or openly rebel

against the government of the master was to declare insolent hostility against all restraint. Negroes were under no law but the master, and amenable to no authority but the over-seer. They could, therefore, commit no graver offense than to run away. It was treason and open rebellion against the only government that had any authority at all over them. Such an offense, therefore, threatened the stability of all government, the security of all property and the safety of the very lives of the citizens themselves. A few runaway negroes might form a mob; a mob could quickly grow into an insurrection; an insurrection could hardly fail to produce a general revolution; and a general revolution would quickly sweep over the whole country. The question, therefore, involved the weightiest interests of both races.

Professional hunters of runaway negroes were nothing more than modern detectives. Naturally enough, they employed every means known to that age, which seemed calculated to help them in their business. In course of time they introduced slow-trailing bloodhounds, to run the fugitive negroes down.

When a pack of well-trained hounds once found the trail of the negro that was wanted, it was utterly impossible to confuse them or throw them off the track. The fugitive negro would often run through squads of other negroes at work by themselves, with no over-seer present, in the hope of losing the dogs. Sometimes he would exchange shoes with a friendly negro in the hope of throwing the dogs off the track. But all to no avail. The hounds would slowly and tediously, but patiently and unerringly work out the trail and follow up the track of the right negro. Of course it would not do for the fugitive negro to run upon other negroes in the

presence of an over-seer, to escape the hounds, unless
he wanted to give himself up, for all over-seers were
sure to capture runaway negroes at every opportunity.

The negro hunter mounted his horse and followed his
dogs till the negro was run down and captured. Such

HUNTING A RUNAWAY NEGRO.

negro hunters charged liberal fees for their services, and
one of them would often be called many miles to run
down a negro. When a runaway negro was caught, he
was always punished severely. In fact there was no

graver crime or severer punishment in the whole system of slavery.

There were but few white people in the bottoms compared with the immense negro population of the big cotton plantations. The over-seers, in the latter years of slavery, were always apprehensive of an insurrection among the negroes, and every precaution was adopted to prevent such a calamity. It is a low estimate to say that the negroes out-numbered the white people ten to one in vast sections of country. There were probably places, including several plantations and wide scopes of country, where negroes were fifty times more numerous than white people. It is not strange, under such circumstances, that the white people feared a serious uprising and general rebellion among the slaves. The wonder is that nothing of the kind ever occurred.

To prevent a plot or conspiracy among the slaves, every negro was kept in his place and no one was allowed to go beyond the bounds of his master's plantation without a written pass. Some negroes had a habit of secretly visiting the negroes of other plantations by night, and to break this up the over-seers of every section organized themselves and patrolled the country. They took it by turns, and while some of them slept others rode over the country every night and kept a sharp lookout for negroes off their master's plantations without passes. Woe to the guilty negro who fell into the hands of the patrols.

The patrols would ride up within a few hundred yards of the cluster of cabins, called a negro quarter, dismount, leave one man to hold horses, and noiselessly slip from cabin to cabin, to see that everything was quiet and orderly. If they saw a light through a chink in a cabin door, or heard any conversation or other noise about the premises, they cautiously investigated it.

The custom of patrolling the country gave rise to a song which is still very popular among the colored people in some parts of the South, the first line of which is, " Run nigger run, the patrol will catch you."

When a negro, who knew himself to be out of his proper place, found that the patrols were near, he took to his heels and tried to save himself by main strength and hard running. Many amusing incidents are told by the old negroes and patrols of the South, of hard races across fields, over fences, through briar patches. and into creeks, sloughs and swamps—the negro trying to escape a severe whipping and the patrols determined to teach him the folly and the danger of his way.

Speaking of negroes, passes, etc., an old over-seer told me an amusing thing, illustrative of the shrewdness of some negroes before the war.

A widow who owned a large cotton plantation and lived in a fine, old-fashioned, Southern, country mansion, employed an over-seer to superintend her business. The cluster of cabins, called the negro quarters, was about half a mile from the lady's residence. She kept a few domestic servants at her home, and the over-seer lived near the " quarters " and had charge of all her other negroes. Among the servants she kept about her own residence were two boys—one of them a shrewd mulatto who drove her carriage, and the other a thick-headed black boy who chopped wood, cultivated her garden and kept her front yard and lawn in good order.

When any of her domestic servants needed to be whipped, she merely wrote a note to the over-seer and sent it by the one that had been condemned to the lash, saying: " Please whip the bearer and oblige," etc.

The mulatto carriage driver carried one note and took

his whipping, but the second time he was requested to carry a note to the over-seer, he suspected the meaning of it, perhaps because he knew he needed a whipping, and concluded to send a substitute. So he hunted up the thick-headed wood-chopper and said to him:

"See yere, boy! Ole Missus say how you got ter fotch dis yere note to de boss!"

The boy was glad to get off from his work for a trip to the "quarters," supposing the note was merely a

"FOTCH DIS YERE NOTE."

matter of some general instruction which "ole Missus" wanted to give to "de boss" about business matters. But when "de boss" ordered him to prepare for the whipping, the real meaning of it all began to penetrate his thick head. He protested that he had done nothing to be whipped for, and declared it was " dat yaller nigger what ort to be lashed," but the over-seer was accustomed to such protestations of innocence, and hence paid no attention to what he said, but whipped him and sent him back.

# CHAPTER XX.

The field hands on large cotton plantations were, as a rule, the meanest specimens of the race. Slave owners of other countries sold their worst negroes to slave dealers, to be resold in the cotton belt. The treatment they received in the bottoms while in slavery, and their almost complete isolation from white people, still further brutalized them. Hence the negro population in rural districts on those large cotton plantations still differs widely from the negro population of all other sections of the country. This fact must be considered by all who would understand what is now called the race problem in the South.

He who forms his opinions of the negro race from the best specimens found in towns and cities, and in the country outside of the cotton district, knows but little about the race question. With such select specimens of intelligent negroes there is no race problem. Negroes of that class are moral, industrious, cleanly, virtuous and intelligent. Between them and the white people there is the best of feeling and the most amicable relationship, except when bad blood is stirred up for partisan purposes and selfish ends by ambitious politicians. The real race problem is not a question of party politics, legal rights or social privileges. The courts are open to negroes, and able lawyers are at easy command to vindicate their rights in any part of the country. It is

folly to try to enforce anything like social equality by law
or through politics, with such glaring antagonism between the races, touching everything essential to the
social compact.
Nor can the utter
incapacity of the
negro race, in its
present state, to
manage the affairs
of government, be
remedied by politi-
cal platforms or
legislation. I have
tried to describe
the very worst
features of the sys-
tem of slavery.
The abuses of the
system of slavery
and the hereditary
ignorance, vice and
licentiousness of
the negro race,
constitute the
source of a slug-
gish, corrupt, stag-
nant, loathsome
national stream,
and the real race
problem is the pu-
rification of that
stream. To clearly

"AN UNCLEAN FOUNTAIN."

understand the problem, one must not stop at a simple
introduction to the educated, refined, virtuous and well-

dressed negro pastor, lawyer, teacher or society belle of the city. He should see the thriftless, filthy, shameless, unwashed, poorly-fed, half-clad personification of sin, ignorance, poverty and contentment that we call the negro population of the cotton district. Whether there is anything in party politics, or any other kind of politics, sufficiently potent to cleanse this stream of human depravity, may well be doubted. The moral record of the apostles of politics who so confidently urge their party principles as the only remedy for this polluted race, is by no means reassuring. The stream of politics has never been rated high for moral purity even by politicians themselves, and to tunnel it into the dead sea of negro vice would hardly do more than produce a stagnant slough of human depravity and political corruption. The negro should be protected in all his rights as an American citizen, of course, but such protection does not solve the race problem. The only solution of the race question that will ever be worth anything to the negro, must provide for the purification and enlightenment of the colored race. As a theory, it must be based upon the real condition and wants of the negro race, and in its application it must have adequate means and sufficient time.

Much of the treatment slaves received was far more humane than that which I have described. There is much of the negro race now that is by no means so far sunken in ignorance, poverty and immorality as the stratum of society I have described. Still, all I have written is true. I am not an apologist for the inhuman treatment slaves received before the war, nor do I believe the ignorance, poverty and immorality of the race should be perpetuated. The inhumanity of slavery cannot be harmonized with the spirit and genius of

Christianity, nor is the present condition of the race consistent with the mission of the Christian religion.

Somehow I have always felt in a measure responsible

THE RACE PROBLEM.

for the wrongs the poor negroes suffered under the system of slavery, and yet I never added the weight of a needlessly unkind word, thought or deed to the burdens of a slave. I deeply sympathize with them now, and earnestly desire to bear an humble part in elevating, purifying and refining the race. I never look upon a crowd of ragged, ignorant, homeless, careless and rolicking negro vagabonds, that I do not pity them in my heart and fervently pray that a loving Father will guide me and help them in the great work of Christianizing the whole race. I never hear them chanting their plaintive music beneath star-gemmed and moon-lit Southern skies in the lonely watches of the night, that I do not long for wisdom to help them improve their condition. I do not believe that the South alone is responsible for all the evils of slavery, or that the people of the South should be pushed aside by holier-than-thou apostles of self-righteousness from other sections of the country, as unworthy to bear any part in the solution of the race problem. The Southern people did not bring the negroes into bondage. They bought them mainly from New England slave ships. It is not for those who sold Joseph into bondage for a few pieces of silver, to rebuke those who paid the stipulated price of his liberty. I say this in no sectional spirit. The South is not free from guilt, neither is the North without sin. Slavery was a national sin and the race problem is the burden of the whole people of the United States. We are all brethren in sin, and should be fellow-servants in works meet for repentance. The way of our salvation does not lie through angry recriminations and sectional bitterness. He who can see nothing in the race problem but vantage ground for his political party is neither a statesman nor a philanthropist. *Christian* people in all parts of the country should be *brethren*, not only in their efforts to solve the race problem, but in every other good work. In no case should they be over-confident of their own wisdom in anything. There is a governing Intelligence in this universe who "moves in a mysterious way his wonders to perform." Human plans often fail, but divine Providence always over-rules the wisdom, folly and wickedness of man to the solution of all the problems of the world's progress.

I have not a doubt but that God through slavery

HARD ON THE NEGROES.

worked out the solution of some great problem in the way of the world's advancement. If there were great suffering to man in the solution of the problem, it was only because the problem itself was the creation of man's wickedness. Probably the African race had, by neglect or disobedience of the laws of man's being,

19

reached a condition from which the easiest if not the only way of escape was through the system of slavery.

Slavery was hard on the negro and a disgrace to the nation, but it solved the problem of converting forests into farms in a large district of the United States. It is difficult to see how that problem could have been solved in any other way. It is questionable whether it could have been done at all by white labor. Before those extensive bottoms were cleared, drained and dried, the country was too full of malaria to be habitable for white people. It was adapted to the constitution of the negro. And yet negroes never would have opened the country for cultivation without the coercion of slavery. The negroes were worked very hard in clearing the country, but the work could hardly have been done more leisurely. The limited resources and the rapidly increasing population of the country demanded that the work should be done as speedily as possible. The people had not time to besiege the forests. The jungles in

NAPOLEON CROSSING THE ALPS.

those fertile bottoms had to be carried by storm. It was a sort of forced march on scant rations across a barren desert. It was a clear case of Napoleon crossing the Alps. It involved suffering heart-sickening to contemplate, but it was a military necessity. It cannot be harmonized with the spirit and genius of Christianity, but, like war, it may have been one of those necessary calamities through which God often leads rebellious people to the solution of great problems.

The hardships of slavery were scarcely greater than the sufferings of the Grand Army of the Republic. Could a soldier in the army claim any more liberty than a slave on a cotton plantation? Was not the authority of the master as absolute in the army as on the cotton plantation? Was not the life of a soldier as absolutely in the hands of the officer, as the liberty of the slave in the keeping of the master? Were not soldiers often driven through heat and cold, storms and floods, with short rations and scant clothing, even to death itself? Were not family ties disregarded by drafting officers for the army? The soldiers' suffering and death, and the country's desolation, wrought by cruel, bloody war may be called a military necessity, but it cannot be harmonized with the spirit and genius of the Christian religion. So slavery is not consistent with the universal fatherhood of God and brotherhood of man, but through all these things an over-ruling Providence was working out the solutions of the problems of the world's progress. Slavery and war may have been necessary to remove the obstacles which the wickedness of man had placed in the way of the world's development. Like the suffering which results from disease contracted by violations of sanitary laws, such evils are to be deplored as inevitable results of man's disobedience to the laws established for the government of the universe.

If God solved the problems of converting forests into farms and slaves into freemen in such ways, to man mysterious, why may he not solve the race question in some way to man unforeseen? O, ye of little faith! Ye blind guides! Be not bitter against each other. Do not unduly exalt your own wisdom in efforts to solve a problem no man, perhaps, fully comprehends. "Trust in the Lord, and do good; so shalt thou dwell in the land, and verily thou shalt be fed."

# CHAPTER XXI.

Having given a fair and full statement of the abuses of slavery on the plantations of the worst masters and over-seers, it seems proper to describe some of the better things that fell to the lot of the negroes on the farms of the best masters before the war. The best positions in the whole system of slavery were those held by personal attendants and domestic servants in aristocratic Southern homes.

Select servants, carefully trained for special domestic duties under the old system of courtly manners, were kept about every plantation mansion. This was one of the best features of the system of slavery. Such servants had the same high ideas of personal honor and family pride that characterized their masters. They magnified their office, believed strongly in "first families" and "select society," and looked with contempt upon "common niggers" and "poor white folks." They were originally selected from the great mass of slaves on account of their brightness of intellect and moral qualities, and these good traits were carefully nurtured and developed in them throughout their generations. Such positions of honor as they held were somewhat hereditary when once established, and descended in regular succession from parents to children on condition of good behavior and satisfactory service. They were by nature the very pick and flower of their race, and every care was taken to properly train them for their high calling. Slovenliness in dress, uncleanliness of person, awkwardness in manners or unreliability in the performance of any of their duties would not be tolerated by their exacting masters. They were continually associated with the white people, whom they served, in the highest circles of aristocratic society. Such training and association greatly improved them with each generation, and during the period of slavery such a policy developed some noble specimens of the negro race. Those select servants had the advantage of good blood as well as of careful training and high social privileges in their development. Nearly all of them were more than half white, and many of them could claim very brilliant ancestry. They were honest, truthful, dignified and courteous. They were governed by the social code from a sense of honor, and were never beaten. In many cases their relationship to the masters they served was very intimate, and not infrequently it was even closely confidential. By nature and education they were the leaders of their race, and they stand to-day, as they have always stood since the war, as mediators between the two races. In the days of slavery the positions they held were little less than honorable offices, with satisfactory emoluments, in minature governments.

There were many slave owners who treated all their negroes with great kindness. Some planters would not employ over-seers who would abuse their slaves. I have before me as I write a letter from an aged minister of the gospel. He was familiar with every phase of slavery in the South for many years before the war. In describing the best features of the system of slavery, as it came under his own observation, he gives an instance in which a large slave owner who was a personal friend of his, showed a devotion to his own slaves that was both tender and touching. During an epidemic, the planter referred to sat in his own negro cabins, tenderly nursing the sick and comforting the distressed, for fourteen nights in succession without an hour's sleep save an occasional short nap in the day time. Every delicacy in the way of nourishment, and every comfort in the way of clothing and furniture, that money could buy, were freely provided for the sick. The negroes had the best medical attention the ablest physicians in the country could give them, and the master himself cheered the sorrowing and comforted the dying by Christian kindness and godly conversation. He read the Scriptures to them, prayed for them and talked with them about the glory land of love and life undying. All work on the plantation was suspended, and those who were not sick were permitted and required to devote all their time to those who were afflicted. All this is vouched for by one who was an eye witness of the case. Nor was that man an isolated exception among slave owners. I have known many planters who treated their negroes with as much kindness as is here described. Such men were in the minority among slave owners, I admit, but they were numerous enough to constitute an important element of humanity in the system of slavery.

Those good men among Southern planters took great pride in keeping their negro cabins neat and attractive. Ordinarily their cabins were built of hewn logs, or plank, and finished off with neat brick chimneys and vine-clad porticos. The usual style was double cabins with an open hall between. The cabins were built in rows, and often there were as many as thirty roofs on a plantation. Each cabin had a back garden well culti-

PICKING COTTON.

vated in all kinds of vegetables, and a neat little front yard set with flowers, vines and ornamental shrubbery. The negroes were allowed ample time from their work on the plantation to cultivate their gardens and keep their front yards in order, and they were required to be neat and cleanly, as housekeepers, in their own homes.

On those plantations the negroes were well supplied with wholesome food and comfortable clothes. They were also amply provided with plain, but substantial furniture for their cabins.

Good masters respected the religious convictions of their slaves and took pains to provide for them church privileges and religious instruction every Sunday. There were many preachers among the negroes, and their labors were supplemented by sermons from the ablest white preachers in the country whenever the negroes requested it. It was no unusual thing for a planter to bring a distinguished preacher from a distant city at his own charges, to preach to his slaves and to the few white people of his vicinity. At camp-meetings and in times of great revivals, the negroes were always allowed to select from among all the white preachers in attendance the one they preferred to hear on Sunday, and their choice was always respected by the committee of arrangement. In such cases, it was esteemed by the white preachers themselves as no small compliment to a man's pulpit ability, for the negroes to request him to preach for them.

Marriage relations and obligations were sacredly respected by good masters among their negroes. In the arrangement of their home life in their cabins, matrimonial happiness, family ties and parental authority were sacredly guarded. Marriage was commended and encouraged, the sin of adultery was rebuked, and any reasonable sacrifice was cheerfully made, by the good master, in the matter of buying and selling slaves, to preserve the families and marriage relations intact. Children were taught to obey their parents, and parents were required to take the government of their offspring.

On the best regulated plantations, negroes were allowed reasonable time for diversion, recreation and social enjoyment. A pic-nic, or even a barbecue, with the usual accompaniment of speaking and a bran-dance, was not an unusual thing. A general gathering of the negroes, on such a plantation, for a dance by moonlight without losing any time from the regular hours of work, was of more frequent occurrence. At such gatherings, those who were not disposed to join in the dance spent their time

COTTON BOLLS.

in social conversation and in such games as suited their taste. The boys and young men would show off their accomplishments in jumping, running, turning handsprings, standing on their heads, wrestling, boxing and lifting heavy weights, and the girls and young women would watch such performances with the interest and admiration of mingled love and jealousy.

Such gatherings were never held without the master's permission, which, however, was easily obtained under ordinary circumstances. In many cases seats for the white folks were arranged at those gatherings, and the young ladies and gentlemen from "the big house" would come and be interested spectators of all the performances. Those gatherings were always held under the trees in some grass-carpeted woodland near the plantation residence when the nights were pleasant and cloudless, and the moon was at its full. It is difficult to imagine a scene more weird and romantic than a lawn party and bran-dance, conducted by slaves, under moon-lit Southern skies in balmy spring or melancholy autumn.

Very few slaves manifested any interest at all in even the elementary principles of education, but, on the best regulated plantations, those who wanted to learn were taught to read and write, at least. The teaching was usually done by the sons and daughters of the good master, and the dusky pupils nearly always pursued their studies with a view to qualifying themselves for the ministry. In fact there was no other calling open to slaves, and their ideas of an educated "nigger preacher"—"one o' dese yere high l'arnt bucks"—never included more than ability to read indifferently in Bibles of very coarse print, and to write an illegible hand. Those preachers among the negroes who couldn't read, and they were probably in the majority in all churches, would come regularly to hear the Bible read every Saturday evening by some member of the master's family. It was no unusual thing to see a gay and flattered belle of society reading the Bible on Saturday evening to one of her father's old gray-haired negro preachers, to post him up for his Sunday sermon.

In such cases the reader would often be moved by the
attentiveness, dignity, reverence and solemnity of the
listener, till she would utter the words with a seriousness of manner and pathos of voice strangely out of
harmony with her usually gay and frivolous life.

But the negroes greatly preferred the reading of "ole

LISTENING TO "OLE MISSUS" READ.

Missus," as they called her, and put more confidence in
her version of the Holy Scriptures than in what the

young folks read. In their sermons they delighted to assure their audiences that "dat's what de big Book say, jest zactly like ole Missus done read it to me." And when the big Book was quoted, just like "ole Missus" read it, that settled the question and ended all controversy.

The best masters gave their slaves holiday every Saturday afternoon. Many masters encouraged slaves to make money of their own, and gave them fair opportunities to accumulate personal property. On many plantations it was the custom to give every slave a little patch of ground to cultivate for himself on holidays, mornings and evenings before and after work hours, and at such other times as the negroes were not at work on the plantation. It was left optional with each negro as to whether he would spend such odd bits of time working for himself, and many of them preferred idleness to work for themselves. But I knew several slaves who would make many dollars worth of cotton on their own patches in their own time. Such money as they could make in this way they were allowed to spend as they saw proper. Many slaves, in the run of a few years, accumulated money enough to buy their freedom. I know several who bought both themselves and their wives with their own earnings. But a few weeks ago I was assured by one of the most reliable negroes in the country that he made as high as one hundred and fifty dollars in one year. He was saving money to buy himself and his wife, and had over a thousand dollars in "hard money" buried under his cabin floor when the war came up and set him free.

These milder features of the system of slavery developed a type of negroes entirely different from the specimens of the race which were brought up on the large plantations of more cruel masters. The negroes who were trained up by good masters had more intelligence, honor, virtue and self reliance than their less fortunate brethren from the plantations of harder task-masters.

When the war closed, the most intelligent negroes from the plantations of those good masters were the best qualified people in the South, barring the old over-seers, to take the management of the vast herd of liberated slaves, who had never known anything in their lives but to work under the direction of over-seers. They had the confidence of both races, and they were entirely competent to manage a business of considerable magnitude. They were the very salvation of the country in the management of cotton plantations immediately after the war, and I believe they will prove important factors in the further solution of the race problem. Between them and the white people there is good feeling and perfect confidence. They seem

THEIR OWN COTTON.

to intuitively comprehend the real character and magnitude of the race problem. They know how sadly the great mass of their own race, descended from the old-time " common niggers," need education, and honesty, and industry, and virtue. They have no political aspirations to turn their heads, and they never stir up strife between the races by clamoring for social equality with the white people. They have no unpleasant recollections of the system of slavery, and no unkind feelings toward their old masters. They have never received anything but kind and courteous treatment from the white people of the South, and they feel that their rights and interests are perfectly secure in any government that is administered by their old-time, well-tried white friends. They are not lacking in patriotism, and they are as devoted as the white people of the South to their own section of country. Denunciations of the South and abuse of Southern white people create no enthusiasm in them. They have no disposition to exchange the people they have known so long and so favorably for leaders of whom they know nothing. They are too true to their early training in modesty to rush into the common herd and take an active part in political hustings, but their influence is always felt as a great conservative force in times of dangerous excitement. They have no particular ambition to be at the head of affairs in politics themselves, and they have but little confidence at all in the worthiness of those of their own race who do aspire to such positions.

## CHAPTER XXII.

For a few years just before the war the South was a land of cotton, negroes, mules and magnificence. Southern planters were among the richest people in the United States. The South was a country of palatial homes and magnificent estates. A well appointed cotton plantation consisted of several thousands of acres of land, from four hundred to a thousand negroes, and as many mules as could be used to advantage, with other property in proportion.

There were no railroads, telegraph lines, telephone companies, land and improvement companies or street railway companies for people to invest money in. They spent their money mainly in extravagant living. They clothed themselves in fine raiment and fared sumptuously every day. Every country home had its costly furniture, fine horses, magnificent carriages, expensive shrubbery, silks, satins, diamonds, imported wines and costly works of art. A reception at a farm house on a cotton plantation was an affair of state.

Religiously, Southern people, including all classes of society, were firm believers of the Bible. There is but little skepticism among native Southern people to this day. The old-time aristocracy at the South modified the form and spirit of their religion to suit their social customs and political views, of course, but they never for one moment doubted the inspiration of the Bible.

(304)

They did not claim to hold anything in political economy, social customs, religious doctrine or church polity in defiance of the Bible. Their effort was to so construe the Bible as to make it teach, or tolerate, at least, what the people were determined to practice. Pastors and politicians labored to prove that slavery, State's rights and secession were taught in the Bible.

Education in aristocratic circles always included a course of thorough training in society accomplishments. Life among Southern aristocrats was wholly occupied in one continual round of fashionable gayety and social enjoyment, and the education of the young people was always designed to fit them for the life that was before them.

Colleges and universities were conducted on the same general plan of lavish extravagance and courtly dignity which characterized the high circles of society. The curriculum in every aristocratic institution of learning included a thorough drill in polite manners and strict social etiquette. The code of etiquette and honor was as rigidly enforced by public sentiment in schools, seminaries, colleges and universities, as in any other department of high society. To fail to act the part of a highborn gentleman according to the accepted standard of deportment, would have expelled a boy from college or university and disgraced him in society.

They had a queer standard of gentlemanly deportment in those days, of course, but they enforced it rigidly. Drunkenness and gambling were considered harmless diversions, if not enviable accomplishments, but discourtesy to ladies or treachery toward enemies was an inexcusable offense against good breeding. Young men in colleges and universities were expected, if not required, to maintain the dignity of their families in champagne parties and swell sprees. They were furnished money by their parents, to make a display of wealth and good breeding in all manner of extravagant living, and were made to feel that the honor of their families depended largely upon the amount of money they squandered in display and style while in college.

Southern planters spent much time and money, traveling for pleasure, on Mississippi steamers. To gratify the fastidious tastes of aristocratic travelers, money, time, labor and ingenuity were united to make the old-time steamers on the Mississippi absolutely perfect, as to comfort, convenience and elegance, in the matter of accommodations for passengers. They were nothing less than floating palaces. They furnished every convenience for social enjoyment, such as could be found in the best appointed mansions in the South. The world has probably never produced anything more extravagant and sumptuous in all of its appointments, in the way of a public conveyance, than one of the best-equipped, old-time Mississippi steamers. Kings' courts have rarely been the scene of more reckless extravagance or regal bearing in general manners of life, than one of the best appointed steamers on the lower Mississippi just before the war. It was simply magnificence gone wild. It was the quintescence of extravagance, dignity, formality, courtesy and debauchery combined. That brief period of Southern wealth, magnificence and aristocracy was an epoch in the history of the world, such as we may never see again.

High society everywhere was fashioned on a courtly scale. Admission to the circle of select society was a guarantee of good character, as measured by the recognized social standards, and implied an obligation to conform to all the requirements of social etiquette. A

breach of etiquette was punished by prompt and irrevo-
cable ostracism from the best society.

Men stood upon their honor as unflinchingly as women upon their virtue. Social etiquette tolerated

A DUEL.

greater immorality in men than in women, of course,
but the requirements of good breeding were rigidly enforced without regard to sex. When the code of honor
required a man to fight a duel, society enforced the re-

quirement on pain of social ostracism. In such a case man could no more decline to fight a duel than woman could compromise her virtue without exciting the contempt of society.

*Ante-bellum* Southern aristocracy was made of highly tempered metal. It could be *broken*, but it would not *bend*.

Southern planters were Statesmen and politicians by the nature and necessities of their business. In the days of Abraham they would have been called kings. In the congress of aristocratic society each planter represented a constituency of no mean proportions. The management of an extensive cotton plantation was practical statesmanship. In those days of rude implements, limited resources and great obstacles in agriculture, it required considerable political and financial ability to successfully manage a cotton plantation.

To love life more than honor was the sin unpardonable. Confidential gossip, which reflected upon the character of any person in good society, was not tolerated. No man was allowed to malign another in a whisper. Back-biting was beneath the dignity of a gentleman. If any man felt disposed to speak disrespectfully of another, society demanded a straight-forward, out-spoken, personal reflection, which the parties interested must settle between themselves on " the field of honor." Society never took the trouble to trace up tales or hear evidence respecting personal character. Personal reflections were not settled that way. The man who would go behind the reflection itself, to raise any question as to the grounds upon which it was made, forfeited the respect of his peers in society and showed himself a man of low breeding. Nor could a man justify a reflection, so as to excuse himself from meeting the usual and almost inevitable consequence of it, which was a personal encounter, by proof even strong as holy writ. The ground upon which the imputation was based cut no figure in the case. The offender must retract and apologize, or fight.

Questions affecting personal character were rarely referred to courts of law. All such questions were settled in the higher court of society. To carry a personal grievance into a court of law degraded the plaintiff in the estimation of his peers and put the whole case beneath the notice of society. The party defendant in such cases declined to appear before the court, suffered judgment by default, paid the findings of the court in dollars and cents and stood upon his right of personal vindication. If his enemy declined to meet him in personal combat, society reversed the decision of the court, ostracised the successful plaintiff and lionized his enemy.

To take an enemy unawares or at a disadvantage was an offense against good breeding which society would not excuse. A man unarmed was as safe in the power of his deadliest enemy, as in a garrison of his truest friends. The man who would not hazard his own life in defense of his bitterest enemy when unarmed, was a craven coward. To seek or accept any advantage of an enemy in a duel to the death, was an offense against good breeding which would disgrace any man in good society.

The highest authority in aristocratic society was a sort of unwritten law called "the code of honor." It was far more respected than either the laws of the land or the mandates of religion. It was of no avail to interpose the acts of the legislature or the precepts of divine inspiration against "the code of honor."

A duel was called "an affair of honor." When one man insulted another, the aggrieved simply notified the insulter that he held him personally to account for the insult. Such notice was called a "challenge." The man challenged had his choice to either retract and apologize, or fight. If he decided to fight, it was his privilege to name the time, place and weapons. Each combatant selected a friend, and these chosen "seconds" arranged all the details of the duel. Pistols were usually selected as the weapons, though swords, and even knives, were sometimes used. The combatants met at the time and place appointed, the "seconds" examined the weapons, stationed the antagonists and gave the word for the fighting to begin. The "seconds" also stood by to prevent either of the "principals" from taking any advantage, and to carry the antagonists from the field, and see that they had all necessary surgical attention when wounded, and proper burial when slain.

# CHAPTER XXIII.

## GOOD MANNERS.

Society openly engaged in many things contrary to Christianity, but in all such things it never violated the " code of honor " in letter or spirit. The code of social etiquette recognized the right of society to gamble, and defined man's rights and duties in games of skill or chance as definitely as it pointed out the difference between proper and improper deportment in the parlor or ball-room. Men were as stiff and unyielding, touching points of good breeding on the race-track or at a card table, as in a drawing room. One incident will illustrate :

There was a race-track near the home of an old-time Southern planter, at which society magnates assembled every year to wager money freely upon the speed of favorite horses. On one occasion, after the people had all assembled, and everything was ready for the races to begin, it was discovered that certain disreputable fellows had taken a mean and dishonorable advantage for their horses in the arrangement of the preliminaries for the races. The old aristocrat, though taking no part in the races, grew indignant at such disreputable conduct, and promptly took matters in his own hands. Mounting his horse he rode out upon the track, faced the assembled multitude, removed his hat, bowed courteously and stated the case. " And by all the powers above and below," said he, " not a race shall be run on

this track under any such circumstances. The crowd
will disperse at once, and I will hold any man who
favors such meanness personally responsible if he inter-

BREAKING UP A HORSE RACE.

feres in its behalf." The crowd promptly dispersed.
The people were not disposed to countenance anything
dishonorable even among gamblers.

Gallantry was a leading characteristic of old-time Southern gentlemen. There were no women in the eyes of such men; all females of human kind were *ladies,* except slaves, of course. The man who would remain seated while a woman, no matter how poor and humble, was standing, or even uncomfortably crowded in her seat, would have been promptly kicked out of a public conveyance, as an intolerable bore. Boisterous, profane or indecent language in the presence of ladies was an offense against society which any man of good breeding was in honor bound to punish if he could not prevent.

Hospitality was another leading trait in old-time Southern society. The traveler found a hearty welcome in every Southern home, and the wealth of the host was always lavished upon the traveler with a delicacy of taste and sincerity of hospitality such as would insure his comfort and enjoyment. Well-trained servants complied with every wish of the guest, and the entertaiment of strangers and travelers seemed to be the pleasure of the entire household. They were not only delighted to entertain strangers, but seemed actually anxious to have them remain in their homes as long as possible. Every member of the old Southern household welcomed travelers to the best hospitality the home could provide, and bade them adieu with evident reluctance to see them go. No remuneration was expected, or would be accepted, for such hospitality.

Language, both in conversation and current literature, in high circles of society, was remarkable for stateliness, dignity and formality. The commonest occurrences and simplest matters in every day life were spoken of, in ordinary conversation, in carefully arranged sentences and well-rounded periods. Items of news were expressed in the papers in pompous phrases, which savored of the dignity and formality of kings' courts. Vulgarisms and slang phrases were carefully excluded from the vernacular of high society. Nothing in the guise of low wit or vulgar humor was ever attempted in social conversation or current literature. With all the formality and bombast imaginable, in the arrangement of sentences, those old-time aristocrats would round up to the statement of the commonest and most immaterial little facts conceivable. They never employed a simple and direct form of expression when they could possibly think of a stilted and high-sounding circumlocution that would even vaguely suggest their meaning. They never attempted to state themselves, touching any matter, in that jocular, rough-and-ready, vulgar dialect of close, confidential companionship so effectively used on all occasions by newspaper paragraphers, stump-speakers, popular lecturers and even preachers, in these latter days. The language of that old-time aristocracy, whether spoken or written, touching politics, science, literature or religion, was the stiffest, most stately, formal and stilted medium of thought imaginable. Children were carefully trained from their very infancy up, in the use of the bombastic and pompous vernacular peculiar to that stilted generation. Even the slaves who were employed as domestics about plantation residences imbibed the spirit of the age and tried to imitate the lordly airs and stately language of their masters.

In matters of dress and general deportment, the code of social etiquette ruled every individual as with a rod of iron. There was no relaxation, diversion or recreation from the stiffness and formality required by society. From the cradle to the grave, every member of aristocratic society was continually on dress parade when not on duty in actual society engagements. Every soul was constantly in full society uniform, drilling in the manual of social etiquette. Good breeding required an absolute uniformity and slavish formality in style and general deportment, in every department of social etiquette, which was murder in the first degree to all individuality and originallty. Under such a system, progress, discoveries or inventions in any department of human endeavor were absolutely impossible with those who were subjects of such environments. It is no marvel, therefore, that all discoveries, inventions, improvements and progress in science, art, politics, sociology and religion emanated from the brains of men outside of the pale of aristocratic society. Such society was a dead sea of stilted formality, and though the living stream of humanity was continually pouring into it, there was never a rise or a fall of so much as a hair's breadth in the dead level of its eternal monotony. It was the staked plane of barren humanity, across whose dreary waste toiling emigrants from the old order of things marched in solemn, stately file to the new dispensation of modern improvements, without discovering an oasis of so much as one independent, individual action.

The stilted dignity and staid formality of select society in that age betokened a generation of disciplinarians. The whole social atmosphere was redolent with the principle of rulership. Those staid old pillars of aristocratic society in the South were just such specimens of humanity as the famous old Roman senators, whose strength of character and powers of discipline so long resisted the decline and down-fall of the Roman Empire.

Aristocracy and slavery were but different parts of the same social system. Neither could have existed without the other. Nothing but the unbending, unyielding, uncompromising, stiff and stately formality of old-time Southern aristocracy could have disciplined, over-awed and held in abject and oppressive slavery the vast negro population, which, in many sections of the South, out-numbered the white population by ten to one at the most conservative estimate. And nothing but the most abject slavery of the masses could have sustained such lordly extravagance of the classes. If we assume, therefore, that Providence had some wise purpose to subserve by the perpetuation of either slavery or old-time aristocracy, till "the fullness of times," it is easy to understand why both had to continue till the purpose of God was accomplished. And when the time for a change was fully come, it was immaterial whether the revolution took the form of a popular protest against aristocracy or an open attack upon slavery. In either case the result would be the same, for the destruction of either must also prove the abolition of the other.

The rigid social discipline in high circles of society in the South in olden times, trained the leaders of the white people for martyrdom. They were not the kind of people to be conquered, or subjugated. They were the sort who have to be exterminated. They defiantly led "the lost cause" till they were well nigh annihilated, and the whole country was completely devastated. With them the rebellion was "an affair of honor" on a large scale. When once the issue was joined, they couldn't see any honorable way to avoid a fight. They looked at the whole question in the light of the teaching of the "code of honor." And why should they look at it in any other light? "The code of honor" was the highest

RURAL HOME IN DIXIE.

authority they recognized. Many of the leaders in the South, therefore, looked upon the late war as a sort of personal matter. They did not go behind the open declaration of war, to consider the grounds upon which such declaration was based. They had not been trained from their youth up to do anything of the kind. When the issue came, they understood that the only alternative was to retract and apologize, or fight, and they promptly decided to fight.

The independence, self-respect and self-reliance bred and born in the women, children, invalids, cripples and aged men who survived " the lost cause " in the South, served a good purpose in causing them to endure the hardships, privations and desolation through which they passed during the years succeeding the war. The whole course of human training for generations back, was well adapted to prepare a people to endure the poverty which fell to the lot of the South after the war. But for that spirit in the people, the fortunes of the country would never have been rebuilt. With a less measure of unconquerable pride and a greater love for luxury and ease, they would have emigrated from a country so completely devastated by war and so hopelessly burdened with the support of a thriftless negro population. It is worthy of note, as showing the metal of Southern people, that very few families emigrated to the North after the war, to escape the hardships every one could see must be endured before the waste places of the country could be rebuilt in the midst of such poverty and desolation. In some cases those who did leave their native country in ruins, to find better environments in Northern States, were remonstrated with by friends and relatives for their lack of patriotism. Whatever else is true of the spirit and genius of such old-time society in the South, it unquestionably trained a people to endure great hardships rather than compromise their self-respect by fleeing for assistance to the people and country they considered their enemies.

# CHAPTER XXIV.

## HARD TIMES IN THE MOUNTAINS.

Up to this point, the story of " Seventy Years In Dixie " has been in the form of a personal narrative of an old man whose memory of men and things extends back to 1820. For good reasons, which need not here be assigned, I desire to give, in this chapter, the story of hard life among the poor mountaineers of the South, in the form of a personal narrative of a much younger man. I need not give any names. It is only necessary to ask the readers to remember that in this chapter they have the observations and experiences of a boy not yet in his teens when the war began. His whole life, up to that time, had been spent in the hill country of the South several miles back from the rich bottoms and broad valleys where negroes abounded, wealth flourished, cotton reigned and extravagance ran wild.

That once far-back mountain country is now—1891— noted for mineral wealth, thriving cities and extensive mining operations and manufacturing industries, but before the war it was populated by very poor people, who depended entirely upon farming for subsistence. Barring a few thousand acres bordering upon the fertile valleys, these mountains were considered comparatively worthless before the war. Every valley plantation which lay near the mountains extended back into the hills far enough to include a few hundred acres of wild lands for timber, but beyond that the poor people were left in

21                                                      (321)

undisturbed possession of that rugged country. Only a very small portion of the hill country could be cultivated at all, it was so rough and rocky, and the best of it yielded discouragingly small harvests for the amount of labor required to cultivate it. The farms were small, the fields were narrow and lay mainly on hill-sides, and the soil was thin. Newly-plowed ground washed fearfully on those steep hill-sides every heavy rain, and after a few years cultivation little of it remained but a heap of stones mixed with barren clay.

A certain old mountaineer was once referred to as a very peaceable man, whereupon, a noted wag said:

"Of course he is peaceable. He couldn't be otherwise where he lives. His old hill-side farm is so poor he can't raise a difficulty on it!"

The hill country was well watered by living springs and limpid brooks, and the people were blessed with vigorous constitutions and perfect health. The population increased as rapidly as the soil failed, and each year the difficulties of making a bare living multiplied. There was no market for anything but cotton, and that grew but poorly at best in the mountains. To raise cotton on those hills in competition with slave labor in the fertile bottoms, was starvation undisguised. And yet, what else could the poor people do? The large planters produced everything they needed in the way of supplies on their own plantations, by slave labor, and supplied the towns and cities with everything salable in the way of country produce at the same slave-labor, starvation prices. The poor people were, therefore, hopelessly driven out of the markets, and forced to subsist upon the products of their own barren little farms. Nor was there any relief to be found in selling their labor. There were no manufactories in the country, nor was there any demand for labor of any kind except the labor of slaves and over-seers. The demand for over-seers was very small, and hence the great mass of poor white people were hopelessly shut up to lives of unflagging industry and severe economy on their little mountain farms.

Under the laws of the United States, a "homestead" consisted of a "quarter-section" of land, which was one hundred and sixty acres. The mountaineers "took up" land generally under the "homestead law," and this largely regulated the size of the farms. It was an extra good "homestead" that had as much as sixty acres of land that could be cultivated at all, and not a few farms had much less than that amount that could be plowed. Now and then a "homestead" would extend down into a narrow bottom on some small creek or branch, and when eight or ten acres of such land in one body fell to the lot of one man, his farm was the envy and admiration of the mountaineers for miles around. The location of dividing lines through such precious soil was a question in which the community took a deeper interest than in national elections. When the interests of two men were involved in such a squabble, every man, woman and child in the community, for miles around, joined in the contention. When the county surveyor arrived, according to appointment, to "run the line" across the celebrated bottom in dispute, he invariably found the people of the whole neighborhood on the ground, to see that he did the thing fairly. Of course there were always two parties to the dispute, and each one knew exactly where the line ought to be. They measured *distance* by *steps*, and settled the question of *direction* by the sun, moon, seven-stars and other guides equally reliable. What chance

did a surveyor's compass and chain stand against conclusions settled by such infallible methods? The surveyor never settled anything unless by chance his compass and chain " split the difference," in which case the
parties to the fuss generally accepted the compromise
with fairly good grace. And the frequency with which
the compass struck the golden mean between contending extremes, leads me now to suspect that those old
surveyors often found their instruments disturbed and
turned away from the true course by the local attrac-
tions of contending parties. I well remember how my
feelings were enlisted in a neighborhood feud about a
line across a narrow strip of bottom land when I was
but a lad not yet in my teens. It was an old fuss then,
and it was still raging with unabating fury the last time
I was in that neighborhood. Out of that old feud have
grown rival churches, rival schools, rival politics and
rival social circles. It is all a preacher's orthodoxy is
worth on one side of that fuss in that neighborhood to
express an opinion that the other side may possibly be
correct in some of their doctrine. Any school-teacher
who is acceptable to one party in the squabble, would
not be trusted, under any circumstances, by the other
party to teach their children Arithmetic or English
Grammar. I have a distinct recollection that, in my
very early childhood, during the war, I always associated my favorite statesmen and soldiers, in my mind,
with my side of the old neighborhood fuss about the
location of that line. I was too young then to know
much about the Mason and Dixon line, but I remember
how my little mind associated it with the line that had
always been a source of discord in our neighborhood.
I know I thought the Mason and Dixon line must have
made sad havoc of somebody's bottom field, to stir up

such a war, and I wondered whether there would ever be a war over the line our neighborhood was always making such a fuss about! I had some very decided convictions about the Mason and Dixon line, little as I knew about it, and as for that other line which cut the best bottom field in the country to tatters at our very door, I was ready to sacrifice myself upon the altar of my country over it at any moment. It is a weakness of my nature of which I am heartily ashamed, but I must confess that even to this day I feel nearer to those who were on my side of that line in those far-off days of my childhood, than to those who were on the other side. I know this is all wrong, and by an effort of the will I can easily shake off such feelings, but the bent of my nature is that way. And in my dreamy moments at this late day, I find myself, half unconsciously and all wrongfully, feeling that Paul and Peter and the Lord Jesus Christ *must* be on what was *my side* of that line in the blessed days of my childhood. I remember how my little mind doubted the reliability of the compass and chain which, I must confess, were against me. I remember the process of reasoning, if my childish efforts may be dignified as such, by which I condemned the compass and sustained my conclusions. I shall never forget my admiration for the argument first suggested by a wooden-headed old numskull and afterwards repeated by men, women and children on our side of the question whenever the occasion called forth our strongest logic. The surveyor was trying to satisfy everybody, and he therefore took pains to try to explain to us all how he followed the line.

"Now, you see, the needle of my compass, here, always points toward the North," said he.

"But how do you *know* that is North?"

"Why, because the needle points that way, of course."

"Great Jerusalem! Would you call just anything

HOW DO YOU KNOW THAT'S NORTH?

North because that thar little thing happens to p'int to'ards it?"

Then the old nincompoop made an *argument* against

the surveyor and his compass which was considered unanswerable for years afterwards in that neighborhood.

"S'pose the thing *does* p'int North. What's that got to do with this case? This here line runs *East and West !*"

The original parties immediately interested in the squabble have long since died or moved away, and most of the land in dispute is worn out and thrown away these many years ago, but the two parties in that neighborhood still nurse their prejudice against each other. By diligent work in political, religious and labor organizations the division is still kept up, and the humane spirit of love and brotherly sympathy commended in a world-wide system of Christianity and philanthropy makes slow progress against the partisan bitterness which originated in the squabble about that line years ago, and which has been perpetuated by dogmatic leaders through narrow and sectarian organizations in politics and religion. .

# CHAPTER XXV.

## MISERY IN THE MOUNTAINS.

Wheat would scarcely grow at all on those poor, worn-out and washed-away hill lands, and to buy flour was a piece of extravagance not to be thought of. The family that could afford flour-bread for breakfast every Sunday morning, and on special occasions when company of unusual notoriety was present, was counted among those peculiarly blessed. The ordinary diet was bread made of coarse corn meal, strong coffee and fat bacon. And the fat bacon and strong coffee often came in broken doses at distressingly long intervals during the hard years. Whole families would often live for weeks at a time on dry bread made of coarse corn meal without grease or salt.

Notwithstanding the poverty and hardships those people suffered, life had its silver lining for them. They were completely isolated from the world, and but for their occasional trips to market when they caught a glimpse of the magnificent farms and residences of the wealthy planters in the valleys, they would not have known there was any better lot for man on earth than theirs. The small mountain farms yielded, on an average, about two bales of cotton each, which would bring in market from thirty-five to forty dollars, net, per bale. This was the annual gross receipts, in cash, of the farm, and these few dollars had to be divided out so as to buy medicine, coffee, sugar, soda, salt, pay taxes and procure such other articles as were indispensable to life and impossible to make on the farm. The wagon that hauled the cotton to market brought back such articles as must be bought, and the remainder in cash was carefully saved for tax and other emergencies. The head of the family usually rode on horse-back to market, sold the cotton and carried the spare cash. The wagon was drawn, usually, by oxen and driven by "the boys" of the household. Occasionally, after the wagon was started on its return home the head of the family would imbibe too freely, and if he once lost his balance " the surplus in the treasury " would be squandered by reckless and extravagant appropriations before he left the town. Once a man maudlin drunk called lustily at a cabin in the mountains, on his return from market.

"Who is that?" came in sharp tones from the cabin.

"Itsh John Loony."

"What do you want?"

"I want to shee you."

"What do you want to see me for?"

"I want you to (hic) zamin ish meshkit."

The owner of the cabin came out and found John Loony as drunk as an owl, on his old olind horse stupidly holding on to one end of a bolt of brown domestic while the whole web stretched back full forty yards down the muddy road. He had been to market, sold his cotton and started his wagon back home. After the wagon was gone he got drunk and bought a bolt of domestic, which he had undertaken to carry home on his horse. The web had come undoubled, and, too drunk to refold it, he had held on to one end, dragging the bolt behind him in the mud. Knowing it was more domestic than John Loony was able to afford at one time, the man asked:

" What in the world are you going to do with all this cloth ? "

Leaning over and putting his mouth close to the man's ear, John said, in a confidential whisper :

" Don't you shay nothin' 'bout it. I want' to sh'prise my old 'oman. You shee its a new frock for her. Shay! My old 'oman aint had a store-bought frock before shince we been married! "

The soiled cloth was carefully folded, and, tightening his grip on it, John moved off, chuckling to think how he would " sh'prise his old 'oman" with a new brown domestic frock!

A few days ago I had a conversation with a popular preacher about the hardships poor people in mountain regions throughout the South suffered before the war. The preacher had spent some years in his early ministerial life preaching in such regions. His brother was also a preacher and co-laborer with him in the mountains before the war. Seeing I was interested in southern ante-bellum reminisoences, he said:

"SH'PRISE MY OLD 'OMAM."

"My brother and I have often talked to each other about the hard fare we had while laboring in the mountains. I thought I had certainly seen the very severest types of poverty, but I must confess he surpassed me in one case, so far as diet is concerned. He went home with a good brother in the mountains one day for dinner, and the only things on the table to eat were coarse corn bread, sassafras tea and a 'coon's head boiled with polk salad ! "

" Speaking of hard fare in the mountains," said an old surveyor, who had " been there " himself, " I stopped at a little log cabin in the hills to spend a night once when out on professional business. I soon learned that 'the family' consisted of a youthful couple recently married. There was but one room in the house, the cracks between the logs were open, there was no ceiling over-head and the floor was made of roughly hewn puncheons. The roof was constructed of rough clapboards weighted down by young trees and the chimney was made of sticks and bedaubed with red clay. The fire-place was from five to seven feet wide, and the fuel was a huge pile of big, blazing logs lighted up by resinous pine. There was not a chair in the house, and a rough bench before the fire was the only chance for a seat. The only cooking vessel on the place was a large skillet, and the only thing to cook was coarse corn meal. A magnificent spring of pure water gushed from the mountain-side hard by, and a gourd was the only water vessel in the family inventory. The young wife mixed some dough without grease or salt, in the skillet, and baked a huge pone of bread before the roaring fire. When it was ready to serve, the fact came out that there was not a knife, fork, cup, saucer, plate, dish, spoon or table about the premises. The little woman took the sheet from the bed, spread it on the cabin floor, turned the skillet upside down and tumbled the pone of bread out upon the sheet. She then informed us supper was ready. Fortunately, I had a pocket knife, with which I carved the formidable pone, and we sat flat down on the puncheon floor and helped ourselves to the bread ! " The reader now has before him a fair and not overdrawn description of the two extremes of society in the South when the war began— the highest circles of slave-holding aristocracy and the poorest classes of mountain society. Between these two extremes there were many grades of society, but the same unbending spirit of independence and self-reliance pervaded all classes. The old aristocrats and the other classes made an army that was unconquerable and equal to any emergency in the matter of rigid discipline and patient endurance of extreme hardships. The Confederate army needs no further description.

# CHAPTER XXVI.

SECESSION AND THE WAR.

In the following pages I give the story of secession and the beginning of the war in the South as told by one who was but a boy not yet out of his teens during that historic period. This will give a clear idea as to the motives which prompted and governed the actions of the people, without confusing the mind of the reader with the abstruse plans and theories of the leaders. And, after all, this is the true standpoint from which to judge the people of the South touching the part they took in the late unpleasantness. Moreover, this is considering the subject from a new angle of vision. Writers on this question have hitherto given ample attention to the leaders and their theories and plans, but who has told the story of the beginning of the war from the standpoint of the people? The young man gives his recollections in the following words:

It is impossible to describe the excitement which prevailed throughout the country during the canvass before the question of secession was voted upon, and the few weeks following during which volunteers were enrolled for the army. Barbecues, picnics and mass-meetings were held all over the country, the Declaration of Independence was read publicly in every assembly, orators poured out the vials of their wrath upon "tyrants," "invaders" and "oppressors," and boys not yet out of school offered to sacrifice their lives in defense of Ameri-

can liberty and the Constitution of the United States!
To people who passed through those memorable days
in Dixie, it seems queer to hear Southern men and women spoken of as "traitors," "rebels," "enemies of
American liberty" "and foes of the Constitution." I
know not what may have been the secret motives of
wily leaders, if there were any such leaders, which I
gravely doubt, but as for the people, nothing but patriotism pure and simple moved them to vote secession
and to enlist in the army. The people at the South
felt just as confident that the people at the North con-
templated a deliberate overthrow of the Republic as
their fathers in the Revolution felt that King George
was a tyrant. In all the public orations and private
discussions the idea that slavery was the bone of contention never once entered the minds of the common
people. They thought they were contending for genuine old George Washington liberty. They understood
that the Constitution of the United States was assailed,
and that they were offering themselves for its defense.
The question, as they understood it, was whether American liberty should be perpetuated or crushed by Northern monarchy. Fighting for slavery? Think of the
absurdity of the thing! The Southern army was
largely made up of volunteers from the mountain regions. There were no slaves of consequence in that
mountain country, and those poor mountaineers hated
"stuck-up" slave holders as cordially as a saint hates
sin. True, they understood in a vague sort of way
that there was some discussion on the subject of slavery
in a general way, but to them this was only an incidental
and irrelevant topic of public interest which was in no
way connected with the question of secession. The
people understood that the question at issue was simply

their right to manage their own affairs in their own States. If the North proposed to interfere with that right, what assurance had they that it would not take from them their homes and all their property? I know not what the leaders thought, but there was no mistaking the feelings and opinions of the common people. I was but a lad not yet out of school, but I remember distinctly that I understood secession was not rebellion against the American government, but that it was the genuine American government itself, pulling loose from a tyranical monarchy, so that it might defend itself! I understood that in seceding the South held on to the Constitution, and the Declaration of Independence, and Bunker Hill monument, and the life of George Washington! True, I had no definite idea as to what the Constitution really was, but I was perfectly confident we had it, and, what was more, we were going to *keep* it! *We* traitors? *We* rebels against the American government and enemies of the Constitution? Shades of Washington and Bunker Hill! Why, what were the people up in the mountains fighting for if not for the Constitution? Fighting for negroes, were they? "Oh, shoot the negro," said they, "and his master, too, just so we save the Constitution, and the Declaration of Independence and the American eagle!" What did they care about slavery? Hadn't it been as a thorn in the flesh to them from time immemorial? Did not everybody know that the North had set aside the Constitution, throttled our liberty and pulled the tail feathers out of the American eagle? As I write these lines, an echo from the stirring scenes of 1860 seems to come floating over the graves of thirty buried years. The crowds surging around the speakers' stand at a mass-meeting in the woods; the animating music; the stirring speeches of distinguished orators; the cheers and yells of excited audiences; the groups of men in earnest conversation; the flushed faces and sparkling eyes of patriotic women; lovers strolling through the groves—I see it all as plainly as if it were but yesterday. Such were the scenes during the canvass before the people voted on the question of secession. I remember well the speeches, and their effect upon the people. I remember the very gesticulations and inflections of the speakers, and the expressions of indignation which burst from the excited audiences as the long list of our wrongs was recounted. I remember how ladies clapped their hands and waved their handkerchiefs when those masters of assemblies closed their powerful orations by pledging themselves and the patriotic South to the defense of the liberties so dearly purchased by our forefathers in the Revolutionary war. I remember how, with a pathos which I cannot describe, the speakers told us that a centralized power that would presume to invade a State and set aside the right of local government which was recognized and protected by the Constitution when it was adopted, was a tyrant not to be trusted. What better guarantee had we for the protection of our wives, and mothers, and children and sweet-hearts than we had for the protection of our right of self-government in our own State? I remember how I stood, a mere lad, with burning cheeks and clinched fists, near the speakers' stand under a giant oak, as I listened to such words of pathos, and patriotism and love for mother, sisters and home as would move a heart of stone! I remember how screams and sobs from the women electrified the frantic audiences, and I remember, too, how the men sprang to their feet, stood on the rude seats and, wild with excitement, threw their hats into the air and yelled themselves hoarse for freedom and American rights! Vote for secession? Of course we voted for it, and we wanted to get hold of the man who didn't. Were we traitors against the American government? Great Cæsar's ghost! We were just

" 'RAH FOR AMERICAN LIBERTY."

getting ready to fight, and bleed, and die to save the American government. We were not seceding from the government. We were the government itself, the original George Washington edition of it, and we were

22

seceding from a Yankee counterfeit! I was too small
to reason about anything, so I know my feelings on the
subject were simply the prevailing public sentiments
which I absorbed and reflected. I had no idea what
the Constitution and the American Government were,
or where they were, but I understood that the South
had them and wanted to secede to hold them. I didn't
understand where they were just at that time, but I was
confident our side had them concealed somewhere
among the stuff, and that they would be brought forth
just as soon as we could secede and get off a safe distance where we could protect them!

Secession was not anarchy. Those who believed in
secession believed also in a federal government. They
believed in the union of States and proposed to defend
that Union at all hazards. The question with them was
as to whether the Union had a right to disregard the
sacred compact on which it was formed. The people of
the South were willing to stand by the Union with
their lives, and never for one moment entertained
a thought of violating in letter or spirit the solemn
compact on which that Union was based. The principle against which they protested was the right of the
Union to compel a State to do anything which it had
not obligated itself to do in the Constitution on which
the union of States was originally formed, and which
the Federal Government solemnly pledged itself to
observe and defend when the States entered the Union.
Any interference with the rights of a State on the part
of the Federal Government not authorized by the Constitution, the South denounced as treachery in the
Union, an unwarranted assumption of power, a despotic
spoliation of a helpless minority and a violation of the
spirit and genius of American liberty! It has been a

long time since I heard these questions argued, and my memory is but second-rate at best, but the impressions, feelings and motives of the people were too deeply stamped upon my mind and heart ever to be erased. I remember how the speakers told us that if it had been understood, when the vote on the adoption of the Constitution was originally taken, that the Federal Government should have the right at any time after a State came into the Union to abolish any organic law of that State which was recognized at the time that State was admitted into the Union, not a single State in America would have adopted the Constitution.

In voting for secession the people of the South did not understand that they were voting for a war. They were told that there would be no war about it. It was a common thing for a public speaker to say, "I'll drink every drop of blood that is shed on account of secession!" In the excited condition of the people, war was not considered of any great moment one way or another, and the South would probably have seceded anyway if every voter had felt confident a war of extermination would have been the result, but it is nevertheless true that hardly anybody apprehended that a serious war would grow out of secession. There were many conservative spirits in the South who were very earnestly opposed to secession, and who voted against it, but in the excitement of those days they either deemed it useless to speak or the people thought it unnecessary to consider their warnings.

I am neither a statesman nor a politician. I shall not stop to express an opinion as to whether the people were right or wrong in their convictions as to these things. To put it in the very strongest light possible against them, the most that can be said is that they were in error.   Still, they were *honest.*   They acted upon their convictions.   They were prompted by *motives* as pure and as patriotic as human hearts ever cherished. Such people deserve not to be rashly condemned, severely denounced or bitterly persecuted because of an honest mistake, and certainly it cannot be anything worse than a mistake.

# CHAPTER XXVII.

## ENROLLING VOLUNTEERS.

But the greatest excitement came after the States had seceded and war had been declared. Mass-meetings were then held all over the country to enlist soldiers for the the army; speakers turned themselves loose in denunciations of the tyranny of the North, and the people went wild with excitement. The rough mountaineers and the aristocratic planters embraced each other: "first families" forgot all social barriers and mingled freely with the common herd; millionaires enrolled their names beside mendicants for the army; and society belles promenaded with back-woods volunteers who had never seen the inside of a fashionable parlor! One night at a ball, a boy was sent with a message from some society young ladies to their aristocratic mammas in an adjoining room. The ball was given in honor of the volunteers about to leave for the army, and the message was a question as to whether those society girls should dance with the back-woods volunteers whose movements in the ball-room were as the tramping of "the ox that treadeth out the corn!" The boy was promptly told to inform the young ladies that it would be an unpardonable breach of etiquette to either dance with any man who was *not* a volunteer, or to decline to dance with any *gentleman* who *was* a volunteer! And there was a peculiar emphasis and inflection on certain words in the sentence which meant clearly that any male who was

not a volunteer was a "*man*," and that every man who
was a volunteer was a *gentleman*!  The boy faithfully

"BELLES AND VOLUNTEERS."

reproduced the message with its essential emphasis and
inflections, and duly enjoyed the "*grace*" of the moun-

tain "boomers" as they "cut the pigeon wing" in rough cow-hide boots and plain home-spun shirts, minus any color, around the blushing, smiling belles whom they seemed afraid or ashamed to touch!

Society was instantly revolutionized. Volunteers were lionized, and those who were not volunteers were publicly snubbed. The prospective soldiers had a monopoly of social circles, and every man who refused to enroll his name for the army was socially ostracised and publicly disgraced. It may not have been thus all over the South, but in the region of which I can speak from personal knowledge, it was even worse than I can describe. The excitement spread throughout the country. Boys in schools, colleges and universities caught the enthusiasm and deliberately exchanged their books for muskets and swords. Institutions of learning throughout the country were closed in a single day, without warning. Pupils and teachers went in a body to enlist in the army. Some idea may be formed as to the readiness with which men enlisted in the army from the fact that many counties furnished a greater number of volunteers than they had legal voters, which means that there were more boys under the age of twenty-one who went to war than there were men over the age of twenty-one who remained at home. On this basis, remembering the probable number unfit for army duties by reason of old age, infirm health and other causes, it may be said everybody enlisted in the army!

It was not a mere transient feeling of excitement in which they volunteered. They went in to win, and they proposed to "fight the fight to a finish." The enrolling officers were authorized to register volunteers for different periods of service. As the men came forward to enlist, they were always asked "for how long?"

SOCIAL MONOPOLY OF VOLUNTEERS.

To this question a rough-looking mountaineer, with clinched fists and set teeth, expressed the sentiment of the whole country when he said:

"Well, Squire, you may put me down fur life, or durin' the war! I'm goin' to win this fight or die at the hole!" In that spirit they all enlisted. Poor boys! Most of them died "at the hole!"

The difficulty of getting arms and uniforms for the volunteers was a serious obstacle. As there were no factories in the South the uniforms were principally made by hand. Women worked almost night and day to get their husbands, brothers, fathers and lovers ready to go to the front. Even the cloth for the uniforms had to be spun and woven by hand, and then the garments had to be cut and sewed by hand. It was impossible to buy even dye-stuff with which to color the material for soldiers' uniforms. They had to gather barks and roots and boil an ooze with which to color the goods. And when "the boys" were dressed for the army, a ludicrous spectacle they made. No two uniforms were of the same color. But what mattered it? They covered honest, brave hearts for a few days, and then served as grave-clothes for mangled bodies in far-away lands!

I cannot suppress a smile now as I remember the novel way in which "the boys" in a certain mountain district armed themselves for the conflict. Pistols and guns they had none, nor could they get any, but such deadly weapons as they could get they provided for themselves and marched to the front. Those formidable weapons were simply huge butcher knives made of large files by a country black-smith, and "mounted" with "buck-horn" handles! A country cobler made rough "scabbards and belts" to suit those hand-made butcher knives, which he sold at a round price in "confederate money" and very cheap for "hard money." The honest black-smith drove a thriving business making knives as long as he could get files, or other bits of steel, but he was too patriotic to charge anything like the prices his monopoly of the market for "munitions of war" would have enabled him to command. A few enterprising speculators bought up all the files in the country, "cornered the market in steel" and heaped up for themselves riches while the patriotic smith worked for the good of the country and died poor at a good old age, after the war, honored and respected by all who knew him. When this company of mountaineers was equipped for the war, with bark-dyed uniforms

DANGEROUS WEAPON.

and home-made butcher-knives, they looked more ludicrous than formidable. About this time report came that the Federal gun-boats were coming up the Tennessee river, and the captain was ordered to report with his com

pany for duty at New Port forthwith. Hastily summon-
ing his men to rendezvous at the little log country church,
he called together the whole neighborhood for a relig-

MOUNTAINEERS ON THE WAR PATH.

ious revival. This may seem a rather deliberate way of
obeying such a command, but it had the merit of both
originality and piety, and the latter was a strong point

in military tactics with those church-going people. The idea of rushing into anything, no matter what, without "opening with prayer," was not to be entertained for one moment! And should these poor men be rushed into battle, where their bodies would be exposed to death and their souls, if unconverted, to hell without any religious preparation?

The people of the whole country came together—men, women, boys, girls, babies and dogs. The preachers of all denominations joined in a union revival meeting. Wives, sisters, mothers and sweet-hearts labored and prayed as they had never done before, for the conversion of husbands, brothers, sons and lovers. The power of God came down and the blessings of heaven were poured out. The altar was crowded with anxious mourners, and many souls were gloriously converted. The revival swept everything before it, and for several days and nights the people rejoiced together in heavenly places in Christ Jesus. The soldiers were about all converted, the meeting was closed, the last sad good-byes were said, and the line of march was taken up. It was more than a week now since the order came to report at once for duty at New Port, to meet the enemy's gunboats, but no matter. The time had been well spent. The soldiers were fixed so that if they lost their bodies in battle, they would save their souls in heaven. The captain gave the command to march, the women screamed, the babies cried, the preachers groaned in spirit, the dogs howled dolefully, the small boys yelled "'Rah for Jeff Davis and the Southern Confederacy," the line moved, the war began! Oh, the dark, dreary, bloody days that followed! Oh, the dear boys who marched away that day, so brave and yet so innocent and ignorant of the ways of the world and the cruelties of war! I can see it all now in my mind's eye! Their ludicrous uniforms, made by the loving hands of wives, mothers, sisters and sweet-hearts; their new red-leather belts and scabbards with the buck-horn handles of big home-made butcher knives clearly visible; and their solemn, steady tramp, tramp, tramp, as they marched away—all this made an impression upon my childish mind and heart which seems to deepen as the years go by.

When they reached New Port a week or ten days behind time, they learned that the gun-boats had not come, and that other companies of Confederate militia which had preceded them, had left for Huntsville, Alabama. They had but one gun of any kind in the whole company, and it was an old-fashioned, muzzle-loading, double-barrelled shot gun with one tube out and the other hammer broken off! But with that old fowling-piece and their formidable butcher knives they managed to besiege and capture a barrel of new corn whisky, and in a short time they were all as drunk as lords and as happy as new converts, so recently out of a revival, could well be expected to be.

# CHAPTER XXVIII.

The story of the war would hardly interest the reader. It has been told so often, that nothing new remains to be said. It was a gloomy time in Dixie. Only those who lived through those troublesome times in the South can ever know fully what the war really was. I shall therefore hasten over that, to me, ever painful period in the Seventy Years in Dixie. I have no desire to linger upon the memories of the war. Many mistakes were made, vile sins were committed, and not a few deeds of love were done which show the divine nature that is in man all the brighter because of the darkness and gloom of the environments.

During the war I did what I thought to be my duty, but when I was mustered out of service I shed bitter tears of defeat and disappointment over the grave of "the lost cause," and solemnly resolved to fight no more. War is a terrible thing. The life of a soldier was not calculated to increase my piety. My environments in the army were not at all favorable to the development of the better elements of my nature. Fighting, as a regular occupation, is a bad business every way. It calls out all the latent meanness in the human species. It can never be defended or excused on any other ground than as a choice of evils, and in the light of my experience I am disposed to hold that it is the last choice a man should make.

(350)

I enlisted in the army as a preacher of the gospel and was assigned the duty of a chaplain. It was the hardest place to fill in the whole army. I was expected to cut my sermons to fit the pattern of our occupation as soldiers. It was a hard thing to do. It was expected that my preaching, prayers and exhortations would tend to make the soldiers hard fighters. It was difficult to find even texts from which to construct such sermons. I soon discovered that I would have to close my Bible and manufacture my ministerial supplies out of the whole cloth.

Some of my preaching brethren told the soldiers, in their sermons, that our cause was just and that God would fight our battles for us. I never did feel authorized to make any such statements. I believed our cause was just, of course, but I could see as clear as a sunbeam that the odds were against us, and, to be plain, I gravely doubted whether God was taking any hand with us in that squabble. I told some of the preachers who were making that point in their sermons that they were taking a big risk. I asked them what explanation they would give, if we should happen to get thrashed. I told them such preaching would make infidels of the whole army, and put an end to their business, if we should happen to get the worst of the fracas. I wanted to do my duty as a preacher in the army, but I didn't want to checkmate the ministry in case we should come out second best in the fight. I think a preacher should always leave a wide margin for mistakes when it comes to interpreting the purposes of God beyond what has been clearly revealed in the Scriptures. It is not good policy for a one-horse preacher to arbitrarily commit the God of the universe to either side of a personal difficulty anyhow. I told the soldiers plainly that I didn't know

exactly what position God would take in that fight.
So far as I could see, the issue was a personal matter
between us and the Yankees, and we must settle it, as
best we could, among ourselves.

It is not difficult to see how this line of argument led

"THE FIGHTING PARSON."

me away from the true spirit of the ministry, and thoroughly aroused within me a desire to fight.  It became
clearer to me every day that one good soldier was worth
a whole brigade of canting chaplains so far as insuring
the success of our army was concerned.  If I must

preach to others so as to make them good fighters, why not give them an object lesson on the battlefield myself? My premises may have been wrong, but my conclusion was certainly not illogical.

So I asked for a gun, took a place with "the boys "and was dubbed the "fighting parson." At Bull Run I stopped the fragments of a stampeded regiment at the muzzle of a revolver, and led them back into the fight. I have no idea how I looked; I do not want anybody to know how I felt. The imagination of the artist is wholly responsible for the illustration of that scene in my eventful career. I have made no suggestions; I offer no protest; I ask no explanations; I attempt no defense.

I have no evidence that I ever killed or·wounded any one during the war. I sincerely hope I never did, and deeply repent the bare possibility of such a thing. I want no fratricidal blood on my hands. As I now stand trembling upon the verge of the grave and look back over the dreary years of an unprofitable life, I weep o'er my many blunders, look trustingly to God for mercy, open wide my arms to a sin-cursed and sorrow-burdened world, and in the tenderest love for all and with malice toward none, say: " *We be brethren*! " The war was a mistake and a failure. All wars are mistakes and failures. They may sometimes be necessary evils, but if so it is only because man's wickedness makes evil necessary. A heart-weariness and soul-sadness no pen can describe come o'er me when I think of those dark days of bloody war with their tiresome marching, wasting disease, cold, hunger and consuming anxiety!

We went into the war with light hearts and bright hopes. We thought we had the richest country, the bravest men, the finest homes and the prettiest women

23

in the world. We believed we had the wealth and the
chivalry of the United States. Our whole country was
in the highest possible state of cultivation, and every
plantation fairly groaned under the burden of
its surplus of supplies. We were on our mettle,
we felt our importance, and we thought we could whip
anything.

But a few years of hard fighting took the conceit out
of us. There was clearly an error in the calculation
somewhere. The lack of manufactories was the missing
link in our premises, which soon showed the fallacy in
our conclusion. The South was well prepared to *feed*
an army, but it could not equip one. The whole Southern Confederacy combined could not manufacture even
a horse-shoe nail or a belt-buckle when the war began. We
never did have a decent supply of even shoes, hats or
clothing. Not a single regiment in the whole Confederate army was ever thoroughly equipped for the war.
We had nothing to fight with and there was no way to
get it. As a nation, we had neither capital, currency,
credit nor collaterals. We couldn't manufacture arms
and ammunition enough in the whole Confederate government to thoroughly equip one company for the battlefield. Factories were started as soon as possible,
with the resources we could command, to manufacture
such military supplies as were most urgently in demand.
But it takes time to build factories, even under the most
favorable circumstances, and we were as scarce of time
as factories. The war was upon us. Whatever we did
had to be done, to use a strong figure, without fortifica-
tions and under strong fire from the enemy. We were
still further embarrassed from lack of the necessary machinery to start factories with. Manufacturing is a
complicated business. To start a factory for any partic-

ular line of goods or implements, it is necessary to draw upon several other factories for the needful machinery. One factory is needed, to manufacture the machinery, to start another. You cannot start a factory to make cloth, for instance, without engines, boilers, cards, spindles, looms, etc. All those things must be made by other factories. In our efforts to start factories we were puzzled to find any place to begin the business.

We were still further embarrassed from lack of skilled labor to establish and operate factories. Nobody in the Southern Confederacy knew anything about such business. We had always been an agricultural people. Negroes did most of the labor in the South before the war, and they were of no more value, except on farms, than an engine without a boiler. There were not even men enough in the South before the war who had any knowledge at all of factories or machinery of any kind, to have superintended and successfully managed manufacturing establishments enough to supply the demands of the country with the simplest articles needed at home and in the army, even if the government had been amply provided with manufacturing plants.

But why dwell upon such bitter memories? My soul finds no pleasure in them. The whole world knows the story. The end came at last, as we all knew long before, it must sometime come. Those of us who understood the real condition of the country and the utter hopelessness of our cause, knew we were continuing the struggle against irrevokable doom long before the end came, and yet no one was in favor of surrendering even to fate. We held out long after it ceased to be a war or a fight. It was nothing less than standing defenseless, unarmed, naked and without food, to be butchered rather than acknowledge defeat. Ah, the cruelties of war! God pity the stubbornness of a heart in rebellion against fate!

I am glad now that in those dark days of strife and bloodshed, I often ministered to the comfort of those who wore the blue as well as those who wore the gray when they fell into my hands, mangled by shot and shell or racked with pain and emaciated by disease. While I was general hospital agent of the State of Mississippi with a hundred thousand dollars of public money and two hundred thousand dollars of individual donations subject to my order, I labored night and day to see that all who fell into my hands received every attention, convenience, comfort and delicacy that could be provided in a war-swept and famine-blighted land. I saved the lives of many, and tried earnestly to guide the souls of many others, whose bodies were mangled beyond human skill to save, to the rest that remaineth for the people of God. I often stood by the side of the dying, both on the battle-fields and in the hospitals, and many a time I became the bearer of the last tender messages of love, which dying soldiers begged me to deliver to loved ones at home. The hearty "God-bless-you," so familiar to my ears in those dark days of blood-shed and suffering, often comes to me now, after the lapse of more than a quarter of a century, in vivid dreams at night and lingers in my failing memory during the day. I remember well the fervency with which a poor wounded Irishman uttered the familiar "God-bless-you" on the train *en route* to Richmond after the first battle at Manassas. I was in charge of the wounded, taking them to hospitals in Richmond. We had a number of wounded prisoners in a freight car, lying on their blankets spread upon straw on the floor of the car. My attention was arrested by the groans of a man who

seemed to be suffering intensely. I asked if I
could in any way assist him. A ball had passed through
his thigh, shattering the bone, and the wound had
been hastily and poorly dressed on the battle-field four

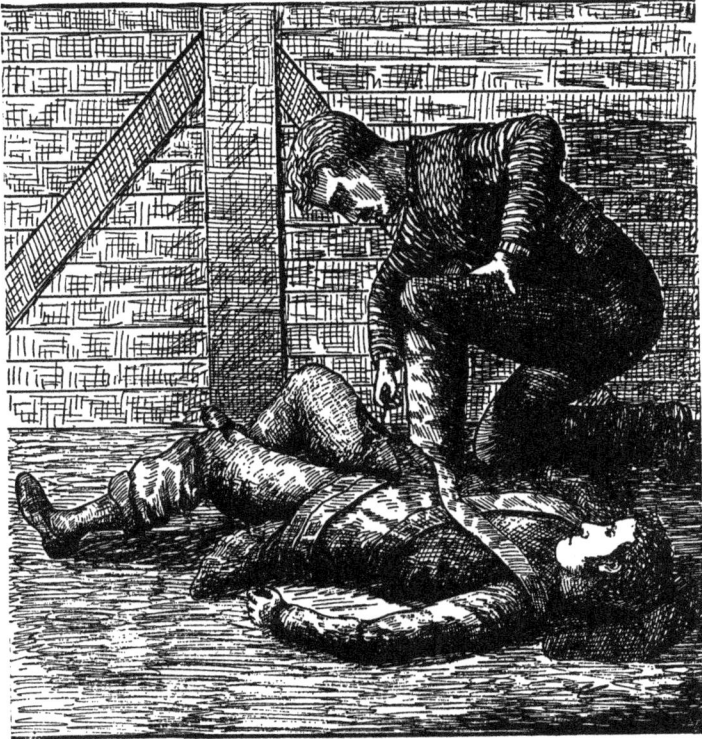

THE BLUE AND THE GRAY.

days before. The dressing had not been changed or
the wound examined since. He looked up into my
face with an expression of suffering on his countenance
I can never forget, and said: " Captain, this is worse
than death. There are hundreds of creepers in my

wound." Poor fellow! He could not assist himself, and no one among his wounded comrades was able to help him! I kneeled by his side, removed the bandage from his thigh and picked the creepers out of his wound with a straw. When I arose to leave him, I can never forget the look of gratitude in the blue depths of his tear-dimmed eyes as he grasped both my hands and said: "May God bless you, sir, forever and ever." I gently placed him in a comfortable position on his hard bed of dirty straw, and in a few moments he fell into a deep sleep. He was a prisoner, and I never saw him afterwards, but the fact that he wore the blue in no wise diminishes the pleasure of the memory of the brotherly assistance it was my good fortune to be able to render him.

# CHAPTER XXIX.

When the war closed, the South was a land of desolation and ruin. There was scarcely a home in all the country that did not mourn the loss of its own dead. In many homes the absent dead out-numbered the desolate living, and in every case the loved, but lost, were the strength and support of the family. It was a land of disconsolate widows and helpless orphans. Every heart was burdened with sorrow and every home was shrouded in gloom. There was no place in all the South but had its evidences of the ruin of war and ravages of famine. With such evidences continually before every eye, no heart could for a moment forget its sorrow.

If the people came to the house of God for the comforts of religion, they probably found the walls of the church pierced by shot and the floor of the very sanctuary itself stained with the blood of their beloved dead. If not so bad as that, they at least found the ashes of camp-fires about the church, or the deep ruts of wagon trains along the road. There was scarcely a horse or a mule in the whole country that did not have the familiar army brand, and the people were compelled to clothe themselves in garments made from cast-off and worn-out army uniforms. It was difficult to find a man in the whole country who had not either lost a limb or received a wound in the army.

The people talked about the war continually. " Of the abundance of the heart the mouth speaketh." Every heart had its burden of war-sorrows, and every tongue was busy with its tale of army reminiscences. It took weeks and even months, for the soldiers, who were fortunate enough to get home alive, to deliver all the good-by messages of love sent by them from dying comrades in arms to sorrow-burdened hearts at home. The imagination of the reader must fill out the picture of those gloomy days. I have neither the power to describe what I saw, nor the desire to reveal what I felt. In our immediate neighborhood, I now call to mind about a score of men who died or were killed in the army, and less than half that number

AFTER THE WAR.

who came back to us alive, but maimed or wounded,

to tell us how they died and what they said. Homes were in ruins everywhere. In many places, where armies camped or where battles were fought, churches, school-buildings and other public houses were converted into hospitals, officers' headquarters and warehouses for army supplies. It goes without saying that in such cases the men in authority did not hesitate to make any changes in the buildings thus appropriated to the use of the army, which would the better adapt them to the purposes for which they were needed. No care was taken to preserve the property for future use after the army was done with it, and the finest groves of ornamental trees were often cut down for fuel for the soldiers without a moment's hesitation. In many cases elegant private residences were despoiled by Federal officers, and not infrequently horses were stabled in some of the best rooms of magnificent country homes. Fences were destroyed all over the country, the rails were often used by the soldiers for fuel, and the farms were all thrown out in the commons without any protection at all in the way of enclosure.

The people were all impoverished and disfranchised. The country was, at first, under provisional military rule, and for several years afterwards it was governed by professional, transient and imported politicians who were as devoid of patriotic principles as they were destitute of personal purity. Offices were created to make room for political place-hunters, and the burdens of taxation were increased to pay the salaries of officers whose services were not needed. State and county taxes ran up as high as five per cent. of the assessed value of property, and boards were created to fix values as high as possible so as to increase the public revenues according to the demands upon the suffering public treasury.

A RUINED HOME.

The boards often set fictitious and unreasonable values upon property, so that the rate of taxation was little else than confiscation. One case will illustrate:

AN ARISTOCRATIC DRAY DRIVER.

Mr. Lee owned one thousand and six hundred acres of as fine land as the country afforded, on the Mississippi river below Memphis, when he enlisted in the army.

When he came out of the army his barns were all destroyed, his cotton gin was burned, his fences were in ruins, his mules were lost in the army and his negroes were all freed. The tax on his ruined plantation, for one year, amounted to $2,100. He could neither sell nor mortgage the entire property for money enough to pay the tax. So he forfeited his estate for taxes, tramped his way to Memphis and hired himself to a transfer company to drive a dray! I know him personally, and have often listened with deep interest to his description of the hardships he endured as a dray driver in Memphis in helping to rebuild the fortunes of the country during the gloomy years immediately after the war.

THEY STARTED TO SCHOOL.

Thousands of negroes lounged about the country enjoying their newly-found freedom and living without work by pilfering the poverty-burdened people. Their chief occupations were voting and conducting religious revivals, and their highest ambition was to live in town. They abandoned the country and drifted to the towns and cities, producing a sort of congestion of negro population in towns, made up largely of poverty, laziness, filth, ignorance, dishonesty and gross licentiousness. The rural districts were almost depopulated, and agricultural interests were badly neglected. Religious enthusiasts began to plan for missionary work among the negroes, and friends of education continually urged the importance of educating the negro race. Meanwhile the negro race was prowling about the country in idleness, rags, filth, ignorance and immorality in search of a square meal! The negro children started to school and the women and men joined the church, but that didn't solve the race problem. In fact there were so many other problems to solve just then, nobody thought much about the race problem.

The greatest problem of those days was how a few widows and orphans could support themselves, feed hundreds of thousands of thriftless negroes, pay enormous taxes, rebuild their homes, repair their fences and sustain a burdensome government without money, horses or agricultural implements.

We hear much of Northern enterprise, but I doubt whether the history of the United States furnishes anything in the way of enterprise to compare with the rebuilding of the fortunes of the South since the war. Where, indeed, will you find anything equal to it in the history of the whole world? When did widows and orphans, with the help of a few invalids, old men and maimed ex-soldiers, rebuild the ruins of a country under such disadvantages in so short a time? In twenty-five years the desert has been made to blossom as the rose, and a new generation of Southern people has grown up to lead the whole United States in material progress. Such is the history of the New South.

In rebuilding the ruins of the country after the war, the people of the South profited by the lesson they learned during the war.   Before the war the South was pre-eminently an agricultural country, but a few years of war taught us that man cannot live by bread alone.

THE NEW SOUTH.

No country is self-sustaining without manufactories of its own.   This lesson was still further impressed upon

THE POLITICIAN'S DREAM.

the South by the utter impossibility of managing negro labor successfully on the farms after the war. The brain of the South, therefore, was directed to manufacting. It soon became evident that the new scheme would be a success, and this attracted capital and immigration.

The South entered upon an era of unprecedented prosperity, and in a few years thriving cities sprang up as if by magic upon the ruins of *ante-bellum* fortunes. The New South has been built by the same race of people that built the old South. The politicians have dreamed and argued about the death's-head of rebellion, and the engines of war, and the race problem, and Southern outrages, and Northern enterprise; but the people of the South have been busy repairing the ruins and developing the resources of the country,

# CHAPTER XXX.

I have now passed briefly, in review, over seventy years of eventful history in Dixie. During that time the wealth and the population of the country have greatly increased, and our environments have been completely revolutionized. Before I lay down my pen, I beg the reader to indulge me in a few pages of moralizing and philosophizing. That these final chapters may not be lightly read and flippantly tabooed, I beg to say that in all that precedes them I have only been endeavoring to lay the premises for these final words as a conclusion.

In the early days, such things as town life and city fashions were scarcely known in all the South, but, as the wealth and population of the country increased, towns sprang up all over the land, and the luxury and extravagance of the new order of things made rapid inroads upon the simple customs and industrious habits of the economical old settlers. Such innovations were not accepted without protest by the conservative old-timers. Those who stood for the old ways stubbornly contested every inch of ground against innovations of all kinds, and those who clamored for something new, boldly advocated every new fad or fancy that human ingenuity could devise. This brought " wars and rumors of wars." Through all these years there has been an incessant conflict between the new and the old. The new wine has been bursting the old bottles. Such antagonisms have

24

raged in every revolutionary period in the history of the world. Many people cling to the old ways, always, simply because they are old ways, while others contend for everything that is new without stopping to inquire whether it has anything but novelty to commend it.

The conflict in such revolutionary periods of the world's history is not an issue between the superior wisdom of progressive minds and the dense stupidity of conservative spirits. Those who clamor for a change have not more foresight than those who protest against innovations. Men have never had any foresight, in any age of the world, save as the God of the universe has specially endowed them with prophetic vision.

We all seem prone to worship the creature more than the Creator. The world has had its heroes among men in every age and in every nation. If we fail to look beyond man for the intelligence that governs and guides the world, we are peculiarly liable to unduly exalt human wisdom in an age of such changes and progress as we have witnessed during the last seventy years. I deem it of the first importance, therefore, to keep in memory the fact that there is a governing and guiding intelligence above and beyond man in this universe.

God moves and guides the world by providence over men. Man is the agent and not the author of the world's progress. Things act only as they are acted upon. Man is no exception to this general rule. Hence God always moves the world by some present emergency in human affairs, rather than by an original ideal in the minds of men. When the world begins to move, it is axiomatic that something is moving it, but it is not so easy to understand what that something is, or whither the movement is tending.

There have been times in the world's history when

countries and people remained stationary in many respects for centuries in succession. The inhabitants of Palestine, for instance, have made no considerable changes in agricultural methods, domestic habits or social customs during the last nineteen centuries. When things are thus at a stand-still there are scarcely such words as progression and conservatism in the human vocabulary.

It is a mistake to suppose that progressive men are those who, of their own inherent force and foresight, move forward, dragging the conservative laggards after them. A progressive man is one who, by reason of his peculiar environments, feels the power that is moving the world. Such men are dissatisfied with things as they are, and they clamor for a change. Conservative men do not feel the need of a change, and hence they protest against innovations. It is doubtful whether progressive men have any more foresight than conservative ones.

It is easy enough to tell when the world is moving, by the fuss it makes, but it is not so easy to determine which way it is going. Whenever the conflict begins to rage between progressive and conservative men, the world is moving.

There have been wonderful changes, in material things, in this country during the last seventy years, and the changes, during the same period, in social customs, political economy, educational methods and religious institutions, have been equally marvelous. The new order of things differs widely from the old, but who will say the former is better than the latter? Is the new order more in harmony with the laws which govern man in his existence upon the earth, and with the eternal fitness of things, than the old? All changes are not improvements. But back of it all is an unanswered question as to who effected the change. Who saw the end from the beginning? Who knew what the new order would be when the changes began? Who led the mighty revolution? Who formulated the plan of the new order of things? We are liable to unduly laud those who continually clamored for changes during the revolutionary period, as *leaders* of the world. They were not leading anybody or anything. They themselves were *driven* by the unseen power which was moving the world, they knew not how nor whither. They had no idea which way the world was moving or where it would stop.

The world has always had its self-appointed leaders, who talk learnedly of plans, and feign great wisdom in the matter of explaining how things must be managed. Their words are but the creaking of the wheels of destiny which are moved by an unseen power and over-ruled by an omniscient providence. The wisest of such men cannot see a day into the future. If they could but know the future of the simplest things of life, what fortunes they could make by investing money in futures?

To me, it is both interesting and instructive, to think about the plans and the predictions of the self-confident leaders who have engaged the attention of the people of the South during the last seventy years. They all had their theories, of course, and they wasted their time and excited the people, explaining what must be done, and demonstrating, to their own satisfaction, what dire calamities would inevitably befall the country if their policies were not adopted. But, for all their pains, they had the poor consolation of seeing an unappreciative⋅ generation ignore their advice and a stubborn universe refuse to fulfill their predictions. The conflict was sharp and incessant in all departments of human affairs. There were discussions in every home, differences in every church, issues in every political canvass, disputations in every neighborhood and contentions in every school district. Society was burdened with plans, and organizations, and parties, and theories, and creeds, and platforms. Preachers explained the trouble and pointed out the remedy; teachers discussed the situation and showed the way out of the difficulty; newspapers diagnosed the case and wrote infallible prescriptions, free; and politicians expatiated upon the dangers ahead, and offered to save the country for a trifle. Every man felt confident that the cause of all the trouble was in the line of his particular business or profession, and that the only way to escape impending destruction was to ride his favorite hobby.

Through all this confusion, the Wisdom that created the universe was serenely moving and guiding the world in its progress. Those fretting, boasting, quarreling and busy little creatures called men were responsible to that great Intelligence for their individual conduct and deportment, but, short-sighted creatures that they were, they were not originating in their own little finite minds the great plans on which the world was moving. Every man had his little sphere of duties and responsibilities, and in that sphere he stood or fell upon his deportment before the great Ruler of the universe. Each man was required to obey the will of the great Governor of the world, as respected himself. So long as men follow the guidance of Omniscience, every problem in the world's progress will be solved correctly and without hurtful conflicts, but when they depart from such guidance, each problem they solve but changes the form of the difficulty without removing or diminishing it.

Will the world never learn that man has no foresight? Must we forever follow blindly after creatures of like passions with ourselves, blind as they are, and who frighten us out of our wits by crying lo, here! and lo, there! Will we never learn that the true wisdom which should guide the world in its progress "is from above and cometh down from the Father of lights, with whom there is no variableness, neither shadow of turning"? Can we never understand that we all are brethren in ignorance, and that one is our Father, our Ruler and our Guide—even God?

The world is still moving. The conflict is still raging. There are great problems still unsolved before us. Men are still planning, and organizing, and explaining, and predicting. The world is not scarce of leaders. Every leader has his plan and every plan has its party. Between these plans and parties there are continual clashings and conflicts. Hence come wars and fightings among us.

Is there no way to get the world to stop and think seriously over the past long enough to catch the idea that we are all stumbling in the dark except the Father of lights lead us? Will we never admit that God is governing and guiding the world by providence over men, and that every work which man can devise is under the providence of God, and that it will be made to praise Him in the end or else it must come to naught?

It is not prudent to be over-sanguine of the success of any of the plans of men. Man is not infallible. The greatest men of earth have made mistakes. "Homer nodded." Neither is it the part of wisdom to despise "the day of small things." God often uses very humble agencies to accomplish his purposes. "The wisdom of this world is foolishness with God." "He taketh the wise in their own craftiness." "The foolishness of God is wiser than men." "The weakness of God is stronger than men." "God hath chosen the foolish things of the world to confound the wise"; and "the weak things of the world to confound the things which are mighty." "Wherefore God resisteth the proud, but giveth grace unto the humble." "Submit yourselves therefore to God." "Stand still and see the salvation of the Lord."

"Thou shalt love the Lord thy God with all thy heart, and with all thy soul, and with all thy strength, and with all thy mind; and thy neighbor as thyself."

"On these two commandments hang all the law and the prophets." If men will but abide in this love, God will guide them to a peaceful and final solution of all the problems that can possibly arise in the progress of the world and the development and perfection of the human species.

# CHAPTER XXXI.

We hear much talk in these latter days about the re-action in public opinion against religion. There has been some change of that kind, I admit, but with respect to old-time religion, churches have probably changed more than publicans and sinners. I am not sure but that the churches are losing power with the people for the very reason that the people are not willing to follow them away from the old-time doctrine and practices of religion. To the extent that the indifference of the world to churches is a protest against the manifest departures of some fashionable churches from the spirit and genius of true Christianity, it is not bad. With strong faith in the providence of God, I am disposed to take a cheerful view of the world even in its worst phases, but with contempt for pious shams and religious cant, I am none too lenient toward some of the ways of modern fashionable churches.

With all the talk about skepticism in these modern times, the Golden Rule seems to have a fairly strong hold upon the public mind and conscience. In a general way, those who have openly rebelled against the churches in these modern days give strong evidence of considerable respect for at least one of the commandments on which hang all the law and the prophets—viz: "Thou shalt love thy neighbor as thyself." Whatever else may be said of the people in these degenerate times, they are usually both ready and liberal in their responses to the calls for help from suffering humanity. In fact it is a question whether some churches and church folks surpass some publicans and sinners in these matters. The truth is, religionists in general have perhaps been giving undue attention to the building up of showy institutions to the neglect of spiritual worship and Christian philanthropy in these latter days, and public sentiment has protested against such departures from the true spirit of Christianity. The people at large seem disinclined to spend time or money in building institutions for outward show while orphans are crying for bread and widows are shivering in the cold. I speak now in general terms, of course. All churches and religionists are not guilty of such departures from these features of genuine, New Testament Christianity. And it is to the credit of the non-church folks of this age that churches and professed Christians who have not made such departures have not lost their hold upon the people. All this argues that this is not the time in the history of the world for churches and church folks to devour widows' houses, and for a pretense make long prayers, build fine houses, hold big conventions, form pompous organizations, flourish high-sounding titles, pass pious resolutions, build the tombs of the prophets and compass sea and land to make one proselyte. This practical age will have none of it. If there is anything the people of this enlightened age may be confidently relied upon to do, it is to detect fraud and repudiate hypocrisy in religion.

As I understand the matter, it is not a bad sign to see a mere handful of religious humbugs trying to hold up a glittering institution and struggling to maintain a costly form of heartless worship, while the rank and file of the people are ridiculing such trumpery, feeding widows and orphans and attending to their own business in open contempt of such hypocrisy. Skepticism among the people of the world is bad, but downright hypocrisy and meanness among the members of the churches are infinitely worse. The errors of the church do not excuse the sins of the world, I know, but the unprejudiced mind cannot fail to see in the present situation two evils that sadly need correction. The people at large have, to some extent, departed from the church. That is one evil in the land which ought to be corrected. The church in general has departed from the true spirit and genius of New Testament Christianity. That is another evil of these latter days which ought to be corrected, too. I do not speak now in terms of sweeping generality. All churches have not departed from the teachings of Christ, neither have all the people of the world departed from the church. But there are evidences of both kinds of departures, and I am in doubt which most needs attention.

Such a life as Jesus lived among men when he was here in the flesh would not be without power now even with the veriest skeptics in the land.

The religionists of this age may as well understand once for all that they cannot drift away from genuine "Christliness" and go back to the expensive religious paraphernalia and imposing ceremonies which flourished in the dark ages. The people of this generation will not be led in that direction. The church which attempts such a thing will part company with the people and commit suicide. This is more an evidence of good sense than bold infidelity in the people. Unfortunately the churches that have made slight experiments along this line have fallen out with the people for declining to follow them, and raised a great hue and cry about the skepticism of modern times. And, what is still worse, the people have allowed themselves to believe they are skeptics, sure enough, and set about defending themselves as such. But I am persuaded that the people are not so skeptical as they suppose, after all. The spirit and doctrine of Christ have a much stronger hold upon them than they themselves suspect. Much of that which they have repudiated in churches, creeds and church folks, Christ himself would not approve if he were here in the flesh.

Christ was by no means popular with the churches and church members of his generation when he was on earth. Some churches and professed Christians of these modern times do not average much better than the religionists whom He so severely denounced more than eighteen hundred years ago. And the religionists of those days denounced Him as bitterly as some modern churches denounce skeptics now. They said He was under the power of the prince of devils and worthy of death. Christ has probably not lost prestige in the world more than in the church in the last half century.

We never heard religious people talking about " how to reach the masses " fifty years ago. In fact we had not so much as heard whether there be any masses then. Such talk in these latter days shows that some churches and church folks are anxious to have it understood that the gulf between them and the masses is so wide that it is a problem which puzzles the wisest heads among them as to how they can reach the masses. Now, if Christ were here on the earth to-day, He would be one among the masses, unless He has changed wonderfully within the last eighteen hundred and sixty years, and all the talk of professed Christians about " how to reach the masses" is but so much talk about how to reach Christ.

I need not go further into details. The church that is away from the masses is away from Christ, and the church that is with Christ is with the masses. The departure from Christ and the people is the prime cause of all the formality, and coldness, and indifference, and proud-heartedness in the churches which are guilty of it and suffering from it. The remedy for it all is to remove the cause by coming back to Christ.

We have not the sturdy faith, and consuming zeal, and deep-toned piety in the churches now which we had fifty years ago. Instead thereof we have a light-heartedness, and worldly-mindedness which was not so much as named among the saints in those days. We have not the spiritual power and doctrinal convictions in the pulpit now which we had then, but instead of those old-time elements of pulpit strength we have a disposition to astonish and please the world by sensational sermons, ethical lectures, beautiful speeches and soft sayings to which the old-time preachers never gave place for a moment. There is need of a reformation in all these things "whereunto you do well that you take heed."

But, after all, some of those who openly array themselves against the church in these latter days are neither good men nor wise teachers. They have not been content to simply enter their protests against the manifest departures from New Testament Christianity. If they had gone no further than that, I might occupy my time wholly in their defense. They have openly denounced the whole teachings of the Bible. This is their mistake. They seem to forget, or perhaps they have never known, that the Christ of the New Testament, were he here in the flesh to-day, would condemn the popular way of doing things in some fashionable churches. They prob- ably do not know that they are but endorsing some of the clearest teachings of Christ in the very attacks they are making upon some features of fashionable religion in these latter days. I have no tears to shed, no regrets to express over the destruction their onslaught is mak- ing among the fashionable churches which have yielded themselves to the evil tendencies already described. Of all such churches I say: Cut them down, why cumber they the ground?

But why should men fly in the face of all history and all experience as to the power of the unseen world? Why attempt what no nation of savages or sages has ever attempted before in the history of all times and all peoples? Why try to usher in the millennium by the destruction of all faith in the origin or destiny of men or worlds? Why repudiate God and all the gods at once, and try to blight all the happiness of this world which comes by faith and hope from the world unseen? Why assert that everything, with man, begins with the birth and must end with the death of the body? It can- not be that man comes from the darkness of an eternal past, opens his eyes in life, looks above, beneath and around, for a few fleeting days full of trouble and dis- appointment, and then drops into an endless sleep. Ah, the gloom of such a grave-shrouded thought!

Man has three natures to develop—viz: Physical, moral and intellectual, and shall he have but one world, and it very imperfectly adapted to his needs, in which to perfect himself? There is little provision in this world for the development of anything but the physical man, and it perishes almost as rapidly as it grows. Be- sides, man has no certain lease of life in this world. In a majority of cases even the body dies ere it matures.

But at the very best, man can never mature as to his moral and intellectual natures if this life is his only chance.

The things of this world address themselves largely to the physical man through the senses—sight, sound, touch, taste and smell. All this is helpful in developing a good specimen of physical manhood, but how do we develop the intellectual and emotional elements of our nature? To this end can we have no thoughts gendered by the intangible, the unseen, the unknowable? Can we never experience any emotions that are kindled by persons, places, worlds, or things as yet unseen? Must we be forever shut up to the things that are patent to the physical senses? Such an idea contradicts all facts, all history and the essential elements of human nature itself.

No personal character has ever been developed, and no national life has ever been inaugurated or sustained, except by the help of the power which comes from the unseen world through faith. And without the help of such power, nothing but mere physical nature or animal life can ever be fully developed. Every creature that rises above mere brute life in any of the faculties or elements of its nature, must draw upon the unseen world by faith for the support and development of all the higher elements of its nature. This is simply a fact, whether the world unseen, is, itself, fact or fiction. From the savages in the forest to the sages in the highest places of the most civilized nations of earth, all men in all ages of the world, have meditated, imagined, wondered and dreamed about the world unseen and the great hereafter. And this mental occupation has been both the food and the exercise by which they developed the faculties which raised them above the brute creation.

Every nation of earth has had three worlds in which to develop the three departments of humanity—viz: One world addressed to the physical senses and two worlds received by faith. One is seen; two are unseen. In one, life and death, joy and sorrow, pleasure and pain, light and darkness, are mixed; In one of the other two, all is life, joy, light and gladness; and in the other all is darkness, disappointment and death. Of the two unseen worlds, one is for the good and pure inhabitants of this; the other for the vicious and impure. Every nation of earth has had its heaven for good people departed, and its hell for bad ones deceased. Faith in such rewards and punishments in the great hereafter has been a potent factor in the development of human character among all people and in all ages. History knows no nation that has not had its hope of heaven to cultivate the higher and better elements of human nature, and its fear of hell to restrain the baser passions of the soul. On this one point the whole human race has agreed with singular unanimity, and that, too, without any consultation. It may, therefore, be accepted as almost axiomatic, that this world cannot offer rewards sufficiently desirable to encourage man to be either good or great; neither can it threaten punishment severe enough to restrain men of evil passions from committing crimes. The rewards of this life are too difficult to obtain, to have much influence over the masses; they are too hard to retain, to be very highly esteemed by many who even have a fair opportunity to secure them; and they are too unsatisfactory in nature to be very highly appreciated by anybody. The punishments this world can threaten are too easily evaded and too light in nature, to have much restraining power over men who are given to evil passions.

The idea that man will live again in a world as yet unseen, and that in that world to come his destiny will be determined by his moral character while here, either came originally .by revelation of Spirit from the unseen world, or it originated in the inherent needs of human nature. But in either case, it is clearly essential to the full development of man's nature, and cannot be lightly set aside without greatly impoverishing the whole human race. The man who cannot meditate upon the dignity of his origin or the glory of his destiny is without nourishment and exercise for his highest and best faculties, and will hardly bless the world with ennobling ideas or refining sentiments. The man who can be content to deal exclusively with the material things of this dull world, and who never rises by faith or imagination to the contemplation of things not seen, is dull indeed. Nay, man can never cease to wonder, imagine, meditate, dream, believe and hope about the world unseen and the great hereafter so long as he is endowed with all the faculties which go to make up a well-balanced mind. To know nothing, think nothing, imagine nothing, believe nothing, care nothing, hope nothing about the great hereafter is an absolute impossibility except with those who lack some of the essential elements of a well-balanced mind.

Men become wise, great, good or bad by the power of faith, hope, love or hatred moving upon their inner natures. Those who devote themselves to noble causes must have love for some definite end or object, faith in their ability to attain it, and hope to encourage them in their efforts to succeed. In deeds of evil, hatred often moves the soul of passions base, and nought but fear restrains from crimes of deepest die, the man whose soul by love, faith and hope cannot be moved to nobler

deeds. Love, faith, hope and hatred, then, are motors of
the human soul, without which we would have universal
stagnation in all departments of human endeavor. Destroy all fear, and the world is without any restraining
power over base natures; abolish faith, love and hope,
and the mainspring of action to all noble souls is
broken.

Thus far in the history of the world, the human family has been under the influence of an abiding faith in a
future existence. The love, faith and hope that have
moved mankind thus far, have pertained both to this
life and the life which is to come, and the fear that has
hitherto restrained the baser passions of mankind, has
been a fear of both present and future punishment.

It is pertinent, in this connection, to ask which of the
two states of existence hitherto believed in by all nations
of earth has probably exercised the greater influence
over the world both in the way of prompting men to
strive for good, and restraining them from giving themselves over to evil. Will faith, love and hope which
pertain to this life only exert as great an influence over
the thoughts, feelings and actions of men, as faith, hope
and love which include both this life and the life which
is to come? On which life has the world hitherto
placed the higher estimate, the one that now is, or that
one which is to come? To ask these questions is to answer them. Whether, therefore, the unseen world is a
fact or a fiction, faith in it is essential to the development of man's entire nature, and through faith in it
the world has made its greatest conquests. If all this
is to be blotted out at this late day, future generations
will be deprived of all nourishment for man's highest
and best nature, the greatest incentives to noble ends
will be destroyed and the most effective restraint and

25

safe-guard against crime will be abolished. The world cannot afford to make so great a sacrifice, even if it were possible to abolish all ideas of the world unseen. But the very fact that such a thing has never yet been done by any nation of earth, strongly argues that it cannot be done even if it were desirable. On these two points, therefore, we can well afford to rest the case : (1) It should not be done if we could, and (2) it could not be done if we would.

# CHAPTER XXXII.

The life of Moses and the history of the Jews furnish illustrations of the providence of God over men and nations well worthy of consideration in this connection.

Moses could not have inherited anything from his parents to distinguish him as one of the world's great lights as a moralist, ruler, law-giver, theologian and military chieftain. His parents were slaves and all his ancestors had been in bondage the most abject and menial for about four hundred years. A careful reading of the code of laws he gave the people on assuming the reins of government abundantly shows that the Jews were morally depraved and intellectually benighted when he led them out of Egypt. It must have been a condition of licentiousness among them perfectly shocking to contemplate, which called for the enactment of laws against specific sins, the very name of which is an offense to ears polite. From such an ancestry he could not have inherited, by nature, the ennobling traits of character which so eminently distinguish him among men. Abject slavery of their ancestors for four hundred years, was a poor training to qualify his parents to give birth to the distinguished ruler, law-giver and military chieftain he proved himself to be. In religion, the Egyptains were grossly idolatrous and shamefully immoral and licentious. Four hundred years of oppressive bondage to such masters, was a poor ancestral record for a distinguished moralist and theologian.

Moses was brought up in the family of Egypt's king and, at the very best, he could have had no educational advantages in boyhood and early manhood, so far as human instruction was concerned, save such as the reigning sovereign of Egypt could provide for him.

When he was about forty years old he fled from Egypt as a murderer, and for forty years thereafter, spent all his time in lonely isolation from the world, watching Jethro's flocks in the mountains. Up to the time he left Egypt, he seems to have done nothing worthy of note save the one bloody deed for which he fled the country, and after forty years spent in isolated solitude, he left Jethro's flocks in the mountains, to lead Abraham's seed out of Egypt.

When the Jews left Egypt, they numbered over six hundred thousand men, able to go forth to war, from twenty years old and upward. The whole number of Jews led out of Egypt by Moses could not, therefore, have been less than three millions.

This man Moses, then, delivered three millions of people from a bondage of hundreds of years. When he led them out of Egypt he was pursued by the king's army and confronted with formidable and almost innumerable difficulties. He at once entered a wilderness filled with deadly vipers, surrounded by hostile nations, reeking with the elements of disease and death and poorly supplied with food, water or raiment for his people.

Just delivered from a bondage which had oppressed them for centuries, as a nation, these three million people were ignorant of science, art, literature and military tactics. They were wholly undisciplined as soldiers or citizens, and utterly lacking in everything which goes to qualify a people for independence and self-government as a nation. They were rebellious as citizens, riotous as an army, corrupt as a people and idolatrous in religion. They were continually at war with hostile nations, plagues and pestilences often raged among them, they were bitten by deadly vipers, harassed by famine, weary of wandering and tired of existence. They murmured against Moses and openly attempted insurrection. Yet Moses held the reins of government over them with a firm hand for forty years. He disciplined them as an army, organized them as a government, purified them, morally, as individuals and instructed them in religion, as a nation. He gave them a code of laws and a system of religion which they have honored and followed individually and as a nation for more than three thousand years without change or emendation. As to morality, those laws are still respected by the civilized nations of earth, and they have received the high endorsement of the Son of God himself. All this was no ordinary achievement for Moses. It may well be doubted whether, under all the circumstances, any man could have done all these things except God had been with him. No wonder Moses made mistakes! The wonder is that he ever succeeded at all. To believe he could have done all this without the help of spiritual guidance and divine providence is a stretch of credulity infinitely greater than to believe in the miraculous and the world unseen. No wonder the name of Moses has been a household word in all the world for more than three thousand years! No wonder it has floated on the wings of the winds and has ridden on the ocean's waves as far as the sun of civilization has shed rays of light on a world lying in darkness.

Moses left an imprint of morality upon the whole Jewish nation which contact with the vices of every nation under heaven for more than three thousand years has not been sufficient to erase. He found the people of Israel in bondage in Egypt, morally depraved and intellectually benighted. He led them out of the land of God's curse, and established them as one of the purest, most intelligent and thrifty of the nations of earth. Is there nothing worthy of note in all this? Is it an ordinary thing for an ignorant son of slave parents to rise up and, without previous training for a work so great, lead three millions of slaves out of the land of their bondage openly, defiantly and in the very face of the king's army, discipline them, govern them, sustain them in a howling wilderness and lay the foundation for a powerful nation to be perpetuated down the ages for three thousand years? Why does not some man, who talks so flippantly about the mistakes of Moses, lead the negroes of the United States out of their difficulties now, and at once solve the race problem by establishing them somewhere as a mighty and prosperous nation? Why not? Ah, the wisdom and the power to solve such problems are not in man save as he is guided by spiritual light from an unseen world, or over-ruled by that Divine Providence which makes all things work together for good to those who love the Lord. Why did not somebody solve Israel's race problem three hundred years before Moses was born? There is but one way to answer: Man, of himself, solves no questions of this kind, and God, in his inscrutable wisdom did not see proper to solve it till the time when Moses was chosen as the agent through whom to accomplish a work so marvelous. Whence came such astounding success to Moses in every department of his great life-work? Are there no evidences of super-human wisdom, spiritual guidance and divine providence in all he did? Could he have done it himself? If he provided for his army and all the nation for forty years in the wilderness, whence came his supplies? If he planned the campaign and the many successful battles fought and glorious victories won himself, whence came the power and wisdom by which he overcame such vast armies and selected the strategic positions with such consummate skill? Whence derived he the military intuitions which enabled him to marshal his warrior hosts with such unerring certainty as never to lose a battle in a forty year's campaign? Ah, be not deceived. The wisdom and power of God were with him.

The military career of this remarkable man is not more marvelous than his moral intuitions as a law-giver. For more than eighteen hundred years the Jews, dispersed as a nation, have wandered among the nations of earth, and yet they cling tenaciously to the laws which Moses gave, and which have not been changed or modified in the slightest particular for more than three thousand years. Fathers have taught them to their sons and mothers to their daughters, and they have been recognized as a perfect standard and code of morality by the most intelligent nations of the world among whom the Jews have wandered in every age. These laws have preserved the Jews as a peculiar people amidst all the revolutions and mutations of the ages since God spake to Moses in the cloud on Sinai's smoking summit. That law to-day has a greater influence over the moral character of the world than all the other laws written by the wise men in every age of the world. It has been endorsed by the Son of God himself, and it is to-day taught to every child of Jewish or Christian parents as the perfect standard and highest authority in morality. The law of Moses has elevated the Jewish race to an enviable position among the peoples of earth. How many Jews are found loafing in idleness about saloons and other places of vice to-day? How many Jews are found on the streets of our cities or highways of our country as beggars, tramps or vagabonds? How many Jews are professional gamblers or habitual drunkards? How many Jews are indicted for crimes in our courts? How many are hung or incarcerated in jails or penitentiaries for violations of the law? How many Jewish women lead lives of open shame? How many Jews commit suicide, maltreat their wives and children, sue for divorce or openly and habitually commit fornication? In the city of New York, where there are perhaps more Jews in proportion to Gentiles than in any other city in the United States, only one per cent. of the cases in the criminal courts are against Jews and those cases are usually for minor offences. The moral code of Moses has thus elevated the whole Jewish nation, and has greatly influenced the morals of every other nation under heaven for more than three thousand years, and will continue to wield its mighty power over the human race till time itself shall grow old and die. Are there no evidences of spiritual guidance and divine providence in all this? Must we believe that the unparalleled moral intuitions which prompted this wonderful law were but the ordinary endowments of an ignorant son of degraded slaves, born and reared in the most licentious age of the world?

Some of the greatest common-law writers of the civilized world distinctly admit that the criminal laws of the most civilized nations of earth to-day are based upon the criminal laws given by Moses to govern the

Jews more than three thousand years ago. Moses, therefore, towers above the law-givers of the whole world as the author of a code of criminal laws which the wisdom of all the nations of earth have not been able to improve in three thousand years and more. Moses, to-day, controls more minds and hearts by the majesty of his laws and the greatness of his wisdom, than any and all other men, the Son of God himself excepted, who have ever lived on the earth. Moses goes into the halls of Congress, the chambers of State legislatures, on the thrones of kings, on the seats of magistrates and judges and into the jury boxes. He sits by the judge who charges the jury, presides over the officer who administers an oath and stands by every witness who testifies in our courts. Most emphatically, " he, being dead, yet speaketh." When the Chief Justice of the United States delivered the opinion of the highest tribunal in the greatest nation under the heavens, in a celebrated case not long since, he only reiterated what Moses said more than three thousand years ago. True, the court based its opinion upon a certain clause in the Constitution of the United States. But how came that clause in the Constitution? Whence did it come? From Moses. And had it not been incorporated from Moses into the Constitution, it is probable that the Constitution itself would never have been adopted, and that there would, therefore, never have been any United States of America. Whence came the wisdom of these wonderful laws? Surely Moses must have been specially endowed for his great life-work. All the facts of his life and the record of his ancestry preclude the idea that such wisdom as he possessed could have descended to him by inheritance, or have been imparted to him by human instruction.

The evidences of God's providence over the nation of the Jews are as clear as the proof of spiritual guidance in Moses. During four hundred years of abject slavery and menial bondage in Egypt, the eyes of the Lord were over the Jews and his ears were open unto their cries. The strong arms of the everlasting God were about them, and human power to afflict and injure them was limited and over-ruled by the immutable purposes of the eternal Intelligence who rules the world and governs the universe. Israel's sins as a nation in the past had created a complex problem in their affairs which could only be solved through a period of four hundred years of oppressive slavery. It was not the pleasure of God, but the needs of the people, on which Israel's bondage in Egypt was based. The problem to be solved was of national proportions and the solution could not be based upon individual interests. The design of the slavery in Egypt was clearly a national education and not personal punishment. It served to prevent amalgamation between the Jews and surrounding heathen nations, and to keep the blood of Abraham's seed pure till the purposes of God could be accomplished in establishing them as a self-governing nation in the land promised to them through Abraham in the centuries long gone by. In Egyptain bondage they could not intermarry with other people, and in a slavery of four hundred years they learned a lesson of humility which increased their faith in the power and providence of God and decreased their confidence in the wisdom and goodness of man.

A careful study of the history of this peculiar people may serve to lift the clouds of gloom from sorrow-burdened hearts, and teach the world of despondent doubters that the hand of God is often concealed in the greatest troubles of life. "Afflictions, though they seem severe, are oft in mercy sent." God's ways are wiser than man's. We often need the education of severe sorrows and grievous misfortunes, as individuals and as nations.

There was a time when faithful Abraham stood almost alone, as the friend of God, in the midst of a crooked and perverse generation. God had respect unto this man of marvelous faith, and purposed good things for his descendants in the ages to come. Never for one moment did that good purpose of God vary toward Abraham's seed. It was a Father's tender hand that led them through centuries of slavery in Egypt, and a Father's loving voice that called them out of bondage by Moses. It was a dark way for a God of love to lead the people of his promise, but it was the only way to the blessings he had in store for them. The wickedness of Israel had reached a point from which the only escape was through the dark ways of oppressive slavery and national humiliation. Still, God did not forget them. He respected their free agency, but by providence over-ruled all their wickedness and accomplished his purposes in them at last.

Through all the centuries God has been fulfilling the predictions of his inspired prophets and working out the plans of his own mind concerning this peculiar people. He was with them in Egypt; he guided them in the wilderness; he blessed them in Palestine; he dispersed them from Jerusalem; and he has watched over them in their weary wanderings among all the nations of the earth for more than eighteen hundred years. Thrones have crumbled; governments have fallen; nations have perished; empires have disappeared; and mighty revolutions have swept over the earth; but the

Jews still remain. There is no power that can defeat the purposes of God concerning these wandering remnants of a once powerful nation.

And can it be possible that the providence of God is over the Jews while all other peoples and nations of earth are as nothing in his sight? Could God exercise a constant providence over the Jews as they are now dispersed among all the nations of the earth, and yet have no eyes to see, no ears to hear and no power to over-rule the nations among which they wander? Is the providence of God over the Jew who sleeps by my side at night, and yet not over me? Does God solve all the race-problems for the Jews, and yet give no attention to the race-problems of the nations of earth among which they are wandering? Why should he curse them, bless them, protect them and guide them, as a people, and yet leave all other nations and peoples of earth without providential supervision? Ah, the deception of such a thought! The providence of the eternal God is continually over us all. He leaves us free to exercise our wills and lay our plans; but He over-rules all our purposes and shapes the ends of all our schemes. He has not vacated the throne as the world's sovereign. He makes even the wickedness of men to praise him. Wherever we go, whatever we do, the eyes that never sleep are over us and the arm that never trembles is around us. What God would bring to nought we have no power to prosper, and what he would prosper we are too weak to hinder. We may lay our plans, and arrange our schemes, and build our theories; but above us and around us and under us there is a power which shapes our ends and determines our destiny. Every plant which the hand of this mighty God has not planted shall be rooted up, and every purpose which he does not approve shall be finally over-ruled to his glory. In this faith I confidently rest. The wickedness of man may be great in the earth, but the power and providence of God are over us all. The hand of our God is on the helm, and the soul which trusts in him shall never be moved. The eyes that watch us are never closed and the ears that hear us are never stopped. The power that guards us can never fail and the Spirit which leads us can never die. In sorrows God will not forget us, and in death he will not forsake us. He is the first and the last, the *alpha* and the *omega* the beginning and the end. We are complete in him, but without him we can do nothing. He is our wisdom, our strength, our life, our all. He will solve all our difficulties, supply all our wants, heal all our wounds, and guide us all the way. Man's whole duty and only safety are to follow his guidance and keep his commandments. Though He should lead us through dark ways and over thorny paths, we should not falter in our faith or murmur at our lot. He has led others in similar ways to joys un- fading, and why may not his purposes concerning us often lie through evil as well as good report? We can- not fathom his wisdom; we know not his purposes; we can only trust him. It is enough for us to know that all things work together for good to those who love the Lord. Nation may rise up against nation; wars and rumors of wars may come; famines may prevail and pestilences may rage; human wisdom may fail and the powers of darkness may rule the world in sin for a season; but no harm can come to the soul which walks by faith in the Father of lights. Blessed is the man who can say the Lord is " always before my face;" he is forever " on my right hand, that I should not be moved." " Let us hear the conclusion of the whole matter: Fear God, and keep his commandments; for this is the whole duty of man. For God shall bring every work into judgment, with every secret thing, whether it be good, or whether it be evil." "Therefore let the heathen rage, and the people imagine vain things," "for if you do these things, you shall never fall."

## A FEW WORDS OF EXPLANATION.

I have now finished the story of "Seventy Years in Dixie." In looking over it, I am puzzled myself to identify all of the ideas and sayings of Mr. Caskey. As to matters of doctrine, I have woven my own faith into the book far more liberally than I at first intended. Still, I thought best to put it as though Mr. Caskey was saying it all. This seemed necessary to preserve the literary unity and harmony of the book. Moreover, this plan was agreed upon between Mr. Caskey and myself, and hence does no injustice to any one. Still, this peculiarity of the book must be remembered, or readers who know Mr. Caskey and who have often heard him preach and lecture, will not be able, perhaps, to reconcile certain passages touching doctrinal matters with his public and private utterances.

As to statements of fact, there are also many things in the book which seem to be parts of Mr. Caskey's personal experience, but which he himself will know nothing of till he sees them in these pages. Some of them are taken from my own experience and some of them from the experiences of others. I put them in because I knew them to be true, and because they seemed necessary to fill out the story of home life in Dixie.

I have put in no statement of fact that is not well authenticated.

But the greater part of the book will be recognized by all who have an intimate personal acquaintance with Mr. Caskey, as simply a reproduction of his quaint sayings and a rather imperfect description of his remarkable experience.

In the main, the story is told in my own words, but I have preserved his peculiar style to the utmost of my ability, and in some places I have given whole pages in almost his exact words.

And now a word as to how I remembered it all. Well, I did not remember it at all. For several years I have made it a habit to write down what I considered strange, peculiar or interesting extracts from private conversations and public addresses while they were fresh in my mind. In this way, and not by memory, did I preserve many of the passages in this book from the lips of Mr. Caskey and others. Other passages I gathered from private letters, and still others I got from manuscripts which at my request he wrote, before I began the work of arranging the matter for these pages.

With these explanations, I submit the work to a discriminating public.                                        F. D. SRYGLEY.

Nashville, Tenn., March 1, 1891.